JOSÉ MARÍA VELASCO

A VIEW OF MEXICO

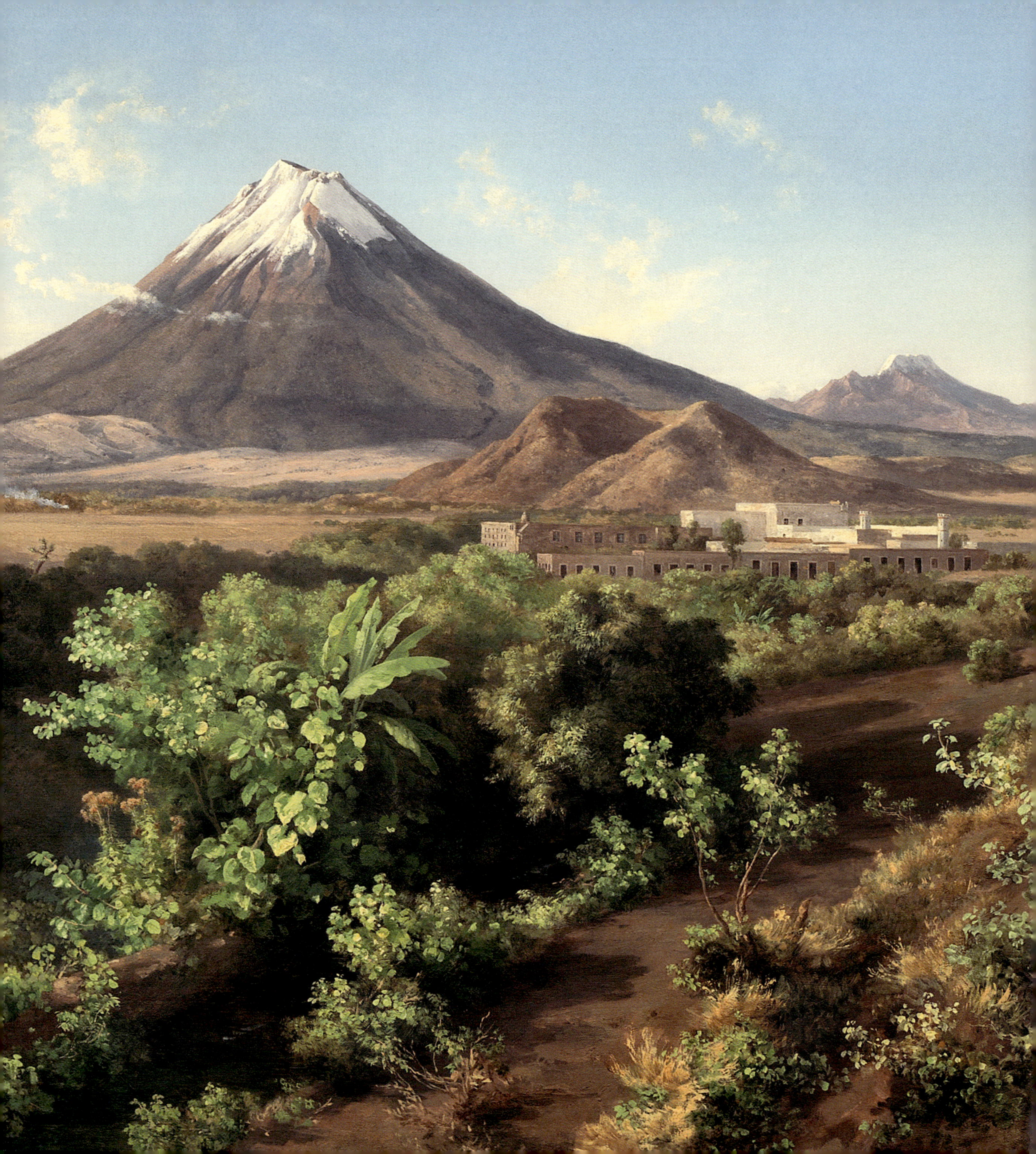

JOSÉ MARÍA VELASCO
A VIEW OF MEXICO

Dexter Dalwood and Daniel Sobrino Ralston

WITH CONTRIBUTIONS BY

Dawn Ades, María Elena Altamirano Piolle,
Pablo Arredondo Vera, Omar Olivares Sandoval
and Valéria Piccoli

NATIONAL GALLERY GLOBAL, LONDON
DISTRIBUTED BY YALE UNIVERSITY PRESS

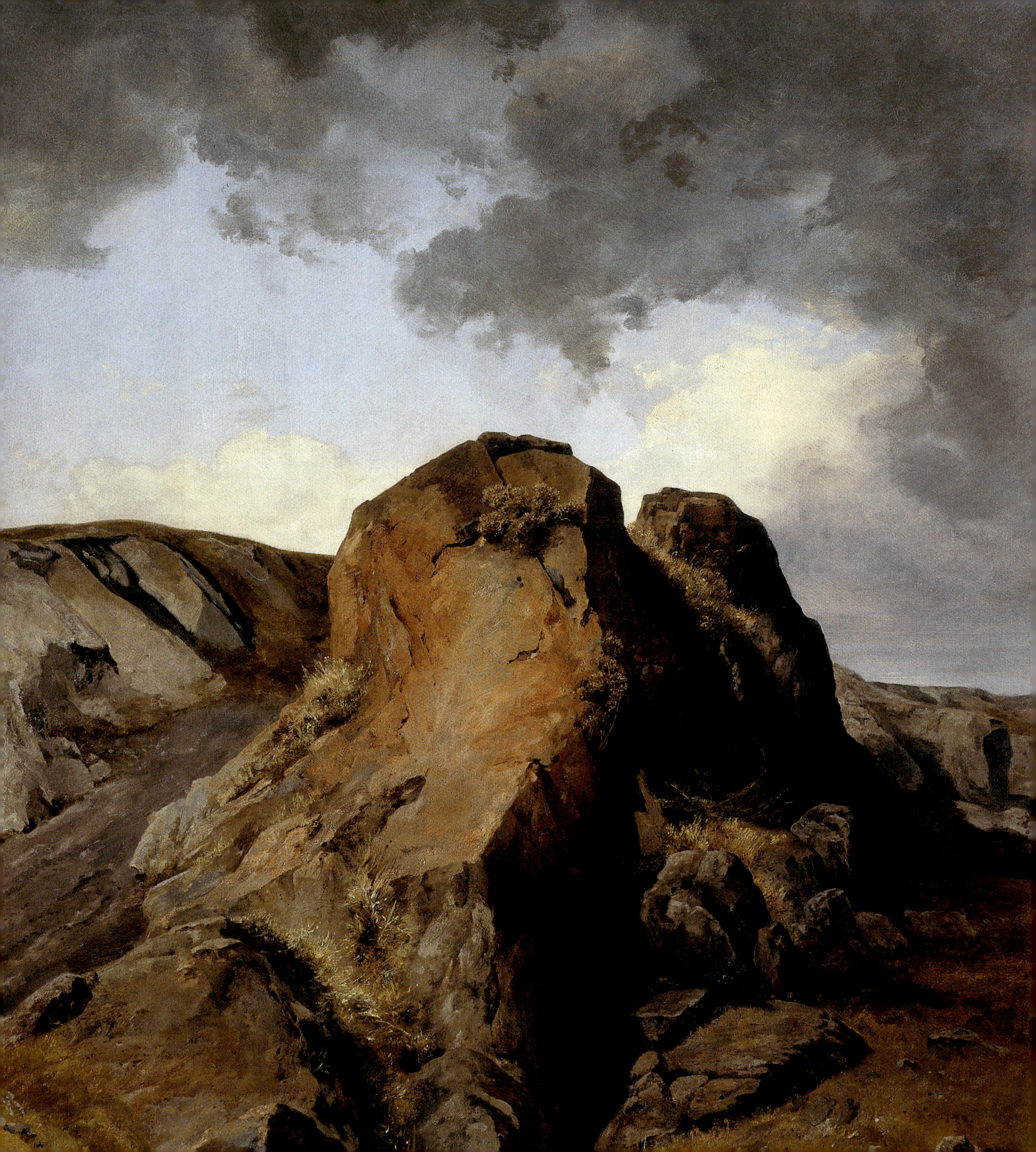

CONTENTS

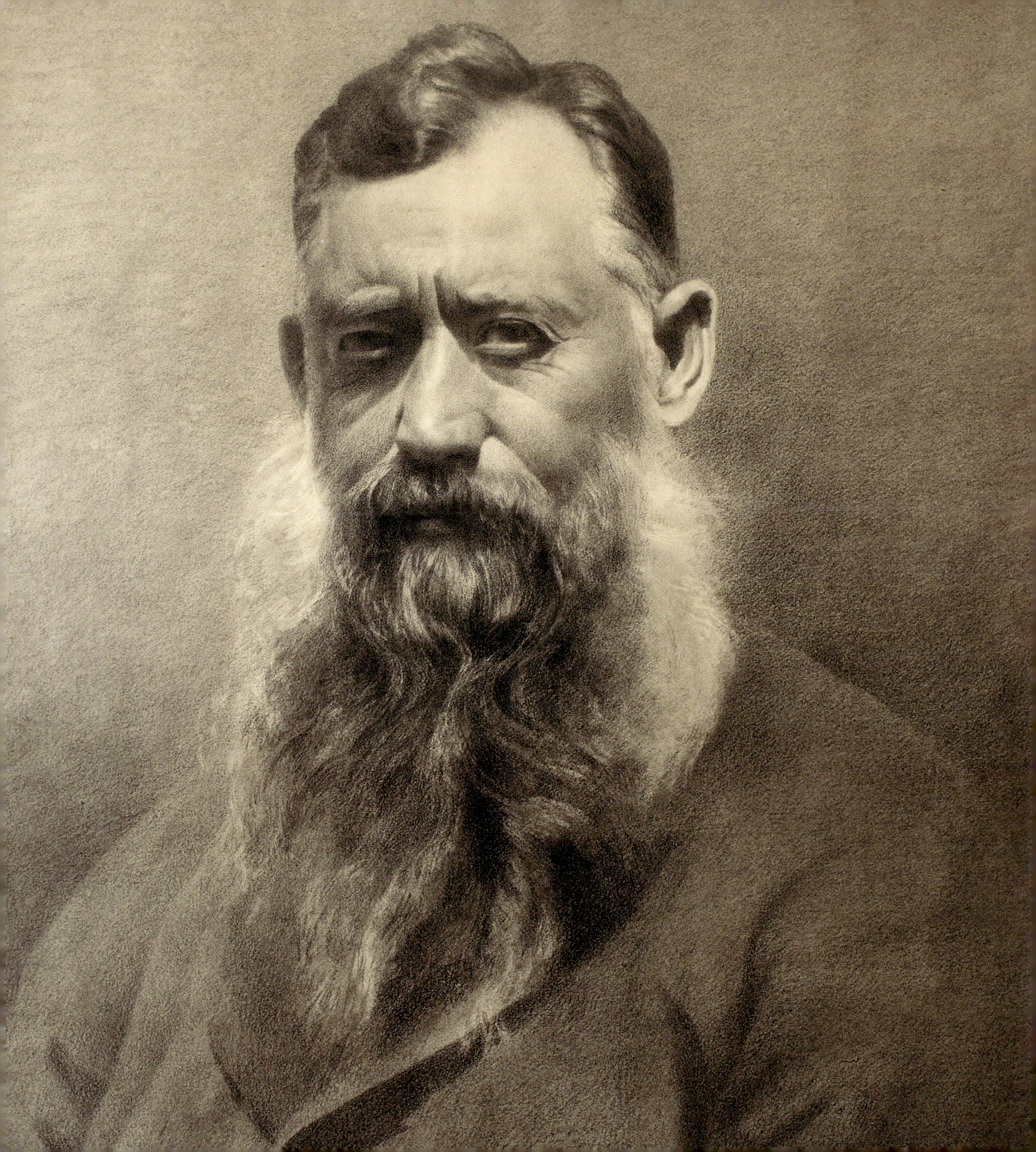

DIRECTORS' FOREWORD

SIR GABRIELE FINALDI
Director, The National Gallery, London

KATHERINE CRAWFORD LUBER, PHD
Nivin and Duncan MacMillan Director and President,
The Minneapolis Institute of Art

Before the Mexican Muralists and Frida Kahlo, José María Velasco (1840–1912) was a celebrated Mexican painter with an international reputation and patrons who hailed from Europe and the United States as well as his home country. His fame outside of Mexico, however, has been obscured in the twentieth century. We are delighted to be hosting the first-ever monographic exhibition of Velasco's work in Britain and the first since 1976 in the United States.

Velasco's principal subject was the landscape of Mexico in all its beauty, complexity and – for non-Mexicans – strangeness. Fascinated with the structure of rocks, the sweep of the Valley of Mexico with its lakes and volcanoes, and distinctive flora, in which he took a modern scientific interest, he made all these his subjects throughout his career. Attentive both to the impressive traces of ancient civilisations and to the forces of industrialisation that in his own time were imposing their presence on the land in the shape of railways and factory buildings, Velasco documented the landscape of the young republic of Mexico with a lyrical precision and a meticulous poetry.

The exhibition was conceived by the English artist Dexter Dalwood, now resident in Mexico City, whose interest in and enthusiasm for Velasco are passionate and infectious. He proposed the exhibition to us, and has co-curated it with Daniel Sobrino Ralston, the CEEH (Centro de Estudios Europa Hispánica) Associate Curator of Spanish Paintings here at the National Gallery, London. We are grateful to them both.

The exhibition could not have been realised without the support of the Mexican Secretary of State for Culture, Claudia Curiel de Icaza, and the Instituto Nacional de Bellas Artes y Literatura, led by Alejandra de la Paz Nájera. The principal lender to the exhibition is the Museo Nacional de Arte in Mexico City and we offer our gratitude to its Director, Mireida Velázquez Torres, as well as her predecessors, Héctor Palhares Meza and Carmen Gaitán Rojo. To the Museo Kaluz in Mexico City we are grateful for both loans and for access to the artist's extensive archive, which the institution under its Director, Miguel Fernández Félix, has recently acquired. The Secretaría de Cultura de Veracruz has lent Velasco's haunting *Great Comet of 1882* and to them and all the other Mexican lenders, public and private, we express our most sincere thanks. To the National Museum of the Czech Republic in Prague, which holds a group of Velasco's paintings donated by František Kaska, a Czech pharmacist who served Emperor Maximilian I of Mexico, we are likewise grateful for lending three paintings.

Our gratitude to colleagues and friends in Mexico is enormous, beginning with María Elena Altamirano Piolle, Velasco's descendant, the former custodian of his archive and a leading scholar of his work, for her enthusiastic support and enlightening contribution to our catalogue. We owe a debt to many individuals for their generous counsel and assistance in facilitating loans, especially Mariana Munguía, Patricio González and Tatiana Peralta. A special vote of thanks is due to Francisco Berzunza, who has been a guide, patron and friend in this enterprise.

At the National Gallery we would like to thank Pictet, The Monument Trust and the individual donors whose funding has helped to make this exhibition possible. The Trustees of the Bernard Sunley Foundation have been long-standing supporters of the National Gallery's Sunley Room exhibition programme and it is a pleasure as well as a duty to say thank you.

In Minneapolis, we are grateful for the work of Valéria Piccoli, Ken and Linda Cutler Chair of the Arts of the Americas and Curator of Latin American Art, whose dedication was instrumental in bringing this project to fruition. We extend our thanks to the individual and corporate sponsors whose generosity has enabled the museum to strengthen and expand its collection of Latin American art. And finally, we are especially pleased that this project has fostered a new collaboration between the National Gallery, London, and the Minneapolis Institute of Art, allowing us to share the genius of Velasco with a multi-national audience.

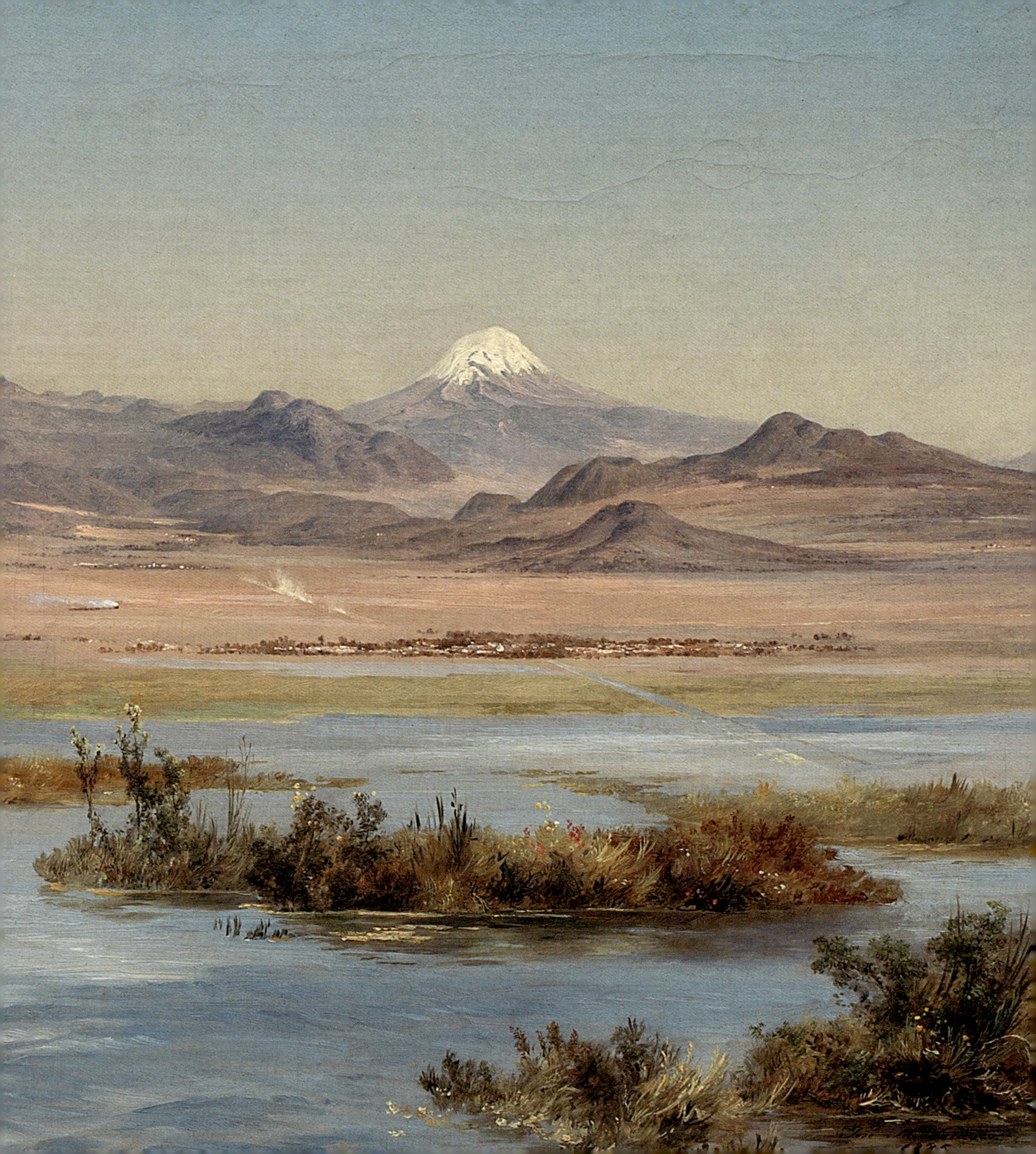

PREFACE

DAWN ADES

José María Velasco is a towering figure in the history of Mexican art, but is little known outside the Americas. His landscapes were shown in depth for the first time in the UK at the 1989 Hayward Gallery exhibition *Art in Latin America: The Modern Era, 1820–1980*, one of a flurry of exhibitions around the 500th anniversary of the 'discovery' of America. In various ways, consciously or unconsciously, the exhibition responded to the perceived model of a centre and a periphery in the art world, with the Euro–US axis dominant and artists from or in Latin America marginalised. My intention, as the curator and author of the catalogue for *Art in Latin America*, was to introduce audiences in the UK to the rich and varied work by these artists and to bring them into the mainstream, as part of a global history of art.[1] But there was also an academic perspective to the exhibition, which locked art in Latin America in specific linguistic, cultural, visual and political conditions and contexts. It simultaneously questioned categorisation in terms of nation while being absorbed in questions of identity. This paradox, in retrospect, marked the exhibition as both an ending and a beginning, in that it helped bring global attention to artists from Latin America while simultaneously making this context redundant, or at least secondary. Many of the now famous twentieth-century artists in the exhibition have long ceased to be the intellectual property of art historians and critics specialised in Latin America, and have entered the general critical arena.

This has, however, largely been the case for modern and contemporary artists, rather than those from earlier periods. In *Art in Latin America* Velasco's landscapes were presented in the context of Mexican history and of the construction of a new identity after Mexico gained independence from Spain in 1821. Although comparisons were made with Jean-Baptiste-Camille Corot, the Barbizon School and early works by Camille Pissarro, the conclusion was that Velasco's love of the grand panorama and, it seemed, complete disregard of the Impressionists' new attitudes to landscape, distanced him from his contemporaries in Europe.[2] His presence in the National Gallery is a welcome opportunity to question this.

In the West we have been conditioned to approach the history of painting formally, through Paul Cezanne, who is Velasco's almost exact contemporary. While comparisons are not always helpful, it is revealing to look at Velasco's work in the broader context of painting rather than of Mexican identity. The 1877 *Valley of Mexico from the Hill of Santa Isabel* (cat. 17), his most famous painting, is understandably treasured as embodying an idea of Mexico, with pre-Hispanic causeways leading in slightly off-centre perspective to the capital city and the eagle and cactus of the national flag re-naturalised in the foreground. But the text accompanying it at the annual exhibition of the Escuela Nacional de Bellas Artes – which Velasco himself either wrote or substantially contributed to – emphasises quite different, very direct and immediate visual aspects of the painting, specifying the season, time of day and weather. The effect of the light is 'from one of the first days of June at three o'clock in the afternoon'.[3] Working in from the foreground, every feature, hill and town is named: 'In the distance are the volcanoes Ixtaccíhuatl and Popocatépetl, the Ajusco cordillera and the ravine of la Magdalena towards the right.' In the sky a cumulus cloud is lifted by the air towards the volcanoes; 'floating in the lower region are nimbus clouds which are appearing to break down.' The combination of precise observation and a mapping that is more related to topography is unusual, and demands an ingenuity which makes us aware of his qualities as a painter and resistance to stereotype: the liveliness of light and shadows, the physical sense of moving down from the grassy scrub of the foreground into the valley past the lake, the individual elements, whether geographical or human, forged into a whole.

Velasco viewed the landscapes of the high sierras and the Valley of Mexico with an uncompromising eye. The critic Ignacio Manuel Altamirano grumbled that he had had enough of 'yellow earth' and begged the artist to look instead at Mexico's exuberant tropical lands; he also complained that everything beyond the foreground 'looks as if it is seen through binoculars'.[4] This draws attention to the pictorial devices which accompany Velasco's acute observation. To make the painted vistas cohere, space is condensed, pictorially speaking, creating the illusion that all this can be encompassed with the naked eye. It is likely, as Altamirano claimed, that he used lenses of some kind, probably binoculars.

As well as vistas, Velasco painted details, with the focus on a single outcrop, as in *Rocks* (cat. 23). This has a parallel in John Ruskin, who believed strongly in a 'truth to nature' that eschewed picturesque, theatrical and ideal landscape models, and combined a virtually religious passion for mountains with studies of striking individual features.[5]

The range of Velasco's treatments of the environment and the natural world, its relationship with modernity and with its histories, is impressive and can be extremely bold. For Velasco trains and railways enhanced rather than spoiled the majesty of the land. In the stunning *Curved Bridge of the Mexican Railway over the Metlac Ravine* of 1881 the gigantic bridge, constructed in 1872, spans a valley where the Mexico City–Veracruz track passes into the tropical lowland – hence the cluster of lush foliage in the foreground (fig. 13). Already a famous site, it appears in many photographs of the period with a similar viewpoint. Velasco, however, turns the track, which in photographs often simply passes across the scene, towards the spectator. The train thus heads straight for the viewer, as in J.M.W. Turner's

Rain, Steam, and Speed – The Great Western Railway (1844).[6] This flouting of
landscape convention, which usually required a clear separation of the pictorial
space from the spectator, contributes to the expression of new sensations of power
and speed. The *Metlac Ravine* predates Velasco's trip to Europe, but he could well
have seen a print of *Rain, Steam, and Speed.*

Velasco's visit to Paris in 1889 and his encounter there with recent painting
made little lasting impression on him, and it is his free treatment of long-standing
academic traditions as much as his independence from contemporary practices that
is remarkable. A canvas of 1885, *Lake Chalco* (cat. 5), presents an extraordinary
counterpoint between old and new, regarding both pictorial traditions and subject.
At first it seems dominated by horizontals, with the virtually unbroken line of the
lake repeated in the edge of the valley below the mountains. Velasco had long
abandoned the Claudian tradition of sloping planes to create the illusion of depth.[7]
However, the starkness is deceptive; the loosely painted waters of the lake catch
the light, its grassy islands recede in space, and there are multiple delicate diagonals
crossing the horizontal planes. The most striking of these is the faint line of the road,
on which a cloud of dust hints at the presence of a coach or cart, horse-drawn,
contrasting with the steam train crossing on the horizontal: the modern world
effortlessly absorbed into the timeless landscape. These pictorially tiny but highly
significant details are characteristic of the ways Velasco skews the conventions of
academic landscape painting to his own purposes. In the unsentimental but deeply
felt response to such scenes the singularity of his vision as a painter is evident.

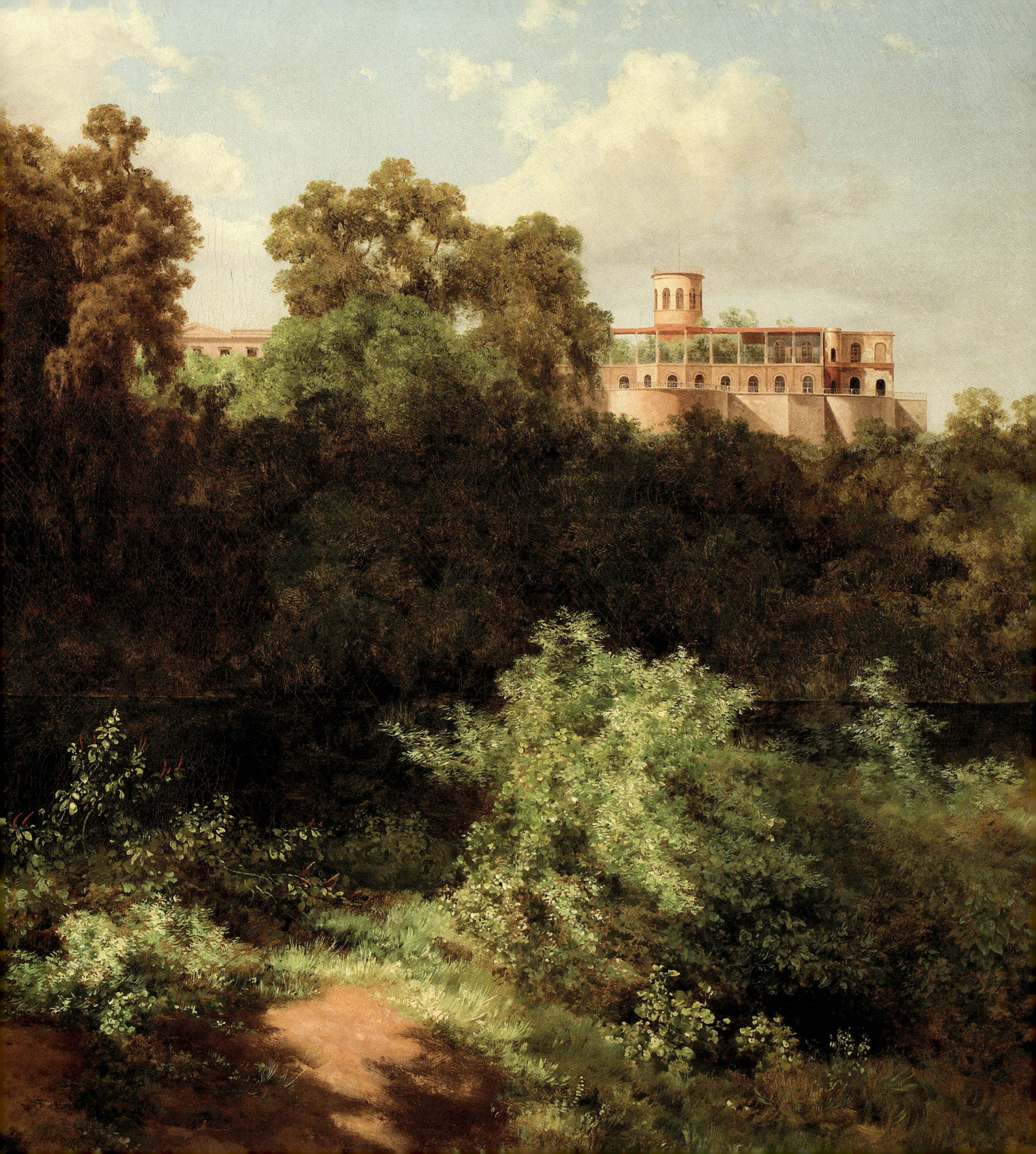

MASTER OF THE FAR HORIZON

MARÍA ELENA ALTAMIRANO PIOLLE

José María Velasco was one of Mexico's greatest painters, winning countless awards not just at home but also in Europe and America. Underpinned by considerable scientific knowledge, nowhere are his remarkable painterly skills better showcased than in his superb landscapes, especially those featuring the Valley of Mexico. He was a master of sweeping horizons, light and nature, all rendered with exceptional accuracy. Having started to draw around the age of 12, he devoted the rest of his life to the twin pursuits of painting and science.

Velasco was born on 6 July 1840 in the quiet village of San Miguel Temascalcingo, 160 kilometres north-west of Mexico City. He and his younger brother Ildefonso attended the local primary school until 1849, when the family moved to Mexico City – where his parents had relatives – in search of work. The boys' father, Felipe Velasco, died of cholera in 1850 and his widow, María Antonia Gómez Obregón, took their three sons (little Antonio was just four months old) to live at Baño de los Pescaditos, a house owned by her brothers-in-law Pedro and José Guadalupe, who worked in the clothing trade.[1] The boys were admitted to a free school, where José María soon discovered a taste for drawing, displaying a talent that from the outset impressed his master, the artist Vicente Villaverde. A classically inspired drawing of a young man, produced when Velasco was in his early teens, has survived from this period.[2]

The Velasco brothers left school around the beginning of 1855 to work in their uncles' shop selling shawls. But José María, unhappy at having to leave his drawing classes under Villaverde, sought his uncles' permission to study drawing at the Academia de San Carlos in Mexico City.[3] That year, while still working at the shop, he enrolled himself there for night classes.[4]

The Academia was enjoying something of a short-lived heyday at the time of Velasco's enrolment, with a new board of governors that had drawn up a curriculum closely modelled on contemporary European counterparts.[5] The director, Javier Echeverría, was keen that each department should be headed by a European artist and approached the prestigious Accademia di San Luca in Rome, which was known for producing recognised artists with a solid academic training. This resulted in the appointment of two Catalan artists, the painter Pelegrín Clavé and the sculptor Manuel Vilar, who arrived in 1846 to head their respective departments. Some years later, when landscape painting was included in the syllabus, Clavé decided to appoint the Italian landscape artist Eugenio Landesio as director of the new department, a post he took up in January 1855.

In January 1858, a few months before his 18th birthday, Velasco completed his three-year night-school course in drawing and resolved to leave his uncles' shop to

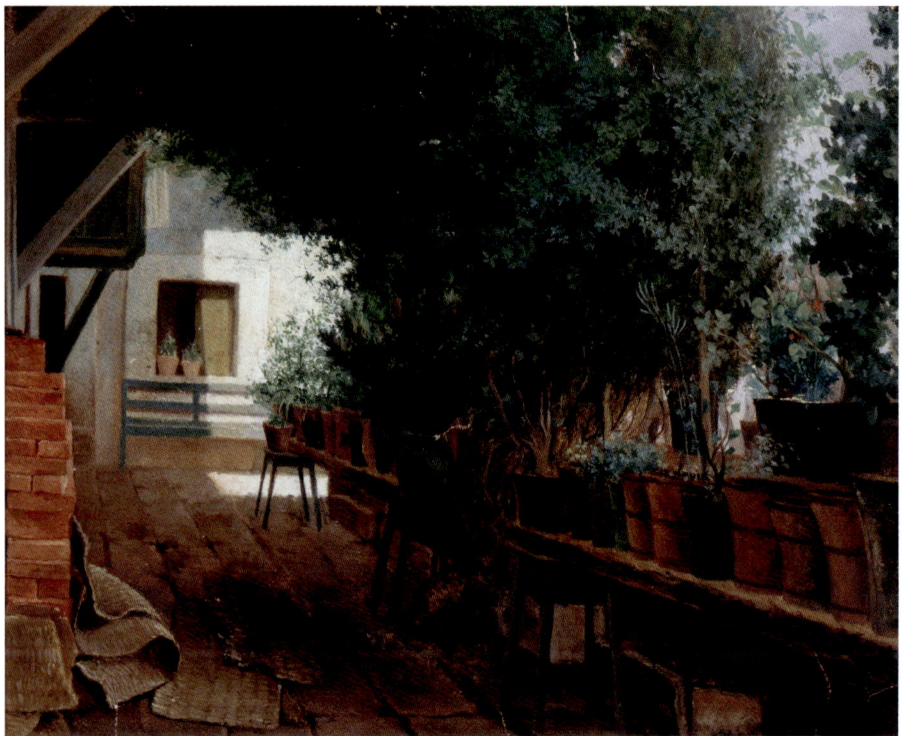

enrol at the academy as a full-time student, specialising in landscape painting. There
he took several drawing courses – including life drawing classes and copying from
prints and plaster casts – taught by Miguel Mata, Juan Urruchi and Santiago Rebull,
and also studied perspective, landscape drawing and painting under Landesio,
whose landscapes were to have a significant influence on his work (see fig. 19).

The landscape painting curriculum, devised by Landesio himself, focused on
the accurate rendering of geographical features, plants and architecture, as well as
skyscapes; students were also required to study and copy human and animal figures.
Velasco produced countless drawings and paintings which would later find their way
into his landscapes: interiors, exteriors, buildings in ruins; foliage in forests and parks,
gardens and avenues; rugged mountainous terrain, plains and caves; clear, stormy or
moonlit skies; still or rippling waters; a variety of animals; and, above all, the human
figure in family, genre, biblical and historical settings.[6]

From the outset, Velasco's remarkable skill and tremendous diligence impressed his
teachers, especially Landesio, with whom he would go on to enjoy a close friendship. Velasco
invariably won prizes at the end-of-term student shows, first for his drawings and later for
his paintings. Landesio taught his students to draw and paint from life in the open air. Later,
back at the studio, they would rework the picture, producing a second or 'studio' version.
For his first foray into plein-air oil painting – to practise reproducing foliage and architecture –
Velasco chose his beloved childhood home, Baño de los Pescaditos (fig. 1).

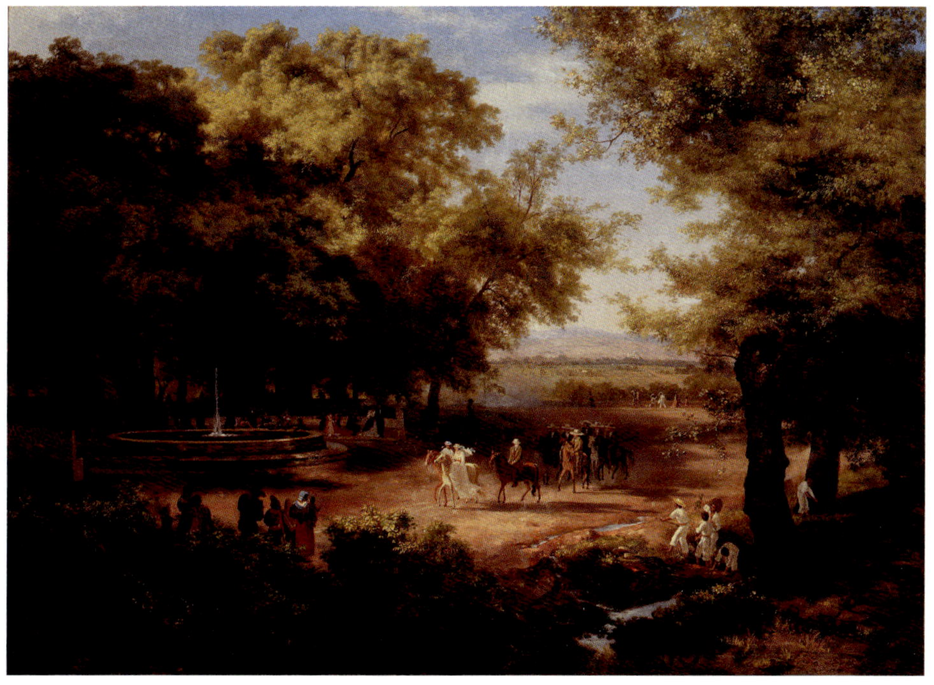

On several occasions during his early years at the academy, Velasco came close
to giving up his studies; his mother's financial situation had worsened and he felt
he should find a job in order to help. Early in 1860, however, he won an academy
scholarship competition with a painting entitled *The Courtyard of the Former
Convent of San Agustín*; this financial aid enabled him to complete his studies.[7]

As soon as he started his drawing classes, Velasco also embarked on the study of
those scientific disciplines which he felt might be of use to him as a painter. Though
naturally keen to learn, his particular interest in the natural sciences was fostered by
the reading list recommended by Landesio, which included all ten volumes of *Los tres
reinos de la naturaleza. Museo pintoresco de historia natural*, published in Madrid in
1852. Velasco felt an immediate affinity with the natural scientist: his growing mastery
of painting techniques was matched by an increasing awareness of the need for a
fuller scientific understanding of what he was depicting in his landscapes.

The governors of the academy had arranged for their students to attend classes
in a range of subjects at the Escuela Nacional de Medicina. Velasco was thus
able to combine his landscape studies with courses in botany, physics, zoology,
mathematics and anatomy. The staff at the medical school demanded as much of
the art students as they did of their own students, among them Velasco's brother
Ildefonso. As a result, Velasco's depictions of the natural world – already in his final
student years – had a sound scientific underpinning. A good example is his last
student piece, *The Alameda of Mexico*, painted in 1866 (fig. 2), in which the trees

and foliage in the foreground are so accurately and meticulously rendered that the species are readily identifiable.

On graduating in 1868 from the Escuela Nacional de Bellas Artes – the name by which the Academia de San Carlos was known from late 1867 until the early twentieth century – Velasco set out on a dual career as painter and teacher that was to last 42 years (fig. 3). On 15 September 1868 he was appointed lecturer in perspective at the Escuela Nacional. That year he married María de la Luz Sánchez Armas Galindo, a childhood friend with whom he had renewed contact in later years.[8] Theirs was to be a long and fruitful marriage: however, only eight of their thirteen children reached adulthood, with two dying at a relatively early age.

Shortly after the wedding, as the year drew to a close, Velasco started work on the lithographs for *Flora del Valle de México* (*Flora of the Valley of Mexico*), a botanical work published in instalments, for which he had been commissioned to provide watercolour illustrations (see fig. 24). He produced a total of 18 plates, describing plant morphology in full scientific detail. As a result of this commission, Velasco was invited to be a founding member of the Sociedad Mexicana de Historia Natural, whose aim was to study the natural sciences – mineralogy, geology, palaeontology, botany and zoology – and to make Mexico's rich natural resources and scientific progress known to a wider audience. Velasco later contributed several articles to the society's journal *La Naturaleza*, including essays on *Ipomoea triflora* (morning glory), *Cereus serpentinus* (dragon fruit), the hummingbird family in the Valley of Mexico and volcanoes. He also later carried out important research into the metamorphosis of a new axolotl species – an amphibian closely related to the tiger salamander – for which the society awarded him a prize in 1879 (see also pp. 47–9).

In the early days of his painting career, Velasco often worked in the Bosque de Chapultepec, a beautiful, densely forested park in the south-west of Mexico City, where he spent long periods sketching, working on compositions and making botanical drawings. He was particularly fascinated by the ancient *ahuehuetes* (Montezuma cypresses), their huge trunks and delicate leaves rustling in the breeze, reflected in the pools fed by the park's many natural springs. He painted several pictures there, including his superb 1883 canvas of *Chapultepec* (fig. 4), showing the *ahuehuetes*, a spring and Chapultepec Castle in the background. In 1864 this splendid castle – ordered constructed in 1785 as the viceroy's summer home – became the official residence of Emperor Maximilian I; from 1884 it was the home of President Porfirio Díaz. For over thirty years, Velasco depicted the castle, its idyllic setting and the warm glow of the ever-present cypresses from a range of viewpoints and in a variety of compositions.

He and his wife often visited her mother in Villa de Guadalupe, a small town to the north of Mexico City. Velasco quickly took to this new setting, and in 1873 began working on the dry slopes of the hill of Atzacoalco, just behind the town. There he spent time drawing and painting rocky crags, plants, clouds and views

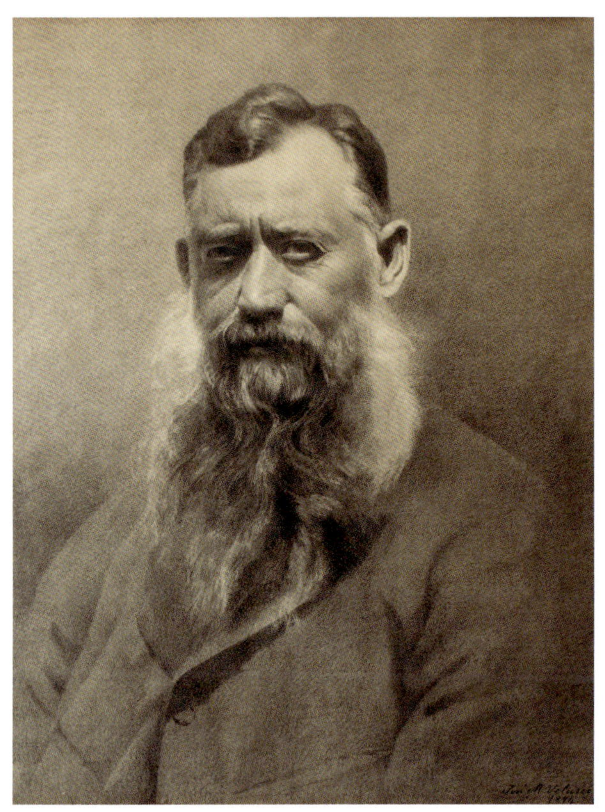

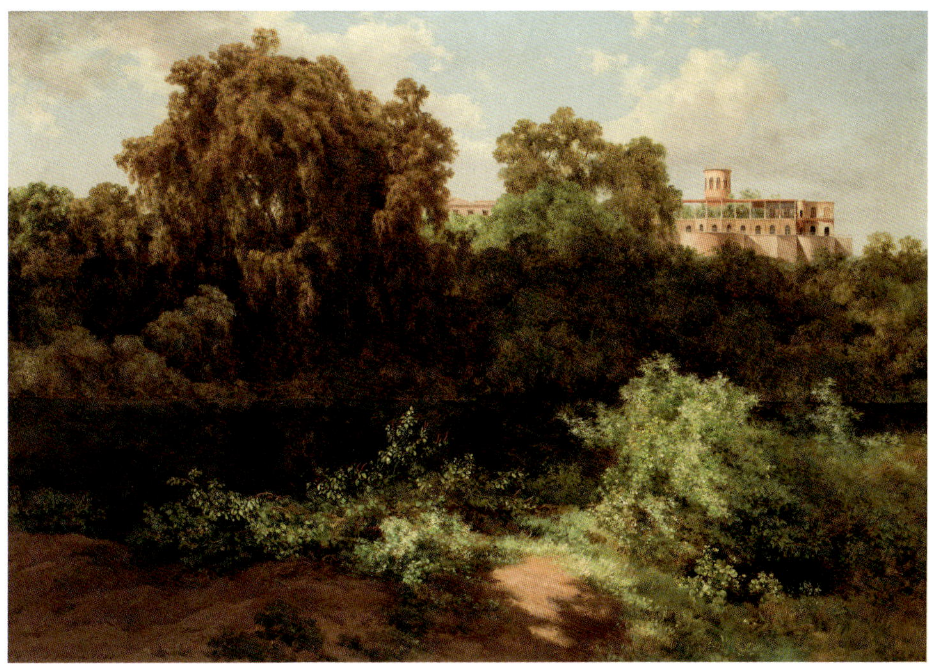

of the valley, preparing for his first great *Valley of Mexico*. On reaching his chosen vantage-point, he would secure a parasol into the earth and adapt his portable wooden paintbox into a table by attaching metal legs, before seating himself on a three-legged folding stool. He liked to make small sketches of details of the view in pencil on paper, followed by pencil studies of the entire landscape. His paintbox housed sheets of cardboard and small prepared canvases and he would attach them to its lid, which served as a vertical support, like a small easel. In this way he was able to produce several small-format oil sketches in one sitting, using the method throughout his career.[9] These numerous sketches in pencil and oils (see cat. 16), together with several compositional studies, provided him with the outline for his first monumental landscape, *The Valley of Mexico from the Hill of Atzacoalco*, painted in 1873 (fig. 5). In this painting, which won a prize at the Escuela Nacional's exhibition in December that year, Landesio's influence is still apparent, especially in the reddish colouring, the marked chiaroscuro and the abundance of both natural elements and human figures.

Velasco also travelled around Tlaxcala and Veracruz, equipped with his pocket sketchbook and portable paintbox, sketching a variety of vistas: ravines and arid plains – where he focused on geological formations and running brooks – as well as dense forests in which he discovered a wealth of tree and plant species. In 1875 he returned to his favourite subject, the Valley of Mexico, this time choosing a higher vantage-point than for the 1873 canvas to ensure a more sweeping vista. This new monumental

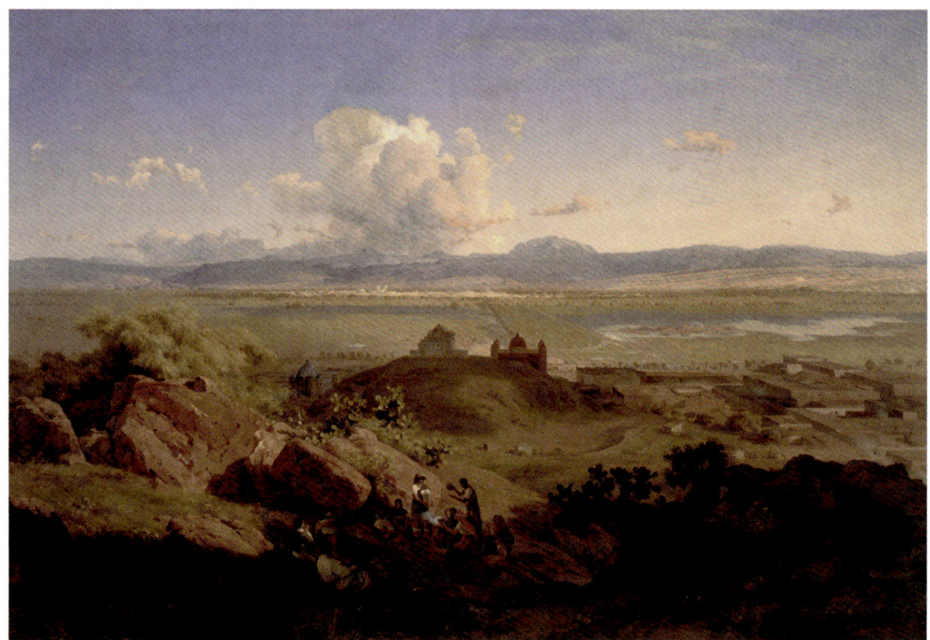

landscape, *The Valley of Mexico from the Hill of Santa Isabel* (cat. 15), included – for the first time – the famous twin volcanoes Popocatépetl and Iztaccíhuatl. Two years later he produced another large-format landscape with the same title (cat. 17); by then, however, the warm red tones and dark shadows borrowed from Landesio had given way to a wholly personal style marked by the synthesis of closely observed detail and subtle historic references, with a less crowded composition than in previous paintings, which enabled him to capture the untrammelled splendour of the valley itself. These two paintings were awarded first prize in both national and international exhibitions, consolidating the artist's professional reputation. At the end of a list of his paintings that he drew up in 1901, which included numerous versions of certain works, Velasco noted:

> I was commissioned on several occasions to repeat certain paintings, and the repetitions are as original as the first version; not just because they were produced by the painter himself, but also because he worked on them quite freely, always seeking new improvements, rather than slavishly copying them; sometimes he experimented with new effects.[10]

In 1873 Landesio gave up his landscape class at the Escuela Nacional de Bellas Artes; four years later he returned to Rome, where he died not long afterwards. Velasco – who had been teaching the perspective class for some years – was appointed lecturer in landscape art in 1877, succeeding his former master, who had taught both subjects for nearly twenty years.

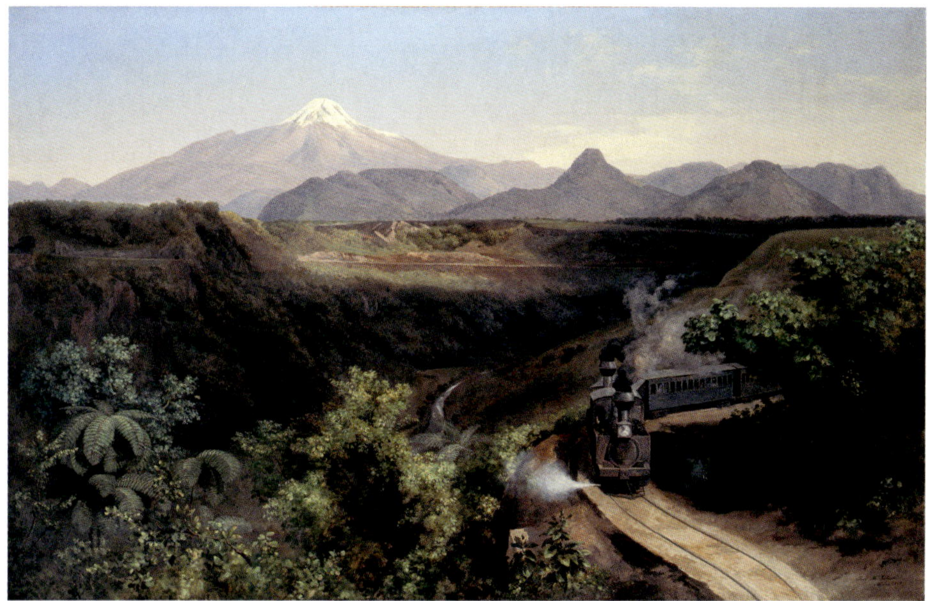

That same year, Velasco also started to work with the Museo Nacional in Mexico City, an institution founded in 1831 for the purpose of safeguarding and studying Mexico's antiquities, crafts and natural history. The museum published a regular bulletin, *Anales*, to which Velasco contributed countless illustrations – drawings, lithographs, oil paintings and watercolours – of archaeological sites and pre-Hispanic objects, as well as reproductions of Mexica codices (pictorial manuscripts).[11] Such was the demand for Velasco's meticulously accurate drawings that for many years he spent his evenings working in the museum.

As well as repeatedly exploring the Valley of Mexico in search of fresh vantage-points for his landscapes, Velasco returned to Veracruz in 1881 to paint *The Curved Bridge of the Mexican Railway over the Metlac Ravine* (see fig. 13), combining a tribute to the modern age with a visual record of the tropical vegetation of the area; several years later, he recaptured the same setting in *The Metlac Ravine* (fig. 6). He also made a long trip through the states of Puebla and Oaxaca, painting landscapes with haciendas, archaeological remains and colonial settlements as well as local topography and flora. In 1893, visiting the Apam valley in the state of Hidalgo, he produced the superb *Hacienda of Chimalpa* (fig. 7), the masterpiece of an artist at the height of his powers. The painting is remarkable not just for its impressive depth of perspective but also because it achieves extraordinary luminosity despite a limited palette and its use of a very light layer of pigment.

In 1889 Velasco – who by now enjoyed an international reputation as a landscape artist – was invited to take part in the Paris Exposition Universelle, joining the Mexican fine arts delegation as head of the painting section (see also pp. 33–4). Four years

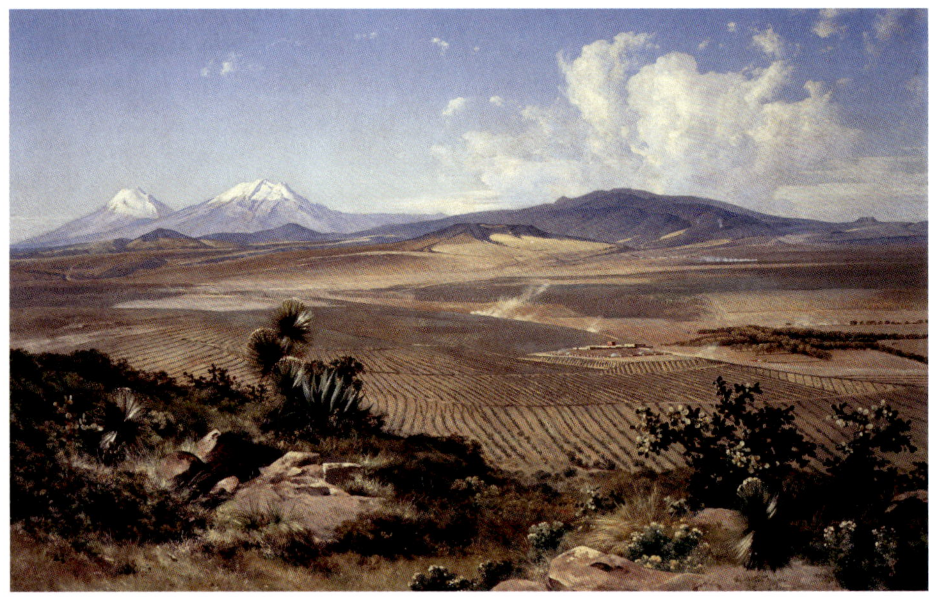

THE HACIENDA OF CHIMALPA, 1893
OIL ON CANVAS, 103 × 159 CM
MUSEO NACIONAL DE ARTE, INBAL,
MEXICO CITY

later he again led the Mexican delegation at the World's Columbian Exposition
in Chicago, exhibiting some of his best works to great acclaim. At both events, his
monumental landscapes of the Valley of Mexico won medals, and in Paris he was
appointed a Knight of the French Legion of Honour. In April 1901 Velasco was
awarded the Knight's Cross of the Order of Franz Joseph for his landscape *The Hill of
the Bells* (see fig. 17), painted as a gift for members of the Austrian nobility when they
visited Mexico. At the turn of the century, heartened by this international recognition,
he was still painting superb landscapes and actively pursuing his scientific research.

On the morning of 28 October 1901 Velasco was on his way to the Museo
Nacional when his train crashed; his right leg was fractured and placed in a cast for
two months. Immobilised, he spent time compiling a list of the landscapes in oils that
he had produced to date. Velasco's list provides an invaluable and detailed account
of his oeuvre, including a brief description of his major works. Though he continued
to paint landscapes after 1901, he ceased to keep any record of them. In the last four
years of his life, he produced a series of small paintings on postcards (see cats 26–8).

In 1908 Velasco – still active both as a painter and as a lecturer at the Escuela
Nacional de Bellas Artes (fig. 8) – blended these twin interests in an unpublished
manuscript entitled 'El arte de la pintura' ('The Art of Painting'), which examined
a range of theoretical as well as technical aspects of landscape painting, applicable
to any artistic style, past or present. In the book Velasco takes the view that 'talent
and imagination cannot be taught, they are innate aptitudes; however, they can be
developed through study, practice and objective learning ... knowledge is the basis
for the development of creative ability.'[12]

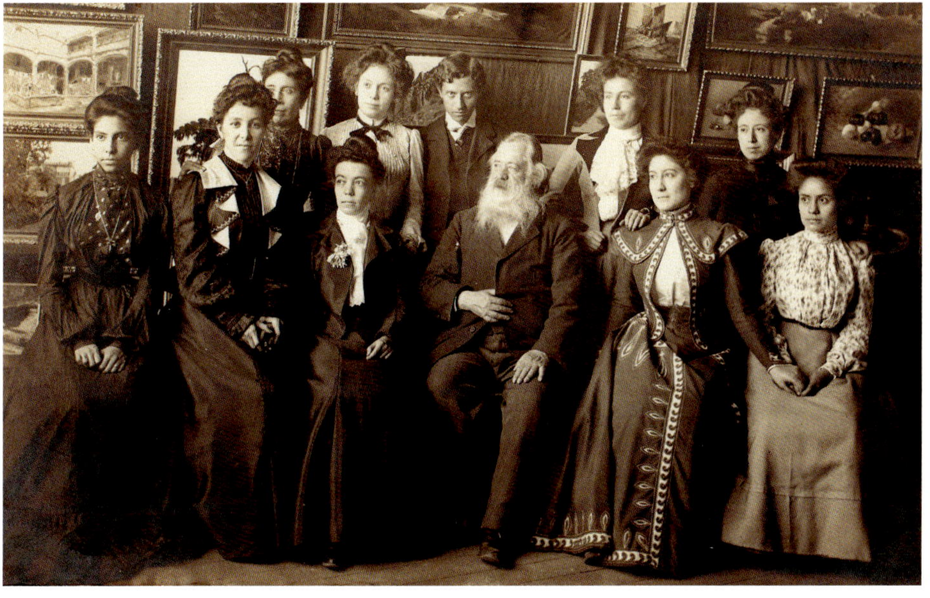

Having devoted so much of his life to the academy – first as a student and then as a lecturer – in 1910 Velasco was dismissed from his post at 70 years old, owing to his age. Summarily relieved of his classes in perspective and landscape painting, he was appointed instead, for just two years, as inspector of painting and sculpture.[13] His perceived unfair treatment triggered a depression that overshadowed his later years and aggravated a long-standing heart condition. Considering himself forgotten and fallen from favour, he died on 26 August 1912, surrounded by his beloved wife and children. He had been working, in his final days, on a small painting that was left unfinished (cat. 28).

Over his career, Velasco produced almost three hundred landscape paintings, along with self portraits and thousands of drawings, watercolours, lithographs and postcards in oils. He is widely regarded as Mexico's finest landscape painter, as well as an inspiration to many twentieth-century painters, Diego Rivera among them (see pp. 56–8). He was remarkable not just for his superb draughtsmanship but also for the dazzling luminosity of his landscapes, his precise brushstrokes, his skilled handling of glazes to achieve a shimmering atmosphere, his impressive mastery of perspective and a choice of palette that perfectly reflects the Mexican landscape. In their scientific rigour his paintings provide a valuable record of the natural world. When exhibited abroad, Velasco's works – sometimes proudly signed 'José María Velasco, Mexico' – focused international attention on the beauty of the Mexican landscape, capturing its vast valleys and lofty peaks, its rocky terrain and its flora.

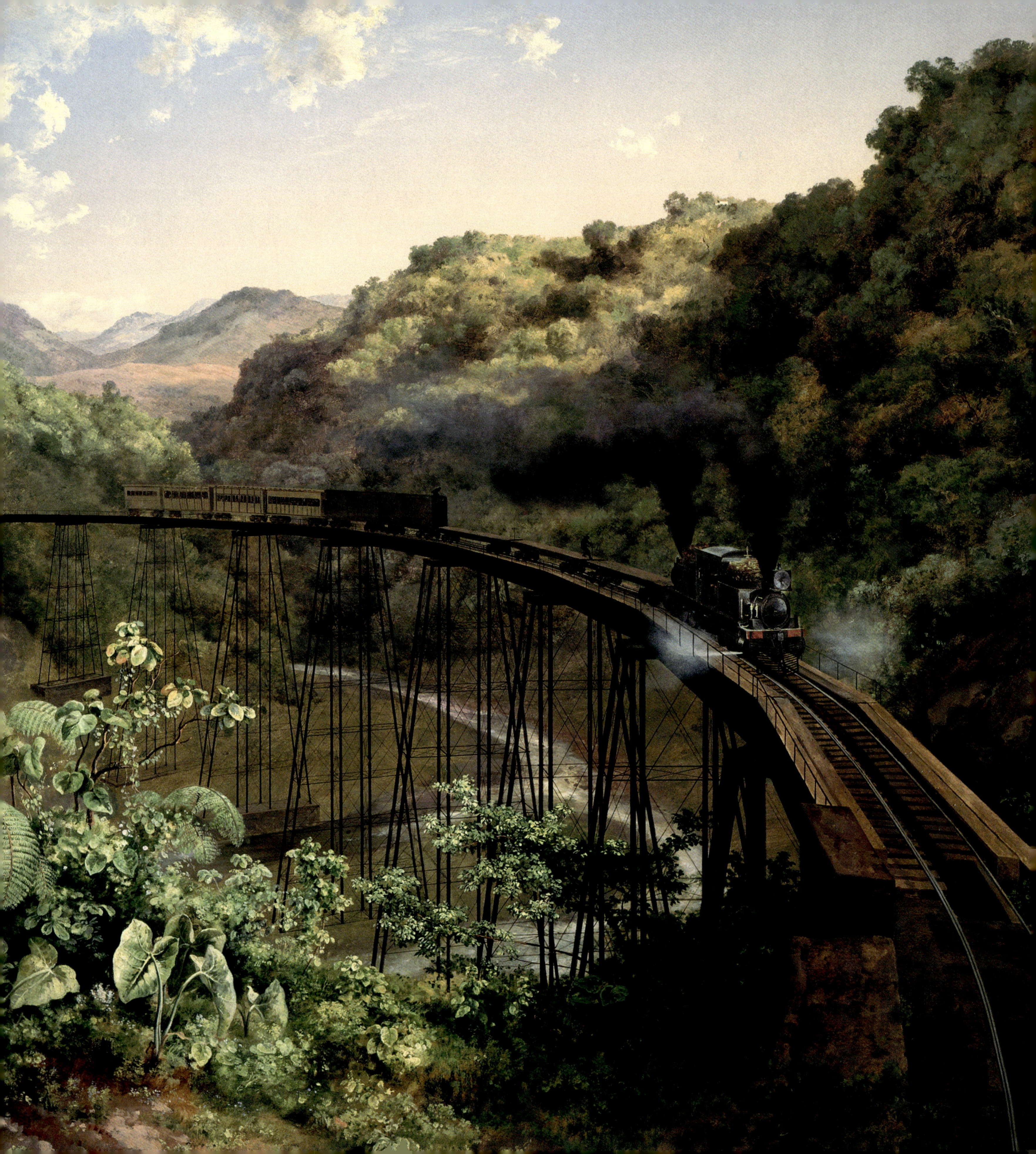

VELASCO BEYOND MEXICO

DANIEL SOBRINO RALSTON

José María Velasco left Mexico only twice in his life. On both journeys he traversed great distances to represent his nation on the sprawling grounds of international expositions, where he oversaw and arranged Mexico's displays of fine arts. Even though he supplemented these long official trips – to Paris in 1889 and Chicago in 1893 – with several painting excursions inside Mexico, notably to Oaxaca and Veracruz, Velasco was, in general, reluctant to leave home. The letters he sent from Europe and the United States to his wife, María de la Luz Sánchez Armas Galindo, are shot through with expressions of sorrow at having to be so long apart from his family. 'I don't know how people can become accustomed to being so far away from home', he wrote after his first month in Paris, 'I guess you need a special temperament that I don't have.'[1] It is unsurprising, then, that the artist's great subject, to which he returned insistently throughout his career and with which he remains most closely associated, was the varied landscape of the expansive Valley of Mexico, where he lived nearly all his life.

That Velasco's oeuvre depicts only his home country, coupled with his aversion to foreign travel, has often precluded understanding his art in anything but its immediate national context.[2] From the very beginning of his career until its end, however, he was inextricably linked to artistic traditions, practices and patrons from well beyond Mexico's borders. Understanding Velasco's unique artistic achievement entails – and indeed demands – considering the artist and his work in relation to the ever more interconnected transatlantic world of the late nineteenth century.

Before the young artist had finished his studies in 1868, Mexico was twice invaded by foreign armies. The country had only liberated itself from the rule of Spanish viceroys in 1821 when, after a decade of conflict, Agustín de Iturbide (1783–1824) proclaimed an independent Mexican empire.[3] In the unstable republican period that followed his brief reign, political leaders came and went with frequency. A dominant figure was Antonio López de Santa Anna (1794–1876), who served as president multiple times between the 1830s and 1850s and took command of Mexico's armies during the Mexican–American War (1846–8).[4] Before this conflict, Mexico still laid claim to vast territories in western North America that included the present-day American states of California, Nevada, Arizona, Utah, New Mexico, Colorado and Texas. In spring 1846 the United States used a border skirmish as the pretext to launch an invasion brazenly intended to annex those great tracts of land. When American troops entered Mexico City in 1847, Velasco and his family had just arrived from the village of San Miguel Temascalcingo, where the artist was born in 1840. With tensions in the capital high,

the family soon decamped, returning in 1849.[5] At the end of the war, the victorious
Americans imposed the punitive Treaty of Guadalupe Hidalgo on Mexico, enforcing
the sale of more than half of the nation's territory to the United States.

Under the heel of its powerful neighbour and with its economy in tatters, Mexico
was quickly plunged into discord. Two broad political groups, roughly divisible into
liberal and conservative factions, vied for control. They were not dissimilar in their
determination to stimulate growth and democratise Mexico, but the conservatives
were adamant that the military and the Catholic Church retain the centrality that they
had long been accorded in Mexican society. When a liberal-leaning constitution was
proclaimed in 1857, conservative forces rose up against the government, which was led
by the indigenous moderate Benito Juárez (1806–1872) from 1858. At the outbreak
of the Reform War, as it was called, Velasco, then a teenager, was working in his uncles'
textile shop in the capital and, in 1855, had begun to take drawing classes in the
evenings (see pp. 13–14). As the fighting persisted, government coffers – which had
been propped up by loans from Britain, France and Spain – were depleted. Juárez
was returned to power at the end of the conflict in 1861 but, unable to raise tax
revenue, he took the fateful decision to suspend repayments on all foreign debts.

In response, the avaricious emperor of the French, Napoleon III (1808–1873),
joined by Britain and Spain, sought to compel the Mexican government to reimburse
its creditors through military force. But Napoleon III had something more in mind: the
establishment of a new and tractable government in Mexico, through which French
power could be brought to bear in the Americas.[6] British and Spanish support fell
away as the emperor's colonial designs became clear, but the French pressed on,
emboldened by the American Civil War (1861–5), which distracted the United States
from the incursion. Despite a surprise defeat at Puebla on 5 May 1862 – the battle
from which the celebration of Cinco de Mayo takes its name – French troops entered
Mexico City in 1863. Once in the capital, they prepared the way for the arrival the
following year of the leader that Napoleon III had plucked from the obscurity of the
Castle of Miramare on the Adriatic Sea, the quixotic Austrian archduke Maximilian
von Habsburg (1832–1867), who would rule as Emperor Maximilian I of Mexico.[7]

Velasco had begun his official artistic training at the Academia de San Carlos in
1858. When it was founded in 1783, it was the first academy of art in the Americas,
with a curriculum derived from the art schools that had been established in Europe
throughout the eighteenth century, especially the Real Academia de Bellas Artes
de San Fernando in Madrid, inaugurated in 1752.[8] It boasted a large collection
of plaster casts of antique sculptures, laboriously imported from Spain, that were
foundational tools for the teaching of drawing and modelling, but also for inculcating
Mexican students with European artistic ideals, often called *buen gusto* in the
discourses of the period.[9] Many of the institution's early directors and teachers
were Europeans, principally Spaniards, and this preference for European instructors

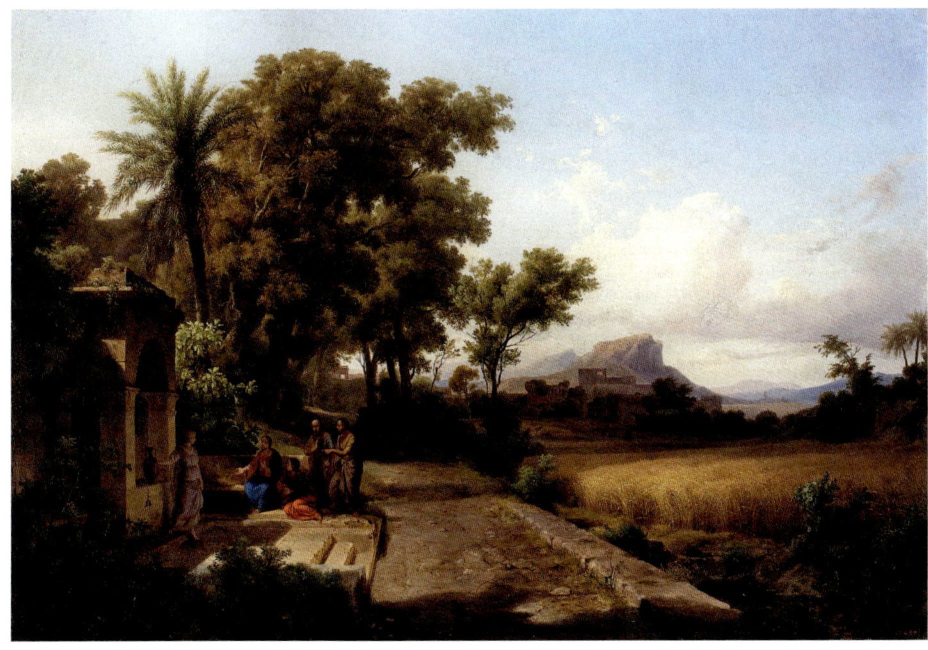

held true long after Mexico's independence. The professor of landscape painting during Velasco's student years, who would become his lifelong mentor and close friend, was the Italian artist Eugenio Landesio.[10] It is impossible to understand the progression of Velasco's art without reference to Landesio, whose ideas and compositional techniques his pupil emulated and, eventually, developed into his own distinctive visual idiom.

Born on the outskirts of Turin, Landesio first studied in Rome at the Accademia di San Luca and then worked in the studio of the Hungarian painter Károly Markó, an exponent of a style of landscape painting that drew inspiration from the orderly, classicising canvases of the great seventeenth-century French painters Nicolas Poussin and Claude Lorrain.[11] The ascent of landscape to the standing of a genre worthy of high artistic endeavour was achieved only in the early decades of the nineteenth century when, in 1816, the French academy established a prize for *paysage historique* (historical landscape). Across Europe in the decades that followed, landscapes began to emerge from the distant backgrounds of large, moralising historical and religious paintings to become subjects in their own right, bearers of narrative and meaning. The works that Landesio made in Italy, like Markó's, evoke the warm Mediterranean tones and rigorous compositions of paintings by Claude and Poussin, sometimes linking them to biblical scenes, as in Markó's *Christ and the Woman of Samaria* (fig. 9). In this painting – sent to Mexico for exhibition in 1854 – the nominal subject occupies only a small segment of the foreground, with the rest of the canvas given over to the representation of a swathe of light-dappled wheat, closely observed trees and

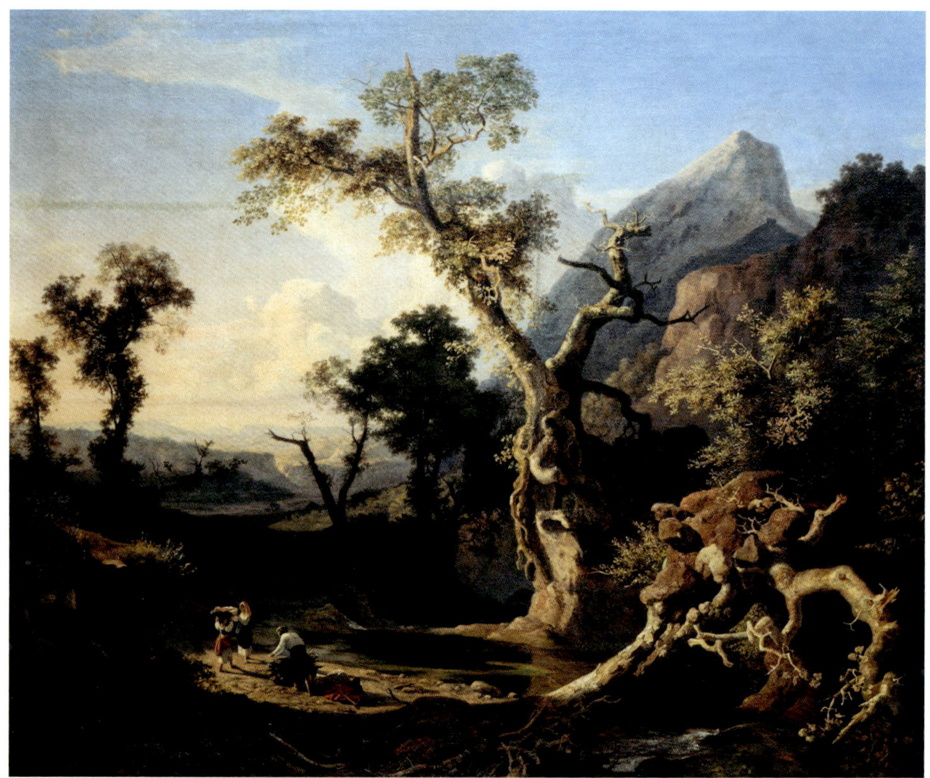

foliage, and scudding wisps of cloud.[12] Landesio, for his part, usually painted works that depicted contemporary life, even if they were idealised, untroubled scenes of pastoral repose or labour, like *The Apennines and Sub-Apennines* (fig. 10), which was shown in Mexico and acquired for the Academia's collection before Landesio himself had crossed the Atlantic.[13] Accompanied by two female figures, a man lashes together a bundle of wood on a sunlit bank in the hills east of Rome, his axe resting on the ground behind him. The undeniable protagonist of the picture, however – and a possible inspiration for Velasco's *A Rustic Bridge in San Ángel* (cat. 7) of 1862 – is a canting, knobbly tree, which presides over the stream descending into the valley in the far distance. The painting is probably the pendant to Landesio's view of Vallinfreda, which Velasco, according to his unpublished autobiographical notes, copied in the late 1850s, around the same time that he made copies of two paintings by Markó that were also in the collection of the Academia de San Carlos.[14]

Landesio became professor of landscape painting and perspective at the Academia in 1855.[15] When he arrived, landscape was still a largely unknown genre in Mexico. Landesio's first biographer wrote that Pelegrín Clavé, the Catalan director of painting at the academy, 'had taught it, but in a very limited way, and the landscapes that up until that time had arrived in the Republic were not sufficiently

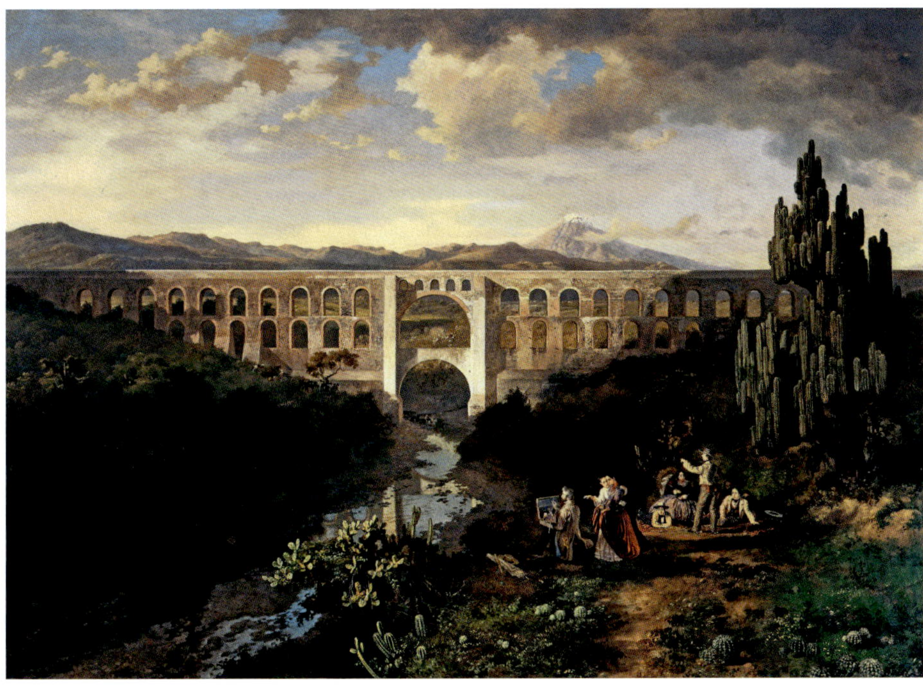

remarkable to attract attention or give a complete idea of the genre'.[16] The Italian's works, rich in detail and painted in deep, saturated colours, represented a significant advance on the winsome views and ethnographic studies made in the preceding decades by the so-called traveller-artists, Europeans who stayed in Mexico for relatively brief stretches, such as the British painter Daniel Thomas Egerton and the German Johann Moritz Rugendas.[17] Confronted with the grandeur of Mexico's natural beauty, Landesio applied the talents he had honed in Italy to the painting of local scenes. He made pencil drawings and oil sketches out of doors before later developing and refining a final composition in his studio, a method that he also prescribed to his students at the Academia.[18] Not long after his arrival in Mexico he portrayed himself at work – brushes and palette in hand and a portable painting box balanced on his knees – in *The Hacienda of Matlala* (fig. 11). This canvas, which features an imposing cactus similar to one that Velasco would paint many years later (cat. 11), was made for the prosperous Spanish-born architect Lorenzo de la Hidalga, who also appears in the picture, gesturing towards the view that Landesio sketches.[19]

Velasco's years of study under Landesio, who can be regarded with some justification as the progenitor of Mexican landscape painting, inflected his early work with a distinctly European sensibility.[20] These paintings, as well as Landesio's, were appreciated by Mexico's Austrian emperor, as well as a coterie of conservative Mexican figures, many with connections to Europe. In 1866 Velasco painted the

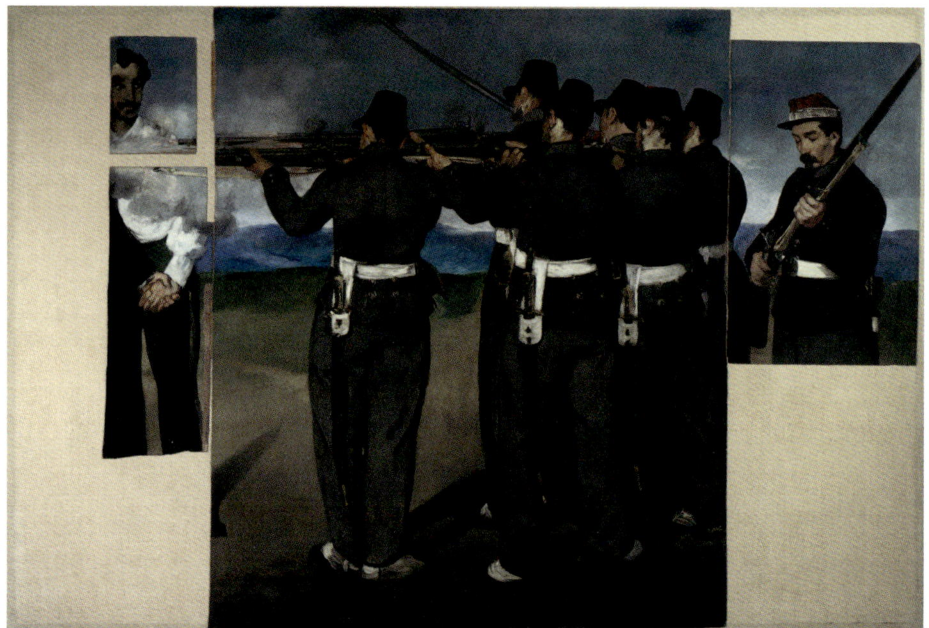

empress Carlota (1840–1927) and her retinue passing through the Alameda, a park in the centre of Mexico City (see fig. 2). He was also reputed to have portrayed Maximilian himself in 1867, though the painting, perhaps based on a photograph, has not come down to us.[21] Velasco's association with the emperor was regarded with suspicion by Mexican liberals, especially after the collapse of his regime, called the Second Mexican Empire (1863–7).[22] During his brief reign, Maximilian attempted to chart a course between the demands of Mexico's liberal and conservative factions while relying on the force of French arms to safeguard his hold on power.[23] When Napoleon III precipitously withdrew French troops and, with them, his support for the puppet leader he had risked so much to install, the Austrian's days were numbered. Rather than flee, Maximilian fought on until he was captured in May 1867 in Querétaro. Despite appeals for clemency from foreign emissaries, he was executed by firing squad, along with his generals Miguel Miramón and Tomás Mejía, on a rise near the city known as the Hill of the Bells (Cerro de las Campanas) on 19 June. The event captured the imagination of Edouard Manet, whose famous series of paintings of the execution, which employed details gleaned from press accounts, offered a sombre reckoning with the tragic consequences of the French imperial adventure in Mexico (fig. 12).[24]

The circle that had formed around Maximilian's court included some of Velasco's most assiduous patrons. In an annotated list of his paintings that the artist compiled towards the end of his career, he named the owners of many of his works.[25] Among those to whom he sold multiple works were two of Maximilian's medical staff,

Federico Semeleder, from Austria, and František Kaska, who hailed from Bohemia, then an Austrian territory and now part of the Czech Republic.[26] After Maximilian's death, both men remained in Mexico, where Kaska seems to have acted as an unofficial diplomatic representative for the Austro-Hungarian Empire. No fewer than eight paintings by Velasco were in the Czech's possession when he died in Mexico City in 1907, making him one of Velasco's most important collectors (cats 3–5).[27]

The names of many other foreigners appear on Velasco's list, suggesting the enduring appeal of his work for those from beyond Mexico's borders, as well as his increasing renown in his own country. The prominent Italian tenor Enrico Tamberlik, who came to Mexico to perform in the 1871 premiere of the opera *Guatemotzin* – which boasted stage decorations inspired by the Mexica *Codex Mendoza* – acquired a painting by Velasco during his stay.[28] Hermann Stiegler, who worked for a business established in Mexico City by the Boker family, a dynasty of German merchants, owned another work, as did Donato de Chapeaurouge, a German banker, who appears twice in Velasco's notes.[29] The recurring references to Leopoldo Weber, a German who ran a jewellery business in the capital, suggest that he was an especially avid collector of Velasco's landscapes. An Englishman, a certain Mr Campbell, also makes three appearances on the list, along with a Mr Barge of Philadelphia, a number of unnamed American businessmen, and Lucien Delacre, a resident of Paris.[30] While the collecting and dispersal of Velasco's work has so far been afforded little scholarly attention, it is notable that so many of his paintings seem to have been bought by people with strong ties to Europe and the United States.[31]

During the 1870s, Velasco flourished. He began to paint the sweeping views of the Valley of Mexico that would become not just his stock-in-trade but the highest expression of his artistic vision. After securing the position of professor of perspective at the academy in 1868, he was able to dedicate himself completely to his art. It was then that Velasco cast off the romanticising idiom of his teacher – Landesio resigned from his teaching position in 1873 and returned to Italy in 1877 – and replaced it with an austere and lyrical style all his own.[32] In an insightful review of the first retrospective exhibition of the painter's work, held in 1942 at the Palacio de Bellas Artes, the Nobel Prize-winning Mexican writer Octavio Paz characterised Velasco's paintings as 'an unmoving reserve, which belongs not to abandonment, but to equilibrium, to that pause in which everything ceases and stops briefly before transforming itself into something else'.[33] The sober architecture of his great paintings of Mexico City and its surroundings have their roots in Landesio's precepts, as can be seen in Velasco's first large-scale painting of the subject, *The Valley of Mexico from the Hill of Atzacoalco* (see fig. 5), completed in 1873. In the foreground a group of indigenous women make an offering to an image of the Virgin of Guadalupe, Mexico's most important religious icon, who was venerated at the late seventeenth-century basilica that rises up behind the hill in the middle distance. Beyond, the plain unfurls towards Mexico City, with a steaming train traversing the flat expanse. As in his later paintings of the subject, Velasco fuses the pre-Hispanic and colonial history of Mexico with the onrush of industrial modernity. While there is no record of its early travels beyond the annotations in Velasco's list, the painting – proudly inscribed with the legend 'José Mª. Velasco painted Mexico' on a sunlit rock outcropping on the lower left – was apparently sent abroad.[34]

By the time he painted his masterful views from the hill of Santa Isabel in 1875 (cat. 15) and 1877 (cat. 17), Velasco owed little to Landesio. Especially in the painting from 1877, he eschews the human figure – so important to Landesio's art – entirely, favouring instead the small but significant episode of the eagle and nopal (prickly pear), an oblique reference to the mythic founding of Tenochtitlan, the Mexica capital that lies beneath modern Mexico City.[35] Velasco's paintings of the valley quickly became well known in Mexico, winning medals at the exhibitions of the Escuela Nacional de Bellas Artes . He also began to send his paintings to international exhibitions. Both of his great views from Santa Isabel were sent shortly after they were made to foreign exhibitions, where, in these decades, landscape had displaced narrative history painting as the most important artistic representation of a nation.[36] After the 1875 painting was displayed the following year in Philadelphia at the Centennial Exposition, where it won a prize, Velasco must have felt that he should aspire to more.

The painting he made in 1877 was expressly intended, he later wrote in his annotated list, to be exhibited in Paris at the Exposition Universelle of 1878.[37] Mexico, however, was still a pariah in Europe following the execution of Maximilian and had no official presence at the great exhibition. Velasco therefore arranged to have his painting transported, at his own expense, to be displayed in the Spanish section of the fine arts pavilion.[38] There, in a review that has escaped previous notice, it was compared somewhat disfavourably but tellingly by Léonce Dubosc de Pesquidoux to the glittering landscapes of the Spanish painter Martín Rico.[39] For the French critic, 'a *Vue de la vallée du Mexique*, by M. Velasco, methodical, ample, polished, gives an idea of the barren, naked immensity of Mexican perspectives. But M. Rico would have seen and rendered the place differently; he would have made the sky glow, the earth sparkle, and found in the tropical desert a dazzling canvas.'[40] While it is improbable that Velasco learned of this appraisal – which contrasts the dispassionate, stolid grandeur of Velasco's art with Rico's charming, fashionable legerdemain – he was hopeful that his ageing teacher Landesio would be able to see the painting in Paris. He informed him in a letter that his most recent painting of the Valley of Mexico was on display at the exposition, and studiously asked for his opinion: 'I would be grateful if you could tell me how you find it, my recent painting. This judgment will be more useful to me than any other, because no one will see this

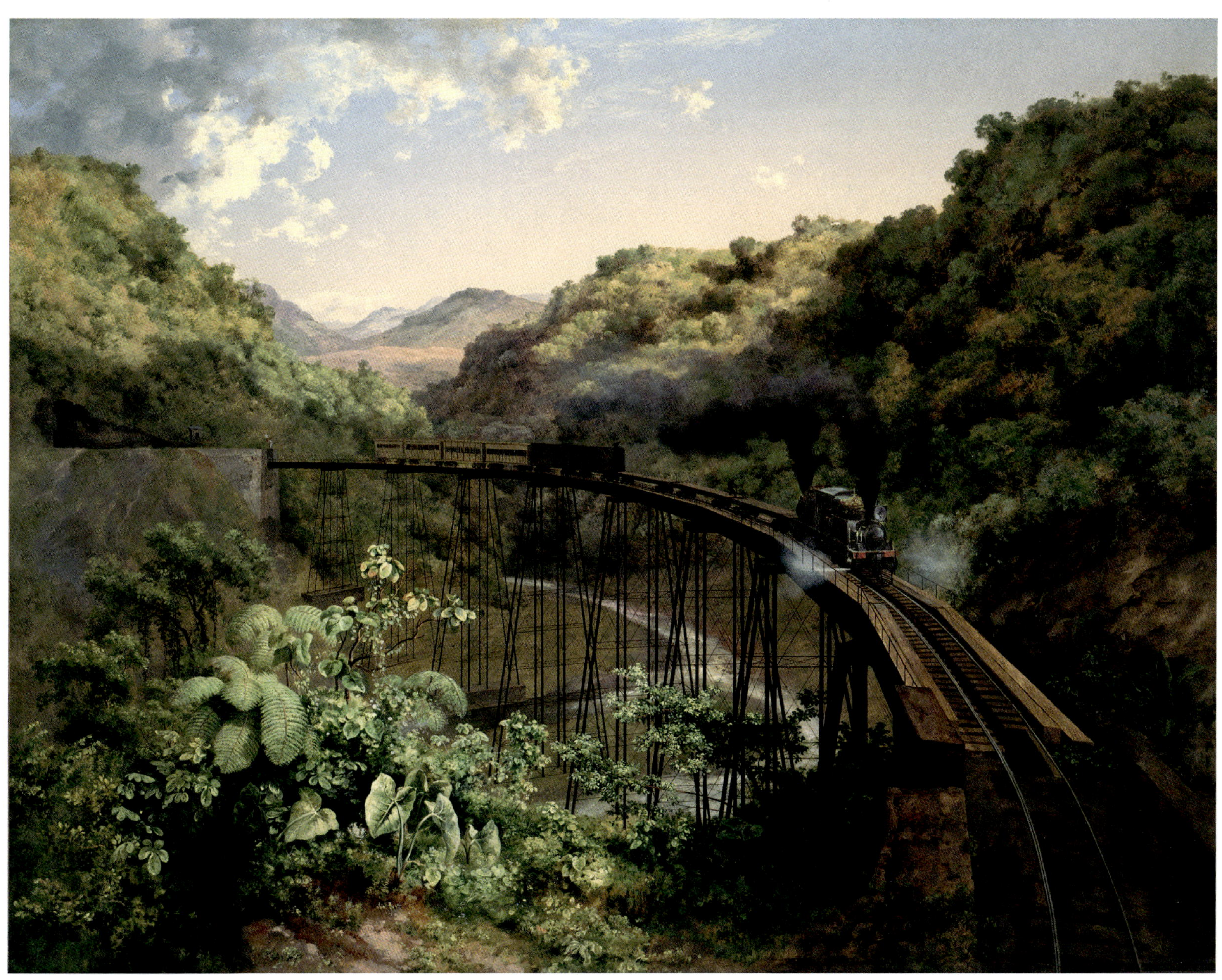

matter with more interest than you.'[41] Apparently Landesio, who had only months to
live, did visit Paris during the exhibition – in the company of his old colleague Clavé,
who had returned to Barcelona from Mexico in 1868 – and approved of his pupil's
great masterpiece, but no record of his reply, if there was one, survives.[42]

As Velasco's reputation grew at home and abroad, political circumstances in
Mexico began to stabilise, though only with the advent of an authoritarian regime.
In 1876 the military leader Porfirio Díaz (1830–1915), who had fought with Juárez,

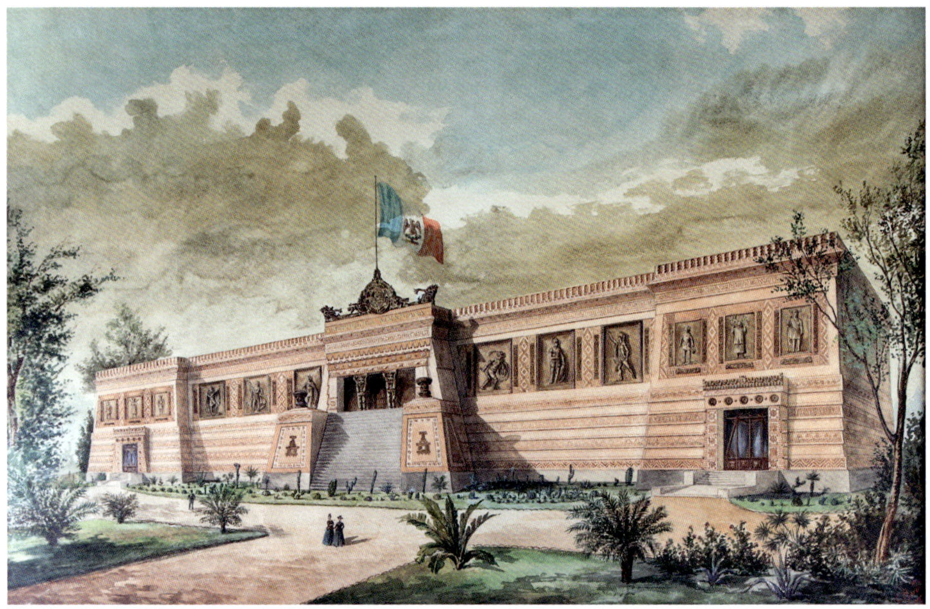

proclaimed his opposition to the sitting president, Sebastián Lerdo de la Tejada (1823–1889). After a series of conflicts, Díaz definitively took the presidency in 1877, which he then held, with several brief interruptions, for more than thirty years during a period that came to be called the Porfiriato.[43] A de facto dictator, he was only driven from office in the early stages of the Mexican Revolution (1910–20). The economic boom of the early decades of Díaz's administration was driven by its receptive attitude towards foreign investment and a positivist faith in economic development as a panacea. High-level Porfirian administrators were known as *científicos* (men of science) for their technocratic approach to governance, which often exacerbated existing social inequities and increased Mexico's dependence on foreign markets. Velasco has occasionally been considered, with some distaste, an adjunct to the Porfirian project, whose paintings might be seen to unreservedly celebrate the advances of the modern age, like the railways that began to criss-cross the country (fig. 13), and its cultural norms, including the regime's ambivalent attitude towards Mexico's indigenous groups.[44] His cerebral, serene art, however, eludes so simplistic an interpretation, even if, as the painter noted in his list, several of his paintings were purchased by Díaz himself.[45]

During the Porfiriato, Velasco's paintings were occasionally used as diplomatic gifts. The celebrated American general and president Ulysses S. Grant (1832–1885) apparently received two of the artist's paintings from the Mexican government.[46] And Pope Leo XIII (1810–1893) was twice presented with his paintings, once by the archbishop of Oaxaca, Eulogio Gillow y Zavalza, who gifted him a view of the city's imposing Baroque cathedral. Kaska sent the pontiff another painting by Velasco, a

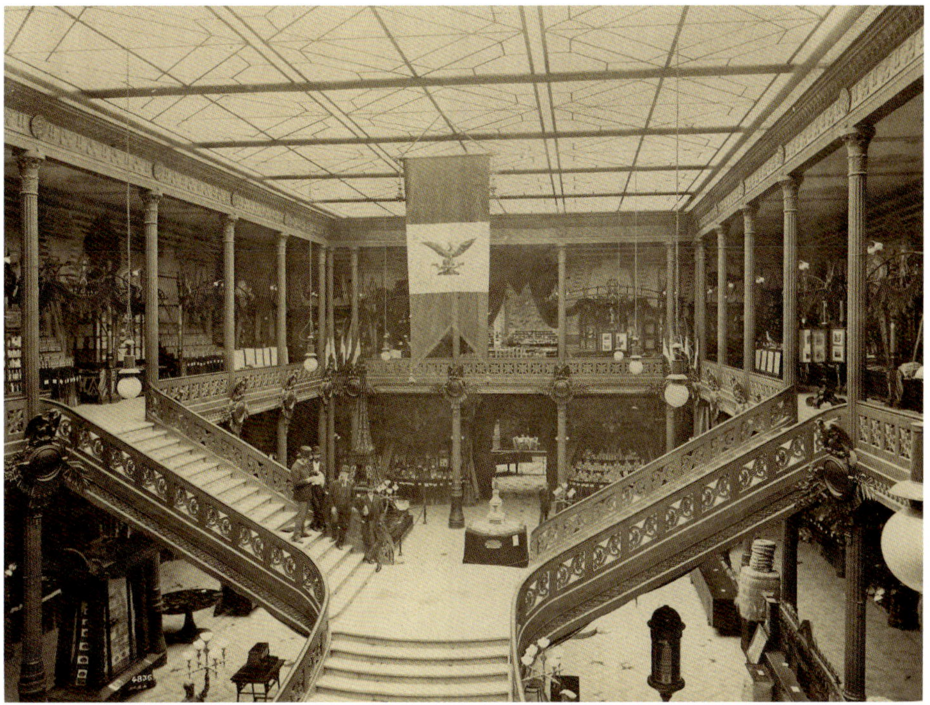

reduced version of *The Valley of Mexico from the Hill of Santa Isabel*. The artist, as was common practice in the nineteenth century, made numerous repetitions of his most famous compositions to be sold to collectors, incorporating small changes in each.[47] In the version in Kaska's own collection, now in Prague, Velasco added a riot of green foliage, not present in the 1877 painting (cat. 17), to the gully on the right, while removing several clouds in the upper left corner, streamlining and simplifying the image.

In these years Velasco's works were stalwarts of Mexico's contributions to international exhibitions.[48] It was only in 1889, however, as he approached 50 years of age, that the painter himself set out on his first-ever foreign journey. At the Exposition Universelle in Paris, where he travelled with his son Francisco Velasco Sánchez Armas, Velasco was head of Mexico's fine arts delegation, responsible for the display of artwork inside the Mexican pavilion, a building designed to resemble an ancient Mesoamerican temple (fig. 14).[49] In a photograph taken inside the pavilion, a bearded Velasco stands on the staircase in the middle of a group of three men, surveying the interior (fig. 15). While none appear in the photograph, Velasco displayed more than sixty of his own works, which made up the vast majority of the paintings on display in the Mexican pavilion. Indeed, he exhibited more works than any other artist at the entire Exposition Universelle.[50] The particular qualities of his work were recognised by at least one French critic, Léon Cahun, who dedicated several paragraphs to Velasco, writing that 'there is a landscape school in Mexico that does not owe anything to anybody, that is not imitating anybody, that has developed by itself…. The art of M. Velasco differs from that of Corot or Rousseau, like a landscape in Mexico differs from a landscape in the valley of the Seine, but it is no less sincerely explained … M. Velasco is a true painter and his paintings are the robust and healthy daughters of his native soil.'[51] Few other notices about how Velasco's work was received in Paris have been preserved, save for a brief comment in a letter that suggested that the eminent French painter Jean-Louis-Ernest Meissonier, who served on the exhibition's jury, had not thought much of the Mexican's paintings.[52] Whatever Meissonier's opinion, Velasco was awarded a silver medal and made a Knight of the French Legion of Honour at the end of the Exposition Universelle.

The homesick letters that Velasco sent to his wife from Paris discuss his duties, the city, and the workings of the Mexican delegation during the eight months he spent in France between April and December 1889. For most of that time he lodged with his son at 68 Avenue Bosquet, in the shadow of the Eiffel Tower, across the street from the exhibition grounds on the Champ de Mars. What his letters fail to mention in any detail, save for passing comments, are his impressions of the paintings that he saw in Paris. His thoughts on contemporary art, however, were recorded in a report he submitted on his return to Mexico.[53] For Velasco, there was much to admire in the high finish and meticulous drawing of some French artists, but he condemned others for 'spreading paint with a spatula and large brushes, sculpting more than painting, disregarding form, correct proportions, and modelling'.[54] While it has sometimes been proposed that Velasco's style changed in the paintings he made after 1889, there is little to suggest, beyond a slight brightening of his palette in certain works, that he took any interest in the innovations of the Impressionists and their imitators.[55] Near the end of his time in Europe, Velasco and his son made two rapid tours, spending two weeks in Switzerland and Bavaria in late summer and, in October, several weeks in cities in France and Italy.[56]

Velasco undertook one more journey before returning to Mexico. In early December 1889, he travelled to London for several days. This short trip, which has received little notice, is confirmed by references in his letters. On 1 December 1889, Velasco wrote that 'tomorrow or the day after tomorrow we will tour London for just four days'.[57] In his next letter, dated 13 December 1889, he predicted that he and Francisco would have no trouble with the transatlantic voyage home, 'because we went to London and we did not get seasick on the crossing from Calé [sic]'.[58] Nothing more is known about the painter's brief stay in the English capital, but it is possible that he visited Juan González Asúnsolo, the father-in-law of his brother Antonio. González, a banker, had previously lived in Paris, where he had taken responsibility for receiving Velasco's painting when it was sent there in 1878.[59] He also owned two of the artist's paintings, which appear in Velasco's list with an annotation stating that they were in London.[60] It is uncertain whether Velasco visited the National Gallery

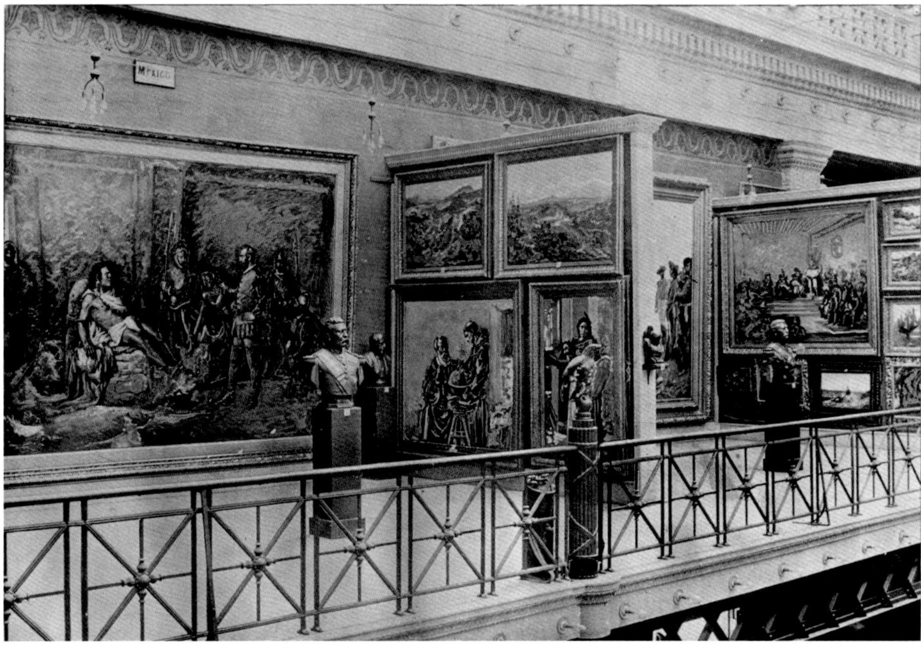

during his stay, but given his insatiable desire to see museums in Italy – which bored his son no end, as Francisco complained in a letter to his mother – it seems highly probable.[61] Soon after his visit to England, Velasco embarked from Le Havre for home, where he arrived in early 1890.

Velasco's next and final trip outside Mexico came in 1893, when he fulfilled a similar role to the one he had played in Paris, this time at the World's Columbian Exposition in Chicago.[62] This much shorter visit, which lasted just over two months and for which Francisco again joined him, was less to his liking, though he won a bronze medal. As in Paris, Velasco was the most-represented Mexican painter, showing 14 paintings, including at least one of his great views from Santa Isabel as well as his striking painting of a *cardón* cactus (cat. 11). In an engraving that records part of the Mexican fine arts display, several of his works are indistinctly visible, including the iconic cactus, which appears on the far right (fig. 16).[63] It is notable that in Chicago, more works by Velasco's students – such as Cleofas Almanza, Adolfo Tenorio and Carlos Rivera – were displayed than had been in Paris.[64] Many works by American landscape painters associated with the Hudson River School, such as Thomas Cole, George Inness and John Frederick Kensett, were displayed in Chicago, as they also had been in Philadelphia in 1876 , where a painting by Velasco was also on view (cat. 15).[65] While there are some superficial similarities between Velasco's expansive vistas and paintings by these artists, as well as their contemporaries Frederic Edwin Church and Albert Bierstadt, no direct connection can be ascertained, though Velasco may have known their works through prints or photographs.[66]

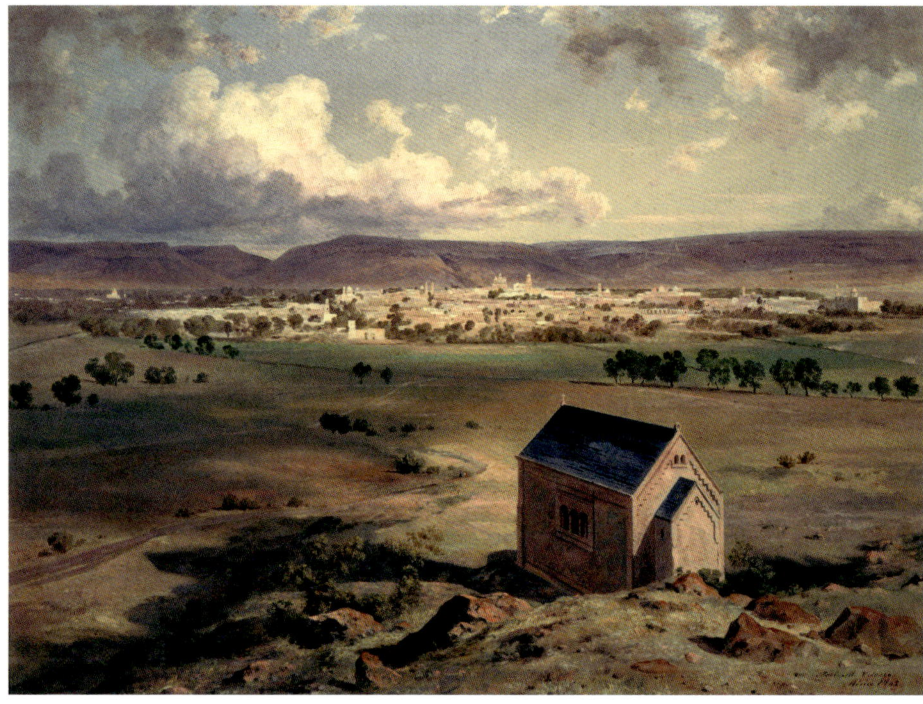

In the years that followed Velasco painted at a somewhat smaller scale than he had previously, but still often depicted the Valley of Mexico, though from different vantage-points than those he had explored before. One painting from this period, seemingly an outlier, represents a nondescript chapel on a hill outside Querétaro (fig. 17). This small memorial chapel, built in 1900 after the reopening of diplomatic relations between Austria and Mexico, was dedicated to Maximilian and erected on the site of his execution. The first version of this painting, now lost, was given to an Austrian delegation that attended the chapel's inauguration in spring 1901. The work, which Velasco made a copy of for his own collection, is a final testament to the international reach of his paintings. Through his friend and collector, the Czech pharmacist Kaska, Velasco met the visiting Austrians, led by a prince who had served in Mexico under Maximilian. They posed for a photograph in Querétaro: Kaska sits on the far left, Velasco's ample white beard stands out in the second row, and the man with his legs crossed is the prince, Carl Khevenhüller (fig. 18).[67] During a dinner that he hosted at his home, Velasco gave the Austrians his painting of the chapel as a gift.[68] Later that year he received word that he had been honoured by the emperor Franz Joseph, Maximilian's older brother, with the Knight's Cross of the Order of Franz Joseph, a decoration he sometimes wore on his breast alongside the medal of the Legion of Honour he had received in Paris.

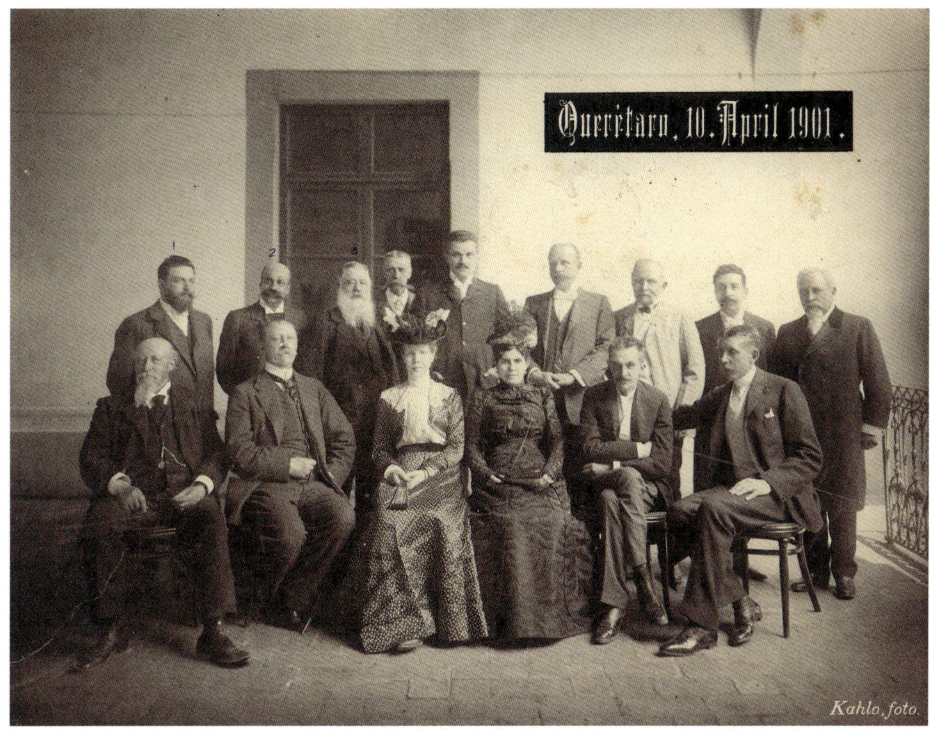

FIG. 18

VELASCO AND THE AUSTRIAN
PRINCES, 1901
JOSÉ MARÍA VELASCO ARCHIVE,
MUSEO KALUZ, MEXICO CITY

Velasco is now regarded as Mexico's greatest nineteenth-century painter. But in the decades following his death in 1912 he fell into obscurity, in part because, following the Mexican Revolution, his work was identified with the conservative culture of the Porfiriato. The next generation of Mexican artists also left behind his meticulous style of painting, taking up the Impressionists' loose handling and the expressive freedoms of Symbolism.[69] One of the artist's first biographers, writing only 20 years after his death, avowed that his account was 'an homage to a forgotten painter'.[70] Velasco's reputation was revived by the large exhibition held in Mexico City in 1942, after which his oeuvre was declared, by presidential decree, a national historical monument. Many of his works were sent to Philadelphia and Brooklyn soon after, in late 1944 and early 1945, and Velasco began to be integrated into the history of the arts of the Americas in the nineteenth century. Several of his paintings were part of large touring shows of Mexican art organised in the 1950s by the prescient cultural administrator Fernando Gamboa, a distant echo of the artist's robust presence at nineteenth-century expositions.[71] Then as now, Velasco's art, whether encountered in Mexico or abroad, conjures up the distinctive landscapes of the Valley of Mexico, identifiable but ethereal. Velasco's paintings, while grounded in the conscientious observation of his surroundings, are elaborated in an artistic idiom that he must have hoped would be seen and understood anywhere. Velasco was a great painter of Mexico. He was also – always – international.

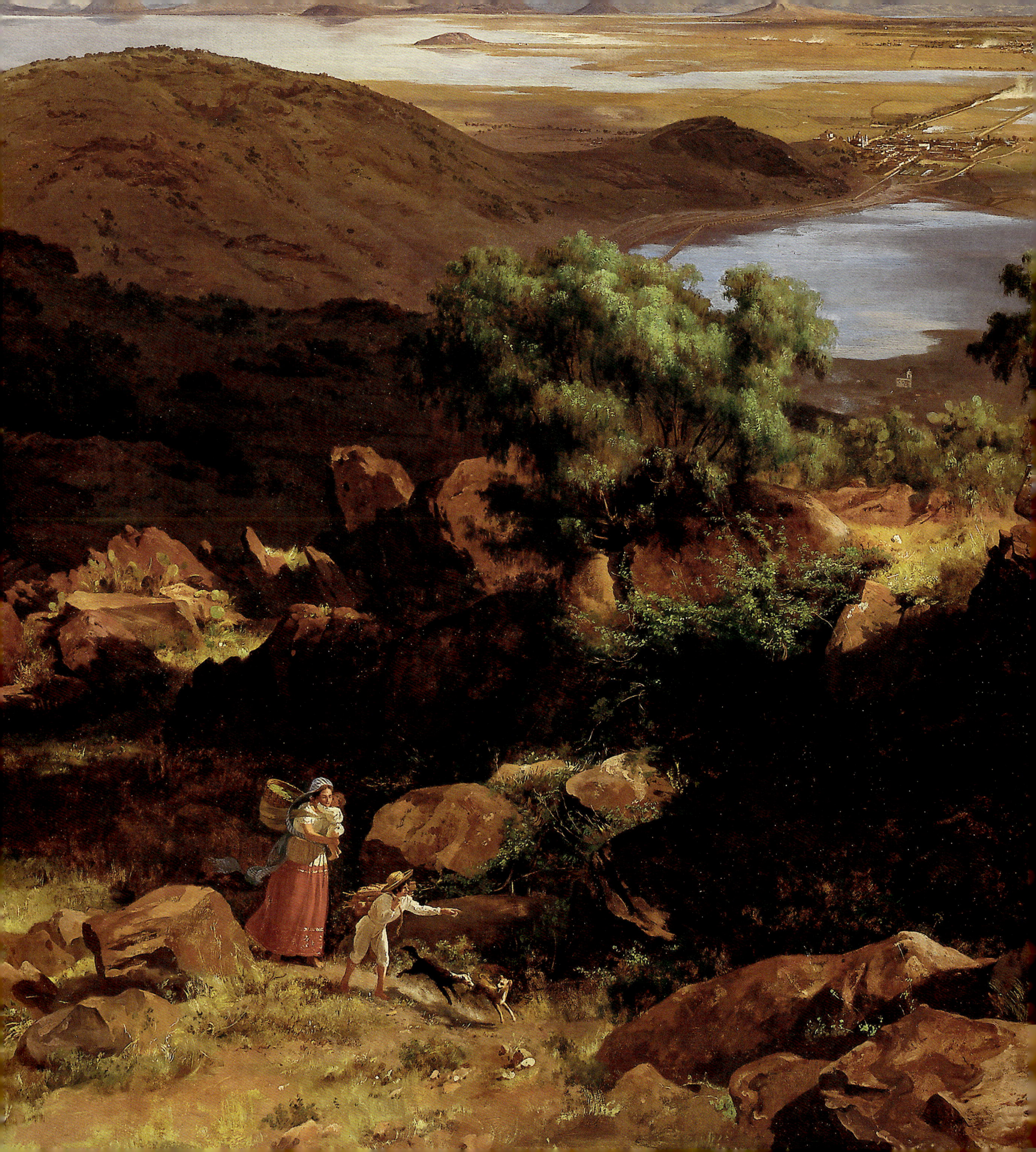

AT THE INTERSECTION OF ART AND SCIENCE

OMAR OLIVARES SANDOVAL

The landscape painting of the Americas during the nineteenth century offers a unique insight into the relationship between art and science, a relationship that is fundamental to modern perceptions of evolution and the natural world. José María Velasco's artworks in particular should be considered in light of the significant scientific developments that took place in his lifetime. During this period the disciplines of geology and biology, as well as the study of evolution, were consolidated in institutions in Mexico and around the world. Velasco's landscapes, along with his extensive production of scientific images, confirm his active role in a thriving culture of knowledge exchange and speak to his achievements as both an artist and a scientist.

Velasco is best known for his grand bird's-eye views of the basin containing Mexico City. A consistent theme, from his landscapes of the 1870s to his decorative programme for Mexico City's Instituto Geológico Nacional of the early 1900s, is the integration of a scientific perspective – drawn from disciplines including geology, biology, archaeology and medicine – with his artistic work.[1] While Velasco made contributions in all these fields, this essay focuses on his landscapes and botanical and zoological works from the 1870s, which positioned him at the centre of numerous research networks and coincided with the expansion of Mexico's scientific institutions as well as a number of related publications.[2]

It is not misleading to say that Velasco was a scientist as much as he was an artist. He studied botany and anatomy at the Escuela Nacional de Medicina and in 1865 he participated in a scientific expedition to the archaeological site of Metlaltoyuca, where he met geologists and geographers including Ramón Almaraz, the surveyor in charge of commissioning new scientific research in Mexico, and Antonio García Cubas, later the most renowned cartographer in the country.[3] Just three years later Velasco became a founding member of the Sociedad Mexicana de Historia Natural.

Velasco's apprenticeship with the Italian landscape painter Eugenio Landesio also helps to explain his deep engagement with science (fig. 19). A close acquaintance of the group of painters around German artist Johann Christian Reinhart, Landesio trained in Rome, where theories around landscape painting and its relationship with the study of the natural world flourished in the mid-nineteenth century.[4] This is evident in the importance Landesio placed in his teaching on drawing from life and his rejection of depicting generic fauna and flora, insisting instead on individual botanical and mineral forms. Many of Velasco's drawings demonstrate a meticulous observation of nature, especially his detailed studies of rocks and plants. Like Paul

Detail from *The Valley of Mexico from the Hill of Santa Isabel* (cat. 15)

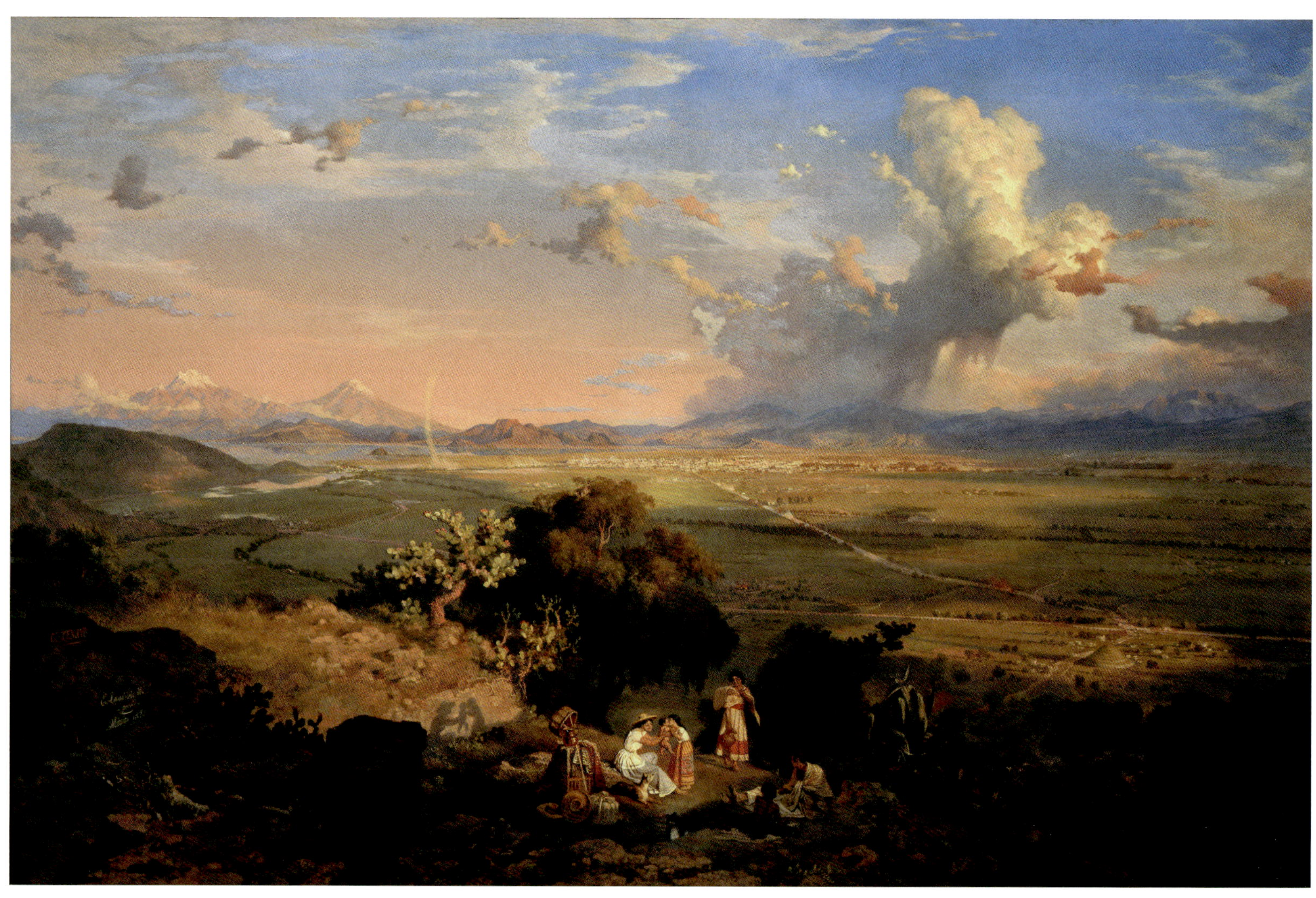

Cezanne in France in the mid-1860s and Thomas Moran in America in the 1870s, Velasco was intent on capturing the geological features of a landscape in his paintings.[5]

In the 1870s and 80s, Velasco developed large-format landscape paintings that fully immerse the viewer in the geological materiality of the space depicted. In his 1875 *Valley of Mexico from the Hill of Santa Isabel* (cat. 15), for example, the dramatic and rugged rock outcroppings of the foreground are clearly discernible. His skilful use of perspective creates a visual link with the distant areas of the basin, where hills and mountains form the horizon line. According to Velasco, this vast canvas was painted on site.[6] Although it is unclear, in practical terms, how he could have achieved this, the artist's avowed emphasis on field observation helps to explain the attention lavished in the final painting on many of the topographical and environmental features of the basin.

In the painting, various geological formations can be identified through changes in the colour of the ground, creating a visual parallel with contemporary geologists' descriptions. For example, in the foreground (the hill of Santa Isabel), we see red soils or 'red porphyries', while the hills that stretch to the lower parts of the basin present different colours: 'grey porphyries' (for the area of Guerrero in the middle ground) and 'yellow porphyries' (for the hills of Los Gachupines and Tepeyac in the background). These distinctions are consistent with classifications made at the time by geologists such as Mariano Bárcena, a significant figure in the field who was key to the promotion of science in Mexico.[7] Also in the foreground, Velasco consciously differentiates between several types of rock; the formation on the left, for example, has been carefully painted to represent pumice. Other geological and environmental features are identifiable elsewhere in the painting. Marks of erosion can be seen in the hills, with their lower slopes occasionally interrupted by areas of loose stones or screes. Further in the distance, patches of swamp at the water's edge indicate the drying up of the lakes in the basin. On Ajusco, the volcano clearly visible on the horizon at the far right of the painting, geological features formed by flowing water can be recognised, including a deposit of sediment known as an alluvial fan.

All these processes were described by geologists at the time as having been essential in the prehistoric formation of the basin. In 1874, the year before Velasco completed his painting, the scientist Juan N. Cuatáparo published a study of the geology of the basin, which in his view was shaped by both 'plutonic' (volcanic) and 'Neptunian' (water action) forces. He argued that the low areas had been formed by the erosion of rocks deposited by 'powerful currents of water', which continued in the present as 'eternal agents'.[8] The resonance of Velasco's landscape with these explanations suggests that the painter was eminently knowledgeable about the geological properties of Mexico City's basin.

This observation is supported by geologists' use of Velasco's painting. In 1876 *The Valley of Mexico from the Hill of Santa Isabel* was exhibited at the Centennial Exposition in Philadelphia, along with numerous works by Hudson River School painters, such as Frederic Edwin Church, Thomas Cole and Albert Bierstadt, many of whom had also engaged with the study of geology. Mexico's participation in the exhibition, with Bárcena as head of the delegation, was intended as a persuasive display of the country's mineral riches: a monolith of silver weighing 590 kilograms was transported to Philadelphia for the occasion. Bárcena used Velasco's painting to illustrate the geology of Mexico City's basin during a conference held at the Academy of Sciences of Philadelphia. He characterised the geological formations of the Valley of Mexico by pointing to Velasco's painting, making it the visual complement to his explanation. He referred to the work as 'a very accurate representation of that picturesque valley', in which 'there are found gathered by nature those most attractive accessories that a good artist tries to associate when he draws and invents

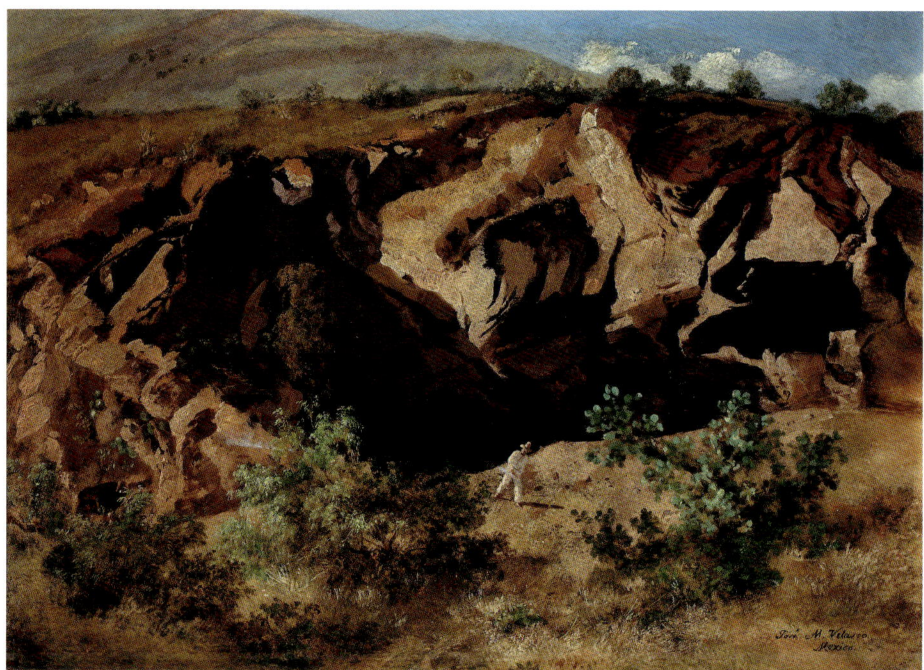

a landscape of the best taste and great effect: the most picturesque lakes, the fertile countryside, and the mountains crowned with perpetual snow.'[9] The most remarkable aspect of Bárcena's lecture is that he expressed his thoughts about geology using the aesthetic vocabulary of landscape painting. For him, it was not the aesthetics of the landscape that generated the picturesque; rather, he saw the geology of the valley itself as picturesque.

In a subsequent large-format painting from 1877 made on the same location, *The Valley of Mexico from the Hill of Santa Isabel* (cat. 17), Velasco elaborated on his earlier composition, symbolising his subject with a hunting bird catching its prey, evocative of the national emblem of the eagle and nopal. Nevertheless, he adhered to the same compositional strategy, assuming a bird's-eye view of the basin and rendering geological features with care.

Velasco did experiment with new compositions, sometimes immersing the viewer in the rocky terrain, raising the horizon line and paying barely any attention to the sky to create aerial views looking down towards the ground. An example is *Quarry at the Hill of Los Gachupines or Atzacoalco*, a view of a basalt mine in which a figure can be seen lighting a fuse (fig. 20). With its allusion to mining and the dramatic treatment of light and shadow emphasising the crevices in the rock, the painting is reminiscent of illustrations created by geologists and published in journals such as *El explorador minero* (1876–7). The foreground scene disappears in other views, such as in the series of paintings created between 1873 and 1876

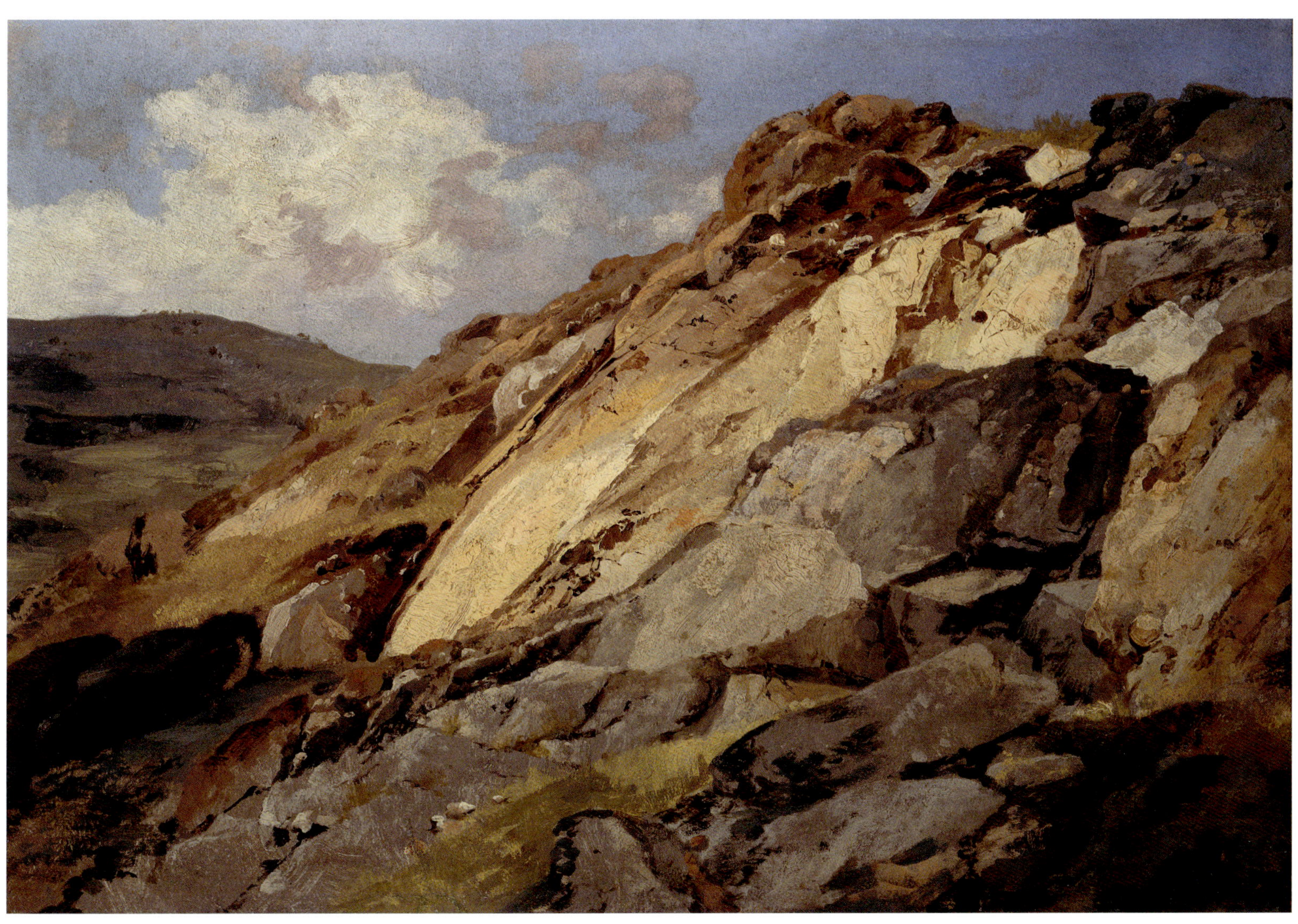

that includes *Rocks on the Hill of Atzacoalco* (fig. 21). Here the painter experiments with compositions that slice diagonally through the view, exposing rocks and vegetation in the foreground and sometimes a glimpse of Lake Santa Isabel in the background. Revisiting this subject with variations on many occasions, Velasco generated a series of observations of the lake's seasonal cycles.

Throughout the century, the management of water in Mexico City's basin was the subject of much discussion. During his stay in the city in 1803, the Prussian traveller Alexander von Humboldt suggested that, instead of completely emptying the bodies of water through drainage (which had been attempted during the colonial period), the construction of a hydraulic system could harness water from

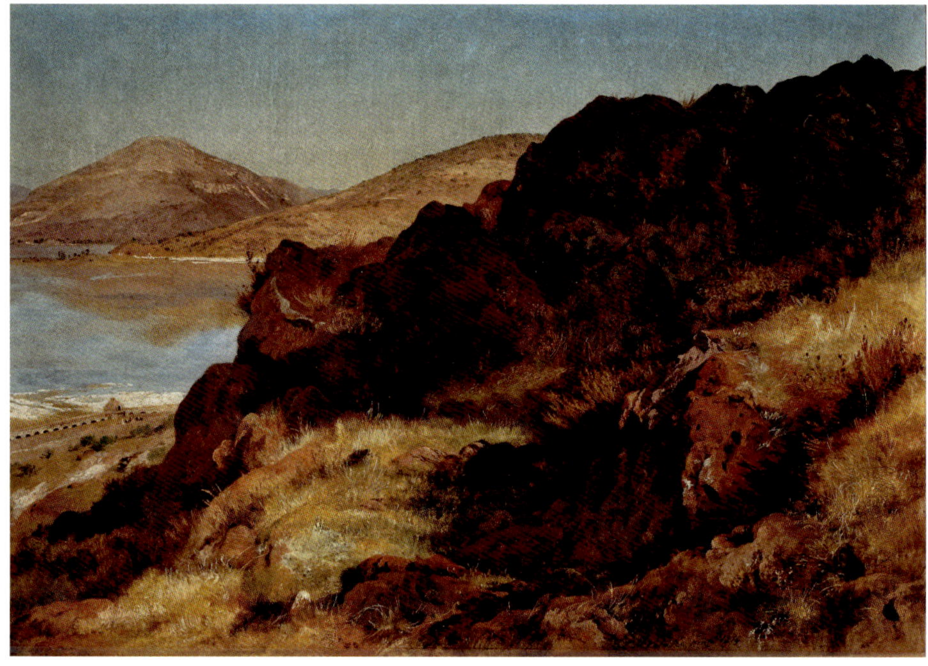

the northern lakes for agriculture.[10] Humboldt approached the issue holistically, pointing to the historic relationship between the climate, flora and inhabitants. In his 'Essay on the Geography of Plants' (1805), he proposed a 'science' of plant distribution, observing for instance that vegetation changed according to altitude.[11]

When the decision was made to build a general drainage system towards the north – which was eventually constructed between 1889 and 1900 – many hygiene experts and geologists held forth, some basing their views on Humboldt's earlier theories. In 1875 the physician José Lobato warned of the problems that completely draining the lakes would pose to the population's health, as the climate regulation provided by the water would be lost.[12] It does not seem a mere coincidence that in his large-format landscapes of the 1870s and his *Rocks on the Hill of Atzacoalco*, where Lake Santa Isabel appears in the background (fig. 22), Velasco detailed the recession of the water, the swampy areas and the lines left by the retreating shoreline. By 1879, when Velasco was studying the axolotl population in the lake, the environmental conditions of the site became an important factor in describing the development of these amphibians. Although made later, in 1885, and taking a lower viewpoint, his painting *Lake Chalco* also demonstrates his interest in representing the lake's seasonal cycles and the different vegetation that sprang up (cat. 5). The composition places the viewer above the lake, looking upwards along a vertical plane that extends from the water to the perpetually snow-capped volcanoes, echoing Humboldt's emphasis on changes in vegetation at different altitudes.

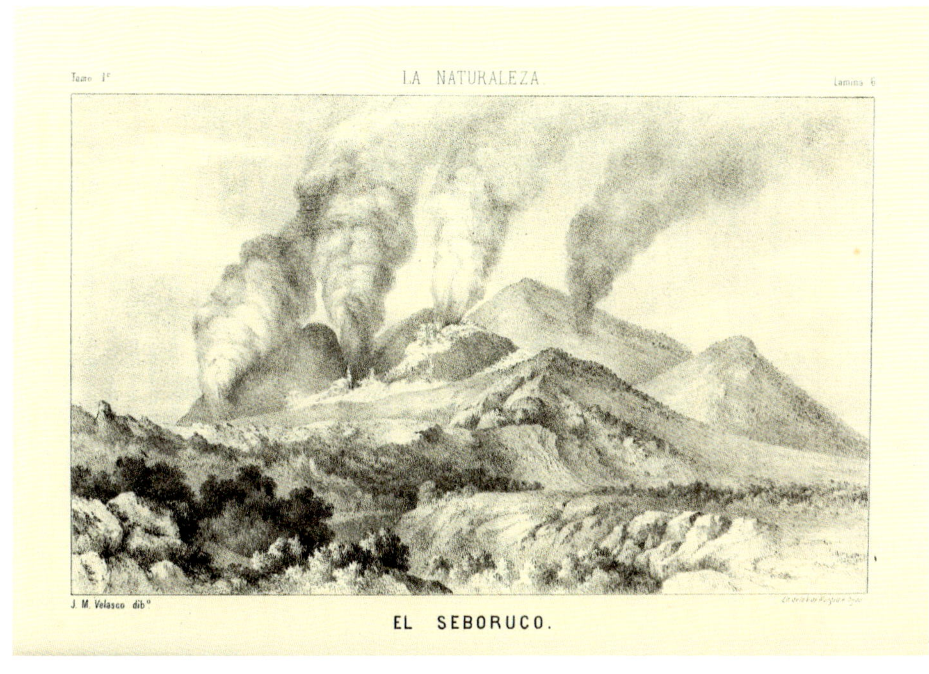

Velasco illustrated studies and reports for the scientific journal *La Naturaleza*, published by the Sociedad Mexicana de Historia Natural. Although these illustrations were often not signed, we can recognise the artist's distinctive touch in many of them. One image that does carry his name depicts the eruption of the Ceboruco volcano in the state of Nayarit in February 1870 (fig. 23). In this case, Velasco's original drawing has been preserved.[13] Over the course of a decade, the various eruptions of Ceboruco and the Colima volcano, near Mexico's Pacific coast, attracted the interest of geologists. Bárcena, for example, made Ceboruco a touchstone in his explanation of the regional nature of volcanic activity in the centre of the country and employed Velasco's images in his publications.[14] Key to the visualisation of the discipline of geology, Velasco's images of volcanoes appeared in both paintings and print media.

In 1869 Velasco devised a publication entitled *Flora del Valle de México* (*Flora of the Valley of Mexico*), which was published that year in instalments, with two plates in each. Despite the project's limited duration – only nine instalments were published – it would be significant for Velasco's later initiatives, notably at the Instituto Médico Nacional, where his students Adolfo Tenorio and Adrián Unzueta worked as botanical illustrators. The short-lived nature of the publication does not reflect Velasco's extensive work in the field of botany – evidenced by his large archive of botanical drawings and pressed plant specimens, much of which is now in the collection of the Museo Kaluz – nor does it do justice to the importance of the subject for his landscapes.

In assessing Velasco's publication, it should be recognised that few attempts had been made to publish the flora of Mexico extensively in the first half of the nineteenth century. The drawings made on the Royal Botanical Expedition to New Spain of 1787–1803 remained unpublished, and only *Nova Genera et Species Plantarum* (1815–25) by Humboldt and Aimé Bonpland included images of Mexican plants.[15] Even though Velasco's project came to an abrupt end, he had intended to follow it up with a comprehensive book on the plants of Mexico, first illustrating those found in and around the capital. While *Flora del Valle de México* records his initial impulse to create a national flora, in 1882 the artist insisted to his colleagues at the Sociedad Mexicana de Historia Natural that he wanted to create a 'Flora de los alrededores de México' (Flora of Mexico's Surroundings) and even a 'Flora universal iconográfica' (Universal Iconographical Flora).

Velasco's objective in all these projects was to illustrate the nation's plants, starting in the capital and spreading to all corners of the country, similar to the botanist William Curtis's *Flora Londinensis* (1777–98). Curtis, who established his own botanical garden in London, was a pioneer in producing publications such as *Curtis's Botanical Magazine* (1787–), which was continued in 1826 by the botanist and director of Kew Gardens, William Jackson Hooker. While it is not certain whether Velasco was familiar with Curtis's work, Hooker's was certainly known at the Sociedad Mexicana de Historia Natural. Like Curtis, Velasco was the driving force behind his own publication, but crucially he was also a field collector, draughtsman and lithographer, as well as a trained taxonomist. The large quantity of pressed plants collected and identified by Velasco himself indicates a thorough knowledge of the process of gathering and classifying plants as scientific specimens. Velasco wrote two botanical studies for *La Naturaleza*, for which he contributed detailed anatomical plant descriptions. One considered cacti in Mexico, while the other, co-authored with his brother, the physician Ildefonso Velasco, and the chemist Manuel Jiménez, explored a new species of Mexican morning glory, *Ipomoea triflora*.[16]

Two further differences can be observed between Curtis's publication and Velasco's *Flora*. By the middle of the century, lithographs had replaced copper engravings for printing botanical images. Velasco's plant illustrations are less linear and two-dimensional than Curtis's, with a more successful expression of volume and so different requirements in the final application of colour. Material analysis of Velasco's lithographs reveals that several hands worked to colour the images, using a mixture of artificial and organic pigments.[17] The illustrations display a careful application of colour that produces multiple tones for the green of the leaves and the colours of the flowers, differentiating light and shade and resulting in a sense of tangibility, as if the plant has been observed in the field (fig. 24).

Another notable difference from earlier works is that Velasco departed from the classification system developed by Swedish biologist Carl Linnaeus, instead using

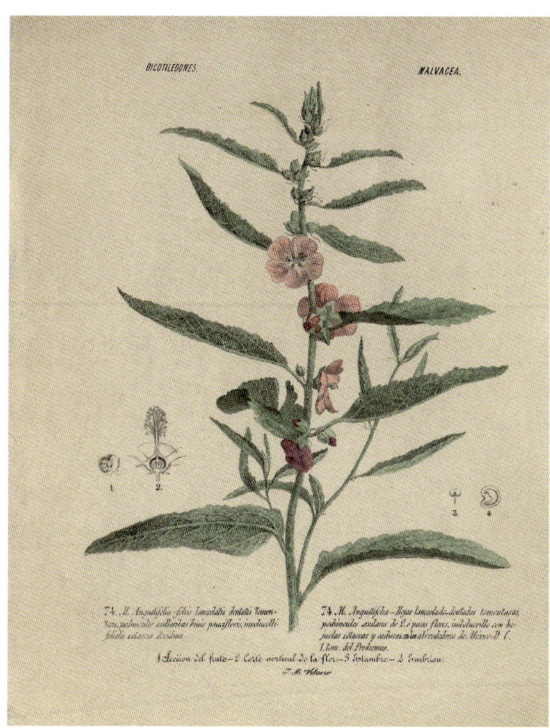

FIG. 24

'MALVA ANGUSTIFOLIA', PUBLISHED IN
FLORA DEL VALLE DE MÉXICO, 1869

the one created by Augustin and Alphonse Pyramus de Candolle in *Prodromus Systematis Naturalis Regni Vegetabilis* (1824–73). The use of this system, which focused on a broad range of a plant's anatomical elements rather than just its visible morphology, as in Linnaean classification, resulted in new visual demands that required greater knowledge on the part of the draughtsman. This increasing specialisation in botany allowed Velasco to exploit his skills as an artist and a taxonomist to the full.

As well as geology and botany, Velasco's scientific interests included zoology. During the second half of the nineteenth century, the axolotl, a gilled amphibian native to the lakes of Mexico City, became a focal point in debates about evolutionary theory. In 1879 Velasco contributed an article to *La Naturaleza* on the animal's anatomy, with three anatomical plates.[18] After its publication, Velasco found himself embroiled in a debate about the interpretation of the axolotl's anatomy and growth from an evolutionary standpoint. Velasco refuted evolutionary explanations, perhaps influenced by his religious convictions. However, it should be noted that his responses to his interlocutors in this discussion were based strictly on anatomical observation. The preparation for his article demanded that Velasco engage in deeper scientific reflection.[19]

To understand the controversy, it is important to bear in mind that the axolotl is an amphibian that begins its life under water before developing into a terrestrial animal. The species found in the Mexican lakes Xochimilco and Chalco, however, rarely undergoes this typical transformation into a salamander form – it remains an aquatic animal and does not transition to a life on land. In the early nineteenth century, naturalists such as Georges Cuvier questioned the axolotl's transformation into a terrestrial animal, but after 1864, when the newly appointed Commission Scientifique du Mexique sent live axolotl specimens to Paris for the Museum of Natural History during the French–Mexican War (1861–7), the transformation became known in wider European scientific circles. The fact that the axolotl rarely transformed raised several questions about its classification, its way of life, and the implications for evolutionary studies of remaining in a sort of juvenile stage of development, an observation that is now included in the field of developmental biology.[20]

Velasco's anatomical illustrations sought to demonstrate the final transformation of the axolotl into a terrestrial salamander. The first plate depicted a specimen with gills, the second a transformed axolotl (fig. 25), and the third presented Velasco's anatomical dissection of the two forms of the animal, which would later be reinterpreted within an evolutionary argument (fig. 26). After Velasco published his anatomical study, the neo-Darwinist August Weismann's views on the axolotl were published in *La Naturaleza* in 1880.[21] Weismann explained that the axolotl did not change because it had reverted to a younger form to adapt to its environment.

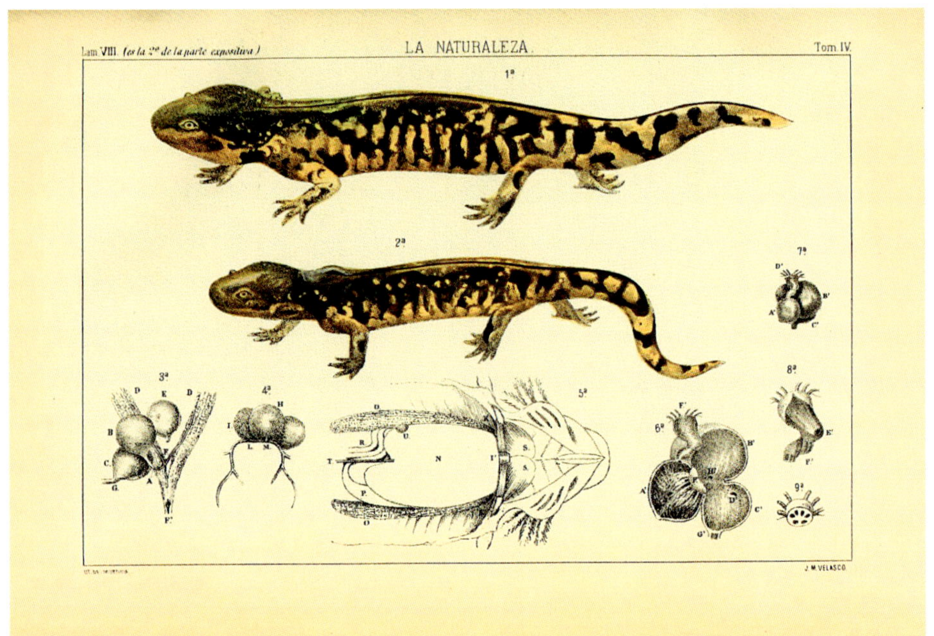

In a subsequent article, published alongside Weismann's text in *La Naturaleza*, Velasco responded to Weismann's views and offered a different opinion based on his research. He argued for a non-evolutionary explanation of the axolotl's transformation based on his anatomical comparison, arguing against Weismann's idea that the axolotl remained juvenile due to an adaptation mechanism and instead attempting to prove through his anatomical observations that the axolotl was always ready to undergo its transformation to a salamander form.[22]

Velasco's research and his images were significant for other reasons. Among the existing anatomical images of the amphibian, his plates were unique in showing a clear comparison between the two states of the axolotl in anatomical dissection. His work did not go unnoticed by zoological societies in Europe. Particularly in France, Velasco's study served as a reference point to either support or refute Weismann's views.[23] Weismann himself commented on Velasco's article in his *Studies in the Theory of Descent* in 1882.[24] He especially valued Velasco's work because it revealed another species of axolotl from Lake Santa Isabel, distinct from those found in other Mexican lakes.

This reception shows that Velasco's work was received in the context of evolutionary theoretical knowledge. One of Velasco's final remarks to Weismann sparked a debate about the difference between knowledge gained by observation and knowledge gained by experiment, in which Velasco argued for the primacy of the former over the latter. Indeed, the investigation of the axolotl marked a turning

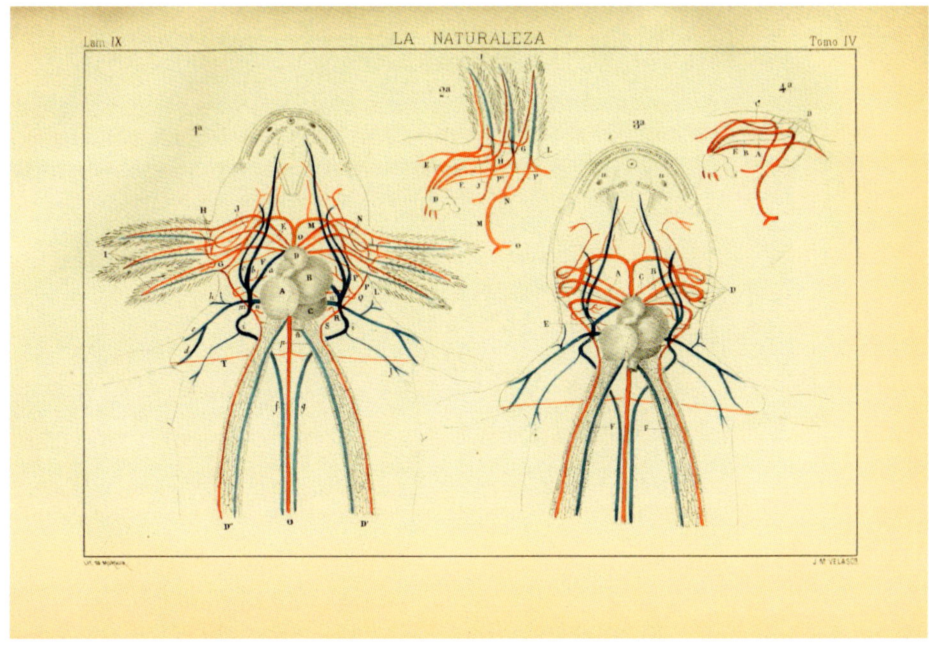

point in the expansion of experimental laboratory research and developmental
biology. Today, the descendants of the axolotls sent to France represent the oldest
self-sustaining population of laboratory animals.[25]

Velasco was immersed in a global network of scientific discourse, both as
a creator of images and as a scientist. His artistic activities and practice were
undoubtedly informed by his scientific interests. In the 1870s he synthesised his
knowledge of botany, anatomy and landscape painting to study the geological and
environmental conditions of the Valley of Mexico in his art. He conducted botanical
studies, proposed publications on local, national and global flora, produced
numerous illustrations and participated in debates on evolution. Rather than seeing
him as a polymath or someone who sought to fuse art with science, he appears
instead as an emblematic figure of his century, part of the significant expansion of
the visualisation of science that took place within institutions in the spirit of universal
and international collaboration. Those institutions needed artists, and Velasco's
remarkable capabilities as both painter and scientist allowed him to create new
knowledge through visual means.

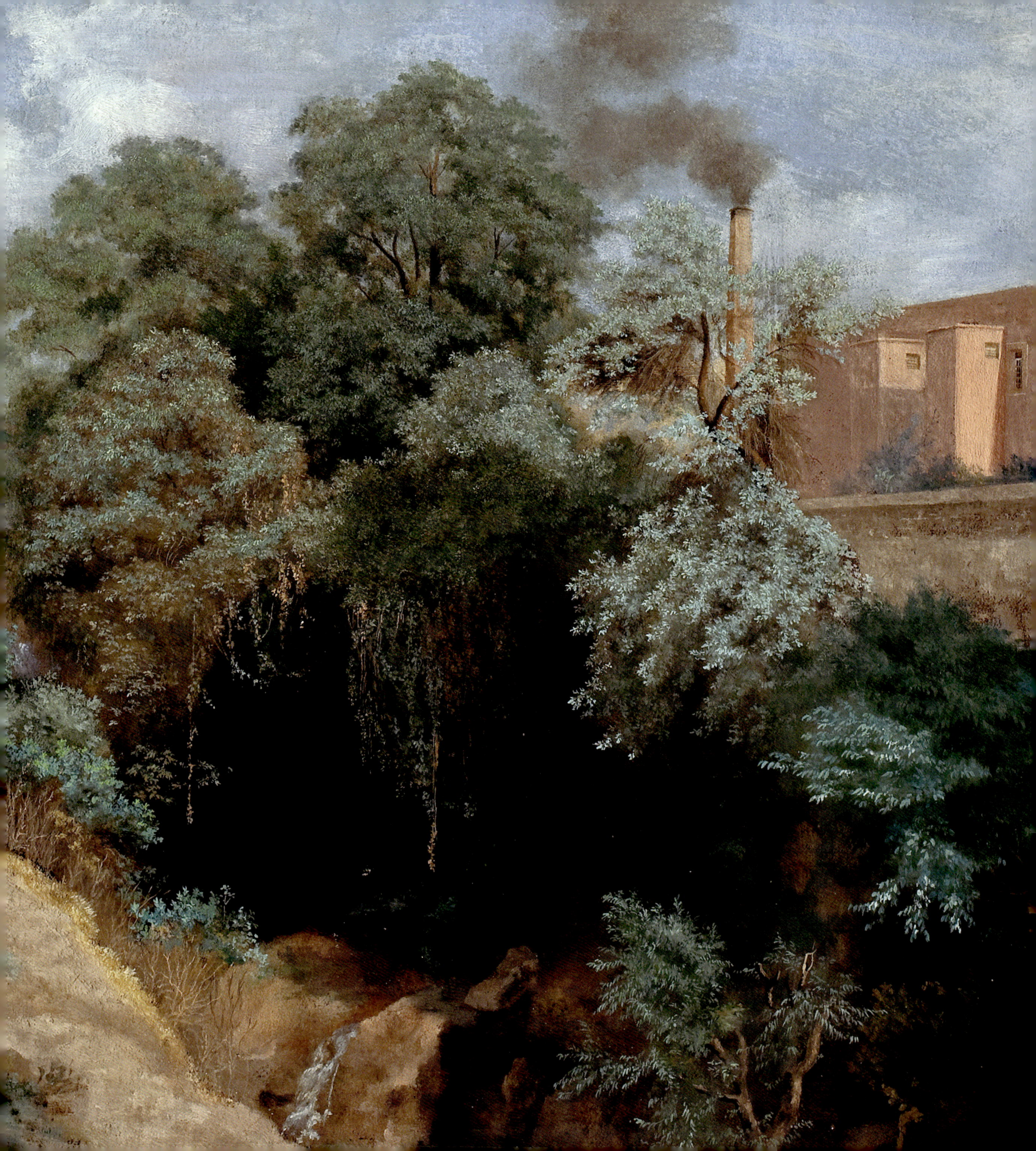

LANDSCAPE AS THE SITE OF CHANGE

DEXTER DALWOOD

If you drive heading north along Mexico City's Avenida de los Insurgentes, the road begins to gently climb as it passes the Basilica of Our Lady of Guadalupe. Within a few minutes, you are steeply ascending into the hills of the Sierra de Guadalupe. It's not easy to find the exact view that inspired José María Velasco to make his monumental 1877 canvas *The Valley of Mexico from the Hill of Santa Isabel* (cat. 17) but, with some effort, you can position yourself to see across the vast bowl of active and dormant volcanoes that border Mexico City today. Across this valley, as far as the eye can see, a man-made concrete carpet now completely obscures the lake that once filled this unique setting.

As in much of Velasco's work, this painting resonates with the rich tradition and history of European landscape painting, yet his rendition goes far beyond mere resemblance. Instead, Velasco used his profound understanding of his native landscape as a site of perpetual change to elevate his depictions of Mexico to new levels of pictorial intelligence. Before and during the regime of Porfirio Díaz, which lasted from 1876 to 1911, Mexico experienced rapid industrialisation, including the construction of railways, factories and power plants. For over a century, Velasco has been deployed as an essential figure in that generation of nation-builders. Still, his work has not been exhaustively appraised in the broader international context of mid-nineteenth-century painting and has rarely been exhibited in Europe since his lifetime. Like many of his peers in Europe and the Americas, Velasco enthusiastically followed the dizzying developments in scientific inquiry, fascinated by the burgeoning fields of geology, archaeology, botany, zoology, and particularly the latest theories on the age of the Earth: the basis of the landscape itself. Though his work has evident roots in the academic romanticism of European landscape painting, Velasco's attention to scientific observation produced a unique, distinctly Mexican realism. He fused a fixed, stable stare with mutable peripheral vision, volume with emptiness, and the suspension of time with the structural portrayal of clouds and landscapes marked by human activity, past and present, that also gestures towards an uncertain future.

During a visit to Mexico City's Museo Nacional de Arte in 2019, I encountered Velasco's work for the first time. While I was already familiar with twentieth-century Mexican painters such as José Clemente Orozco, David Alfaro Siqueiros, Diego Rivera and Frida Kahlo, I had little knowledge of Mexican painting from the previous century. This made me realise that, despite the importance of his achievements, Velasco is little known outside of Mexico. His best paintings draw you into their aura effortlessly, demanding a slower and more deliberate act of looking. It's as if he has the ability to slow down time and capture a moment, freezing it in front of you with a studied and persistent gaze that solidifies the view before your eyes.

The question of how and what to depict in a changing landscape had, of course, occupied painters in other parts of the world at the same time and earlier. Europeans had for years struggled with the question of how to represent the ancient and the modern in the same space.[1] Earlier in the nineteenth century, the British painter J.M.W. Turner captured the transformative change taking place around him in works like *Rain, Steam, and Speed – The Great Western Railway* of 1844, and *The Fighting Temeraire* of 1838, which reflected the demise of the era of tall ships in favour of steam.[2] Earlier still, John Constable painted landscapes of atrophy, possessed with a longing for the recent past. But while Velasco shared Constable's powerful inclination towards order and harmony, he had little interest in either the sublime or the visual invention of idealised, quasi-Edens. Velasco's work focused, instead, on the relationship between humanity and the environment, and between the generations of peoples who have shared Mexico City's sprawling valley over the centuries.

When the Mexica arrived in the Valley of Mexico in the 1400s, they discovered an abandoned city, built more than a thousand years earlier, that they named Teotihuacán (meaning, in Nahuatl, 'the place where the gods were created'). They built a mythology around the ruins, linking themselves to the lost civilisation to justify their new dominance over the existing communities in the valley. Velasco's careful depictions of the high plateau went beyond a visual representation of space to inscribe his historical moment over and within the region's deep cultural and archaeological past. His interest in capturing the passage of time and change in the present also highlighted what came before: an implicit comparison of human influence on the landscape across lifetimes and civilisations.

As an artist, I see in Velasco's work a dedication to refinement and progression arrived at through reworking the same subject over a long period of time. The development of his painting is not guided by a constant search for new subject matter, but rather by a commitment to perfecting his skills while continually exploring a particular motif. For example, his numerous paintings of the volcanic peak of Popocatépetl demonstrate his careful observation and adjustments to the changes in the landscape. He meticulously documents the time of day, date and weather conditions, while also making bold compositional choices – at times positioning the vanishing point below the horizon line to draw the foreground closer to the viewer. These instances demonstrate his deep engagement with the practical aspects of painting, subtly reflecting the progression of his thoughts and concerns within his work.

At the beginning of the 1860s Velasco created two works with the same theme, both reflecting his new interest in juxtaposing the present with the past. The first, *The Goatherd of San Ángel* (cat. 1) from 1861, made on site, marked the beginning of his fascination with a particular way of painting a scene that moved away from

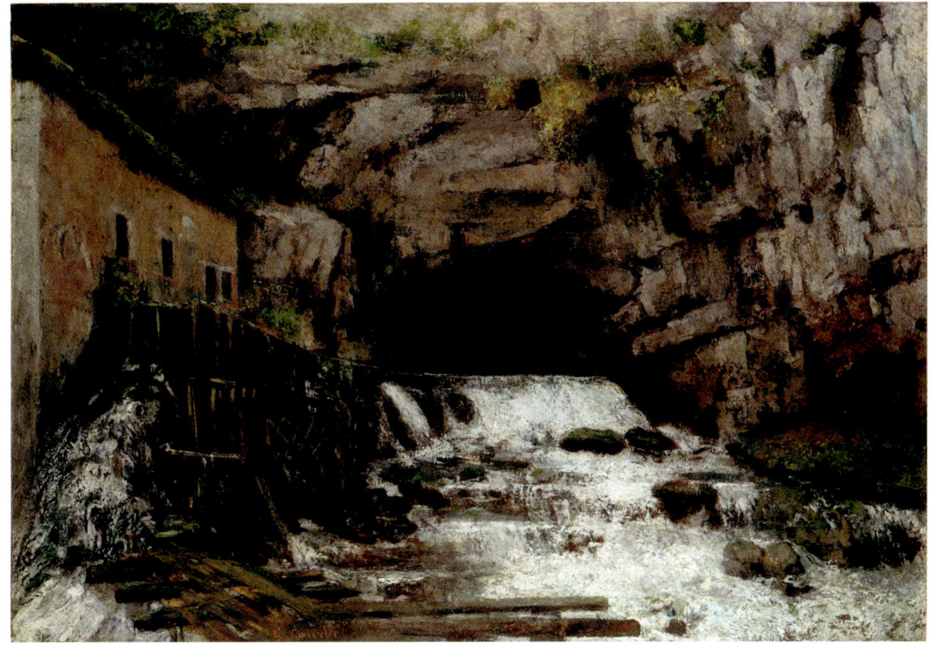

the soft romanticism that his Italian teacher Eugenio Landesio had brought to the Academia de San Carlos in Mexico City. This breakthrough painting heralded a cooler, empirically observed take on the *now*. The solid mass of a factory dominates the right edge of the small canvas, its smoking chimney an explicit contrast with the wild scene along the riverbank below: an encounter between the recent pre-industrial past and modernity. Velasco placed a concave space at the centre of his composition that recedes into darkness, an unusual compositional move that creates a void in the heart of the scene (see the detail on p. 50). He reduces the stream tumbling over a hydraulic dam on the Magdalena River to a trickle, a realistic evocation of the dry season in Mexico's highlands. The painting brings to mind Gustave Courbet's 1864 *Source of the Loue* (fig. 27), which similarly pondered the harnessing of natural power alongside man-made structures. In both works, the dark recess conjures a sense of the uncanny, drawing attention to the unfathomable mystery of nature, even when forced into the service of industry. In Velasco's realist rendering, the natural surroundings of the river lend a sense of bucolic order, while a curl of smoke rising into the sky and an uncoiling path in the opposite corner of the canvas together draw the viewer's attention back to that strange cave-like absence at its centre.

The second *Goatherd of San Ángel* (cat. 2), a larger version completed in the studio in 1863, adds a pair of human figures that provide a genuine sense of scale to the landscape, one perched on the factory roof, the other shepherding goats along the riverbank. Here, Velasco telescopes out for a more expansive view of the scene, rendered now with a natural droplet rainbow thrown up by the force of the waterfall crashing over the dam. White foam bursts through the sluice gates to balance the darkness of the central recess. The factory looms in this broader view, its static mass contrasted with the rhythmic, undulating leaves of an agave, foregrounded on the opposite bank.

In a work Velasco made nearly thirty years later, *Pico de Orizaba from the Hacienda of San Miguelito* (fig. 28), a severe horizon line bisects the painting: above it, the Pico de Orizaba, Mexico's highest mountain, soars over a volcanic range. Below that, a wisp of smoke escapes from a factory's smokestack, embedded in dense vegetation. A swirling spring breaks onto the surface in the immediate foreground: an emergent element. But the work has no fixed surface. Instead, it functions as a geological cross-section, describing different strata from the Earth's crust to the snow-capped volcano that surges upwards from the molten core.

In most museums across the world, collections of nineteenth-century painting adhere to a European canon of art history, with categories that are still easily recognised (Romanticism, Realism, Impressionism, Post-Impressionism). The singularity of Velasco's work becomes immediately apparent within the context of a collection like the National Gallery's, in which so many artists of the period ignored the radical changes taking place in their surrounding environments. It is worth noting that there are very few artists in the late nineteenth-century collection who depicted any obvious sign of the Industrial Revolution. Two examples include Georges Seurat, with his almost robotic workers lounging on a riverbank with smokestacks in the background (*Bathers at Asnières*, 1884), and Claude Monet, with his depiction of smoke spiralling into the cathedral-like vaults of a Parisian train station (*The Gare St-Lazare*, 1877).[3] Of all the Post-Impressionist painters, Paul Cezanne perhaps comes closest to Velasco's scientific frame of mind. Though he would not focus on rocks as a key subject matter until the 1890s, he became fascinated with geology, 'the new science, with Provence as his "laboratory"',[4] as early as the 1860s. 'In order to paint a landscape well', he wrote to Joachim Gasquet in 1897, 'I first need to discover its geological foundations.'[5] While Cezanne redefined the viewer's role in the act of looking, and thereby the game-changing physical form of painting itself, Velasco's ongoing project – empirical depictions of the Mexican landscape derived from science – centred on his profound commitment to a conceptual pictorial truth. The seemingly contradictory nature of these two approaches can be reconciled upon closer examination, as they were both motivated by a common enduring purpose.

Even still, Velasco's work presents us with a challenge: to truly diversify the Eurocentric canon of art history, we must not only recognise overlooked artists based on gender or race and from countries not previously considered of interest by European art historians or public alike, but also reconsider the timeline of modernism itself. By questioning the narratives that relegate academic painting to a lower rank than those included in the trajectory that led to modernism, we can

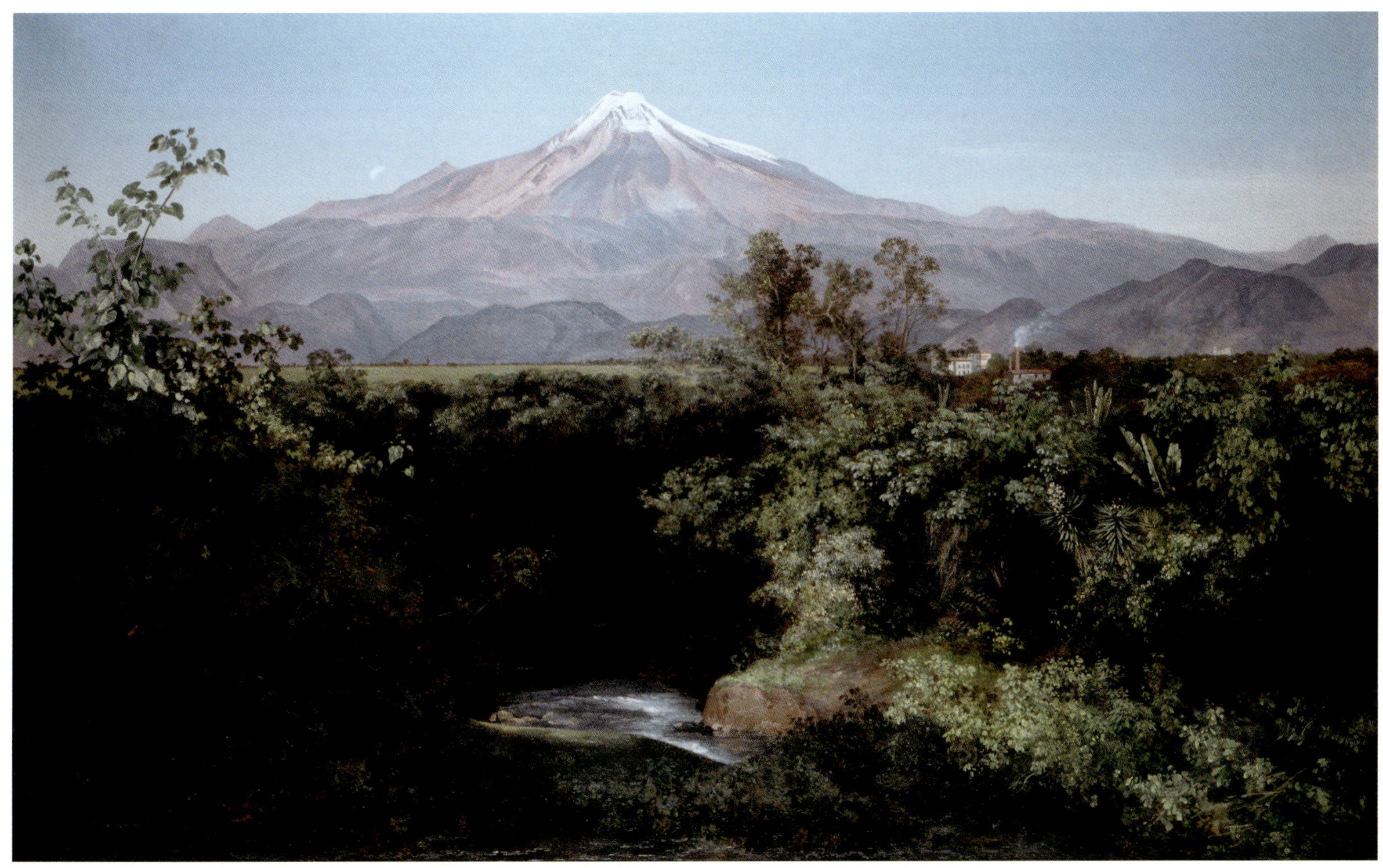

better appreciate the intricate, conceptual practice of realist painters like Velasco. By the early 1900s Velasco had witnessed the rise of Impressionism in Paris, during his time at the Exposition Universelle of 1889, and by 1896 Joaquín Clausell, a prominent artist of the generation after Velasco, had brought his cadet version of Impressionism back to Mexico. In Europe and elsewhere, the movement had quickly gained followers who lacked the artistic rigour of Monet and Pissarro but were delighted to find a form of painting that focused solely on the sensation of light, allowing them to squint their eyes and dab paint onto canvas in front of a charming motif. One reason why the Impressionist style of painting remains so popular today is that it often overlooked the social problems that came with the tsunami of change reshaping Europe.

Velasco was not a scientist who also happened to be an artist; we cannot separate his artistic training from his academic vocation. For him, painting offered a way to communicate his research and therefore became an essential part of it. As the

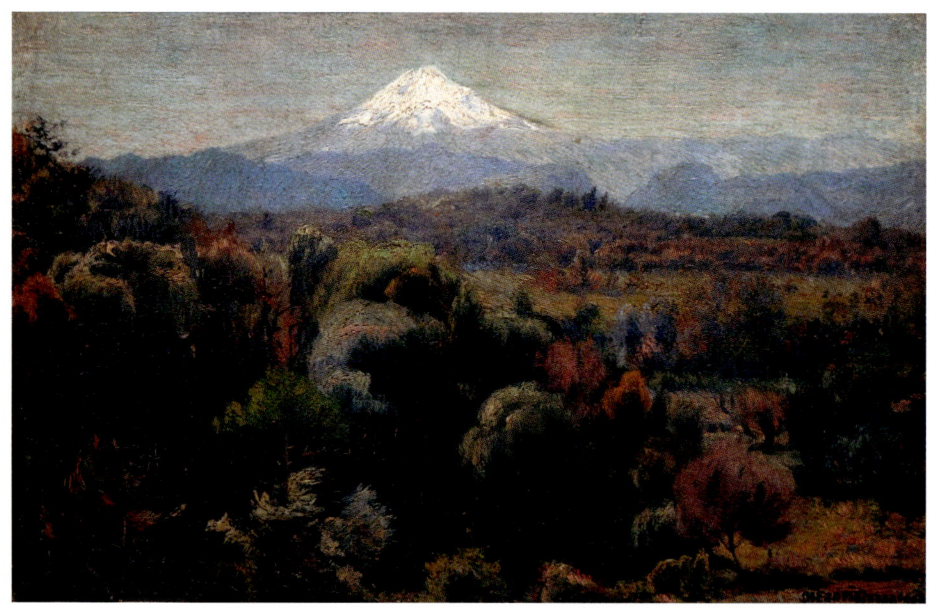

Mexican writer Octavio Paz wrote after having visited the large exhibition of Velasco's work at the Palacio de Bellas Artes in Mexico City in the late summer of 1942, Velasco was 'an amphibian who lived between art and science'.[6]

Formally appointed at the Museo Nacional as a draughtsman in 1880 and then as a photographer in 1890, Velasco worked to document archaeological sites and objects to be archived, such as Mesoamerican codices, meteorites and ceramics.[7] It is unsurprising that Velasco was so drawn to photography given his interest in scientific research. Some of his later drawings show a simplified tonal rendering that suggests the influence of photography; while few photographs taken by him remain, he did make a series of drawings based on photographs from an archaeological dig in Cempoala in 1890.[8] Velasco also began producing landscape studies in oil on small commercially produced postcards that demonstrated a looser technique, allowing him to make quick decisions while recording information rapidly.

In his lifetime, Velasco witnessed his style of painting being overshadowed by new trends in Mexico. In 1902 Antoni Fabrés, a Catalan painter, was hired to lead the painting department at the Escuela Nacional de Bellas Artes. He introduced a kitschy costume-drama style of realism that soon became popular. Velasco's approach to painting was going out of fashion: the new guard of Mexican painters dismissed or overlooked the specificity and deep territorial knowledge that made Velasco's work so original, though his influence nevertheless persisted into the twentieth century. A precocious talent, the 12-year-old Diego Rivera started at the Escuela in the later years of Velasco's tenure; his 1906 painting *Pico de Orizaba* (fig. 29) – which he made around the age of 20, shortly before his first trip to

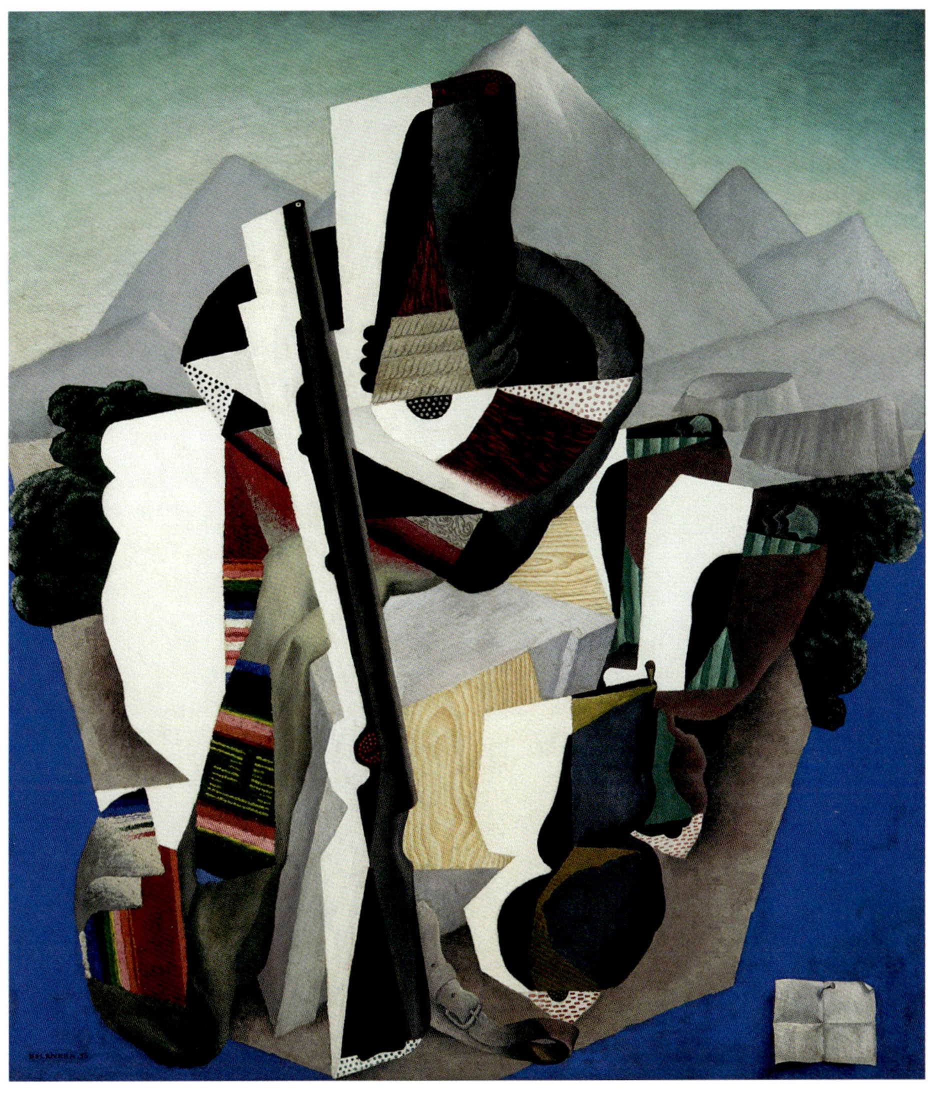

Europe – is Rivera doing his best to emulate Velasco. The palette is similar, and the undulating landscape consists of earth tones with brighter highlights, though it lacks any sense of underlying structure. Rivera would later reminisce about Velasco's advice regarding colour perspective while critiquing one of his attempts: 'Boy, you can't go on painting like that. In the foreground, you put side by side yellow spots for sunlight and blue spots for shadows; but yellow comes forward and blue recedes, so you destroy the very plane you pretend to describe.'[9] Rivera would remain, throughout his career, a great borrower (or, as one might say today, appropriator) of styles. He was still in Paris in 1915 when he produced his most successful Cubist work, *Zapatista Landscape* (fig. 30), which addressed the Mexican landscape in a sequence of snow-capped mountains and volcanoes drawn from memories of his homeland, riven at the time by the brutal violence of the revolution that had begun in 1910.

Perhaps even more distinctive than Velasco's subject matter was his powerful use of the aerial view. In his monumental *The Valley of Mexico from the Hill of Santa Isabel* from 1877 (cat. 17), the landscape stretches away from the viewer, dry and undulating in the afternoon light of the early summer dry season. Mexico City lies far away. Rather than portraying the actual city in which he lived, Velasco keeps it at a distance, piecing together an almost cartographic vision: the city set down like a map over the surface of the earth. In this and other expansive paintings of the Valley of Mexico, he combines his singular talent for observation and detail with a talent for the playful reworking of perspective; the vistas are realistic while subtly reminding us of their artificiality, their status as sophisticated reimaginings of spaces, collaged together from different points of view.

The elevated view also allowed Velasco to explore innocence and exaltation, as in a late-career canvas from 1909 titled *Temascalcingo*, which depicts the small town where the painter was born, nestled into the foothills of a volcano (cat. 24). Seen today, the sense of childlike wonder evoked by Velasco's painting, made just three years before his death, recalls a powerful moment in Juan Rulfo's 1955 novel *Pedro Páramo*, Mexico's most famous work of literary fiction, in which the protagonist thinks back to a day spent flying kites and his feeling of elation as the string tugged him heavenwards: 'I was thinking of you, Susana. Up in those green hills. When we'd fly kites during the windy season. As we played on top of that hill, we'd hear the sounds of life rising from the town below, and the string, pulled by the wind, would get away from us.'[10] In Mexican painting, Velasco's elevated views would prove even more significant, particularly in the expressionistic canvases of Gerardo Murillo, better known as Dr. Atl, who was the most notable Mexican landscape artist after Velasco and is still well known for his paintings of volcanoes seen from above, perspectives achieved from voyages either in hot-air balloons or in light aircraft (fig. 31). He even penned a manifesto claiming that the aerial view would change art forever.

Velasco's preoccupations did not stop there. *The Forest of Pacho*, a small canvas from 1875 (cat. 8), beckons the viewer into the suffocating intimacy of the image; coming in close to the surface – a wall of jungle – feels like being in the artist's actual workspace. It takes time for the eyes to adjust to the half-light; daylight feels reduced, obscured by the green vegetation of the canopy. In works on paper like *Mafaffa Leaves* (date unknown, cat. 10), he reveals his technique of scumbling a background of earth tones and muted greens to begin the painting, then working on top a brighter palette to highlight precise botanical details. Or take *Rocks* from 1894: a monumental portrait of a rock (cat. 23). Although many of Velasco's works include figures, the exclusion of the human figure – inescapably the

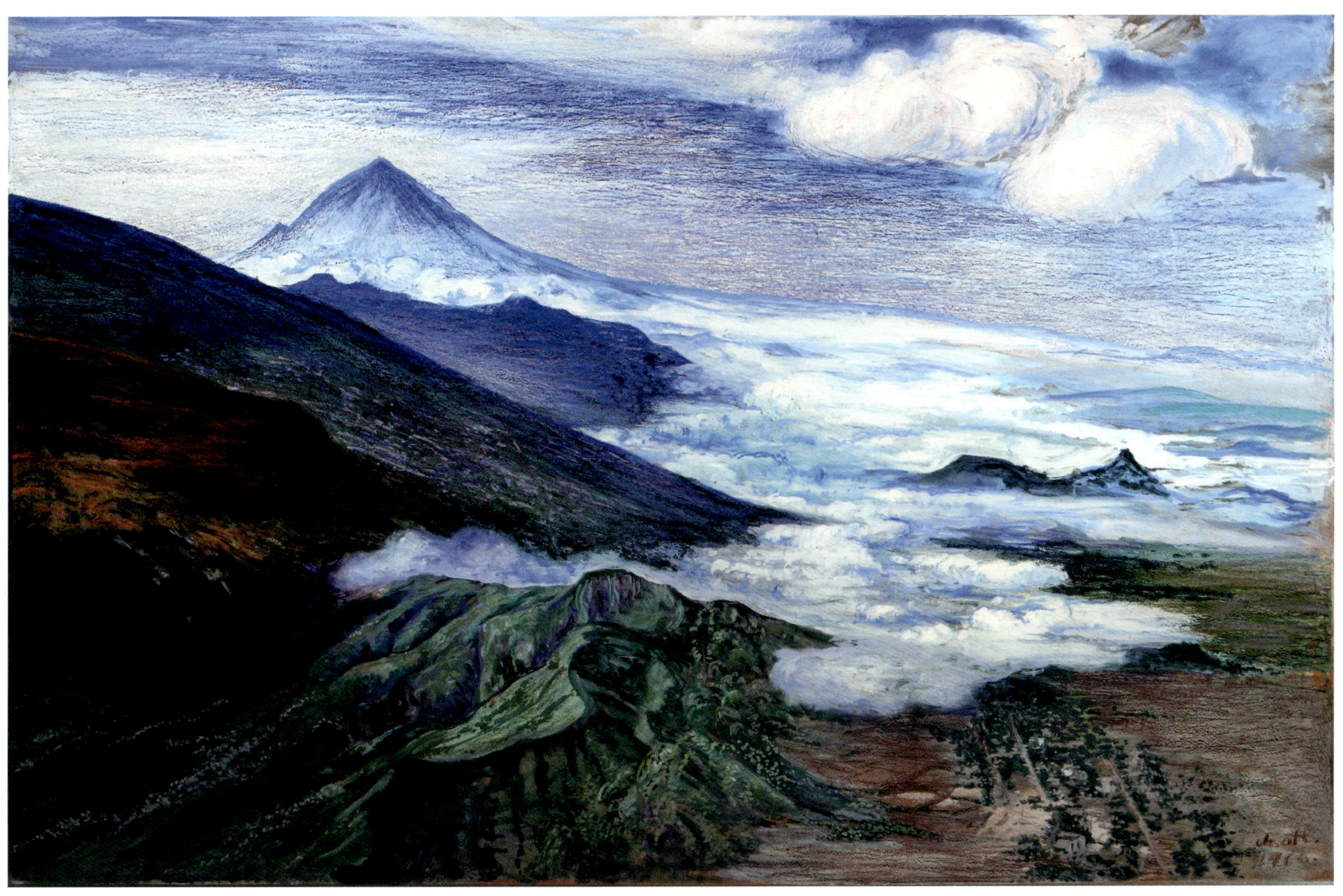

fundamental measure of proportion – activates a meaningful play of scale against size within the painting. In this large-scale work, Velasco confronts us directly with his technique – *Rocks* is built up from thin striations of paint, a method perhaps designed to mimic the newly understood process by which geological layers build over time – and, simultaneously, with the stature of the rock itself. Compositionally, the painting moves your eye vertically along the axis of its subject; the rock resists being understood as a mere feature in the landscape and takes on, instead, the presence of a living character. It is, in its silent power, comparable to great portraits like Titian's *Pietro Aretino* in the Frick Collection (1545) or a late Rembrandt self portrait. And yet, to animate such inert material as rock requires a different kind of painterly intention and skill. Much of Velasco's work negotiates far and middle distance, sending us drone-like across and then back through the landscape, but

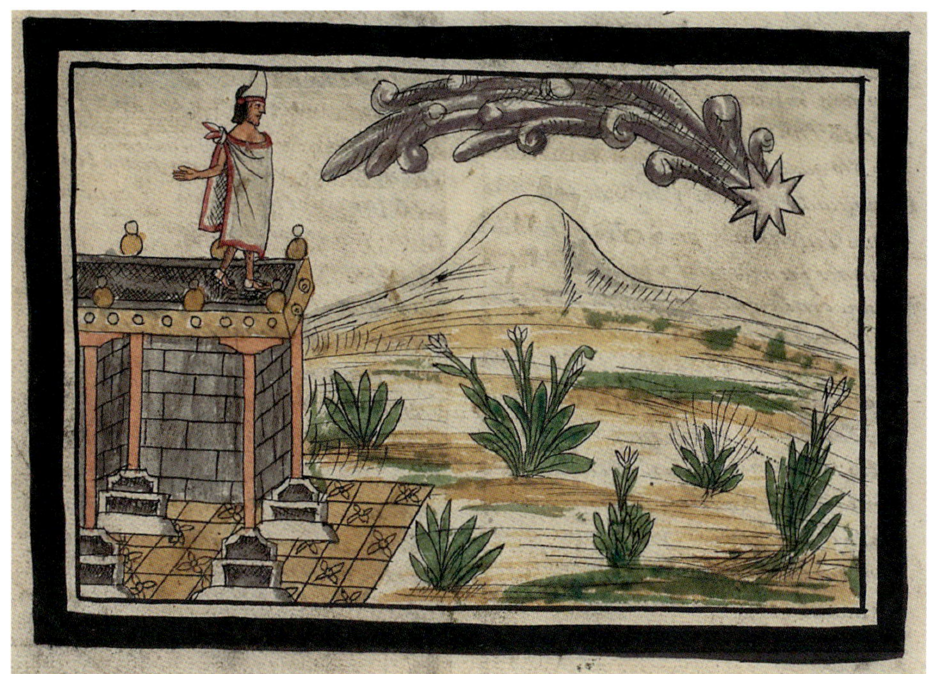

Rocks instead brings an ancient, inanimate object into our presence. While time is unknowably expansive in the silent force of a rock, history takes physical form. The effect is electrifying.

In the late sixteenth century, in collaboration with the Spanish Dominican friar Diego Durán, an artist painted a small, imagined scene of Moctezuma and a comet (fig. 32), with the Mexica emperor standing on the roof of his palace in Tenochtitlan (modern-day Mexico City), watching as a comet passes overhead. The image appears in *The History of the Indies of New Spain*, better known as the *Durán Codex*. The comet arcing across the sky was retroactively explained as a premonition of the impending catastrophe of the Spanish invasion of Mesoamerica. Halley's comet, which passes the Earth roughly every 75 years, appeared in 1910,[11] the same year in which the eruption of Mexico's decade-long revolution brought the rule of General Porfirio Díaz to an end. It was a seismic moment in the history of post-independence Mexico and remains the defining historical moment of the country's modern history.

That year, Velasco painted his own image of a comet, based on a similar phenomenon he had observed in 1882. He made the painting just two years before he died in 1912 at the age of 72, when he was no longer making many large-scale works. Yet the grander scale of his *Great Comet of 1882* (fig. 33 and cat. 25) only adds to the arresting elegance of subtle blue-grey gradations dissolving into the flattened tones of a landscape at twilight. The tail's blaze bursts through the sky

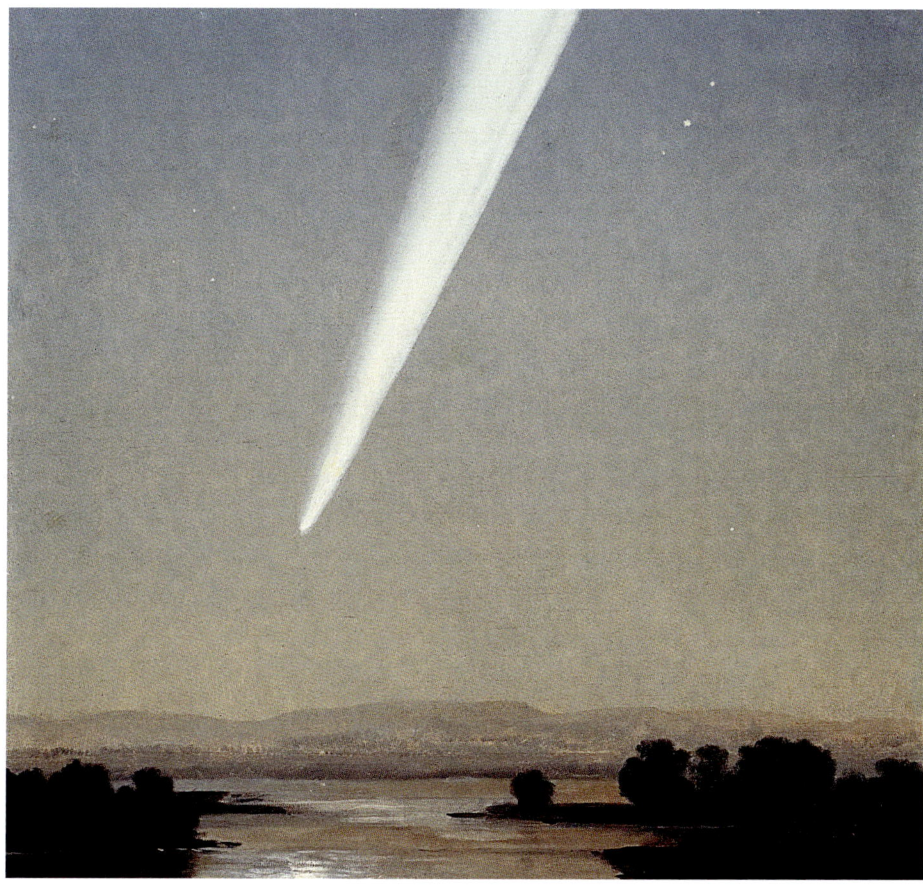

with a dash of bravado, mirrored with a few staccato brushstrokes on the surface of a lake. This work goes far beyond depicting the sky's immensity. It portrays a visitation from beyond. Underlying this image is an almost mystic sensibility, a challenge to the idea that human events – the succession of moments we define as history – are somehow separate or divisible from the cosmic scale of universal time represented by the arrival of the comet.

When one stands on the hill of Santa Isabel and looks out across the Valley of Mexico today, the volcanoes encircling the city provide a timeless backdrop to the rapid human expansion that has taken place since Velasco's time. The experience invites thoughts of the past and future; but it is completely in the present moment. Velasco's unwavering depiction of this location calls to mind another genre of painting – history painting – that memorialises a specific event or place while leaving space for the viewer to contemplate the meaningful embedded references. Establishing a relationship between topography and a state of mind, Velasco paid close attention to his surroundings but left room for the imagination. More than a century later, viewed in Mexico or beyond, the resulting works still feel contemporary.

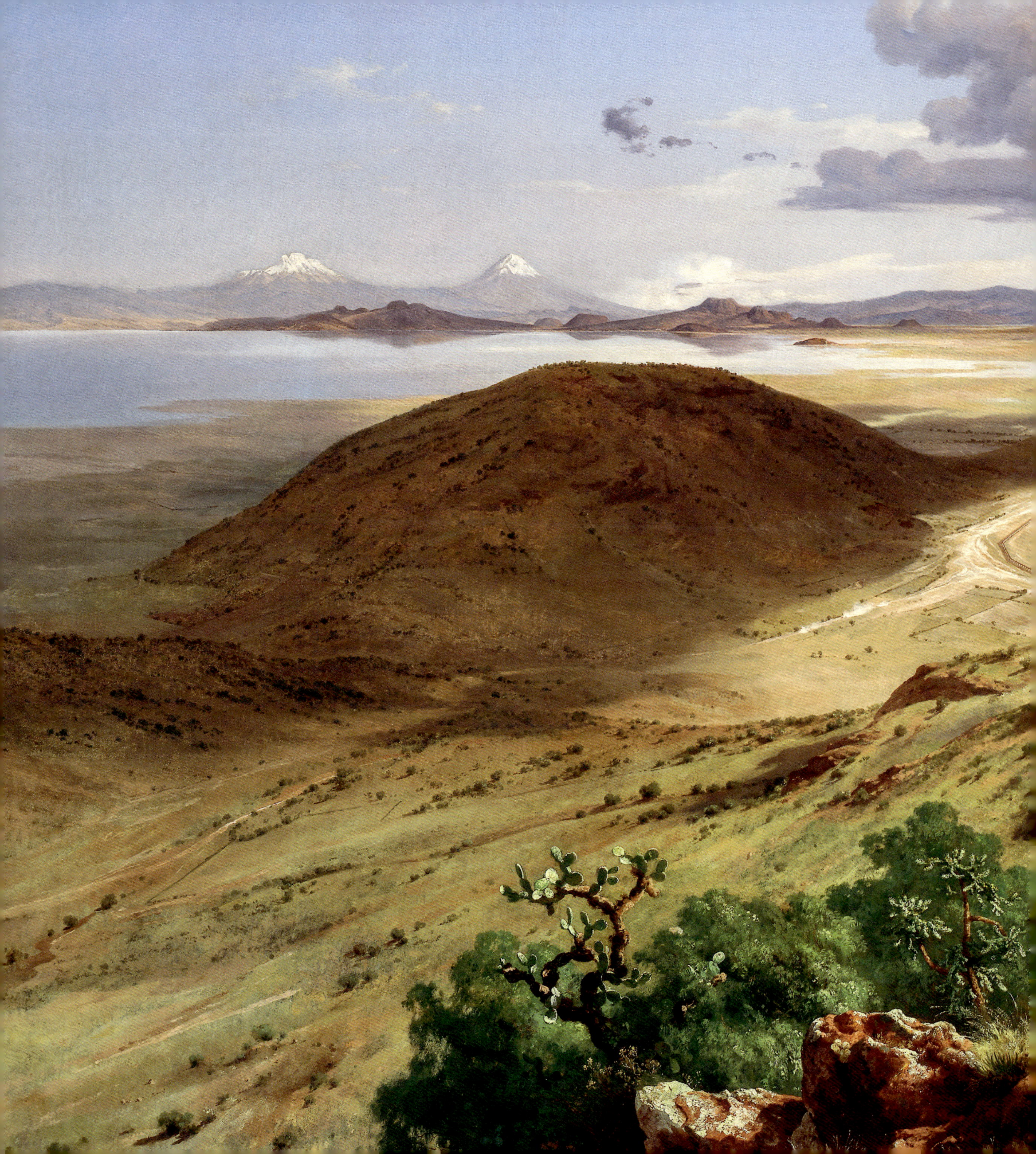

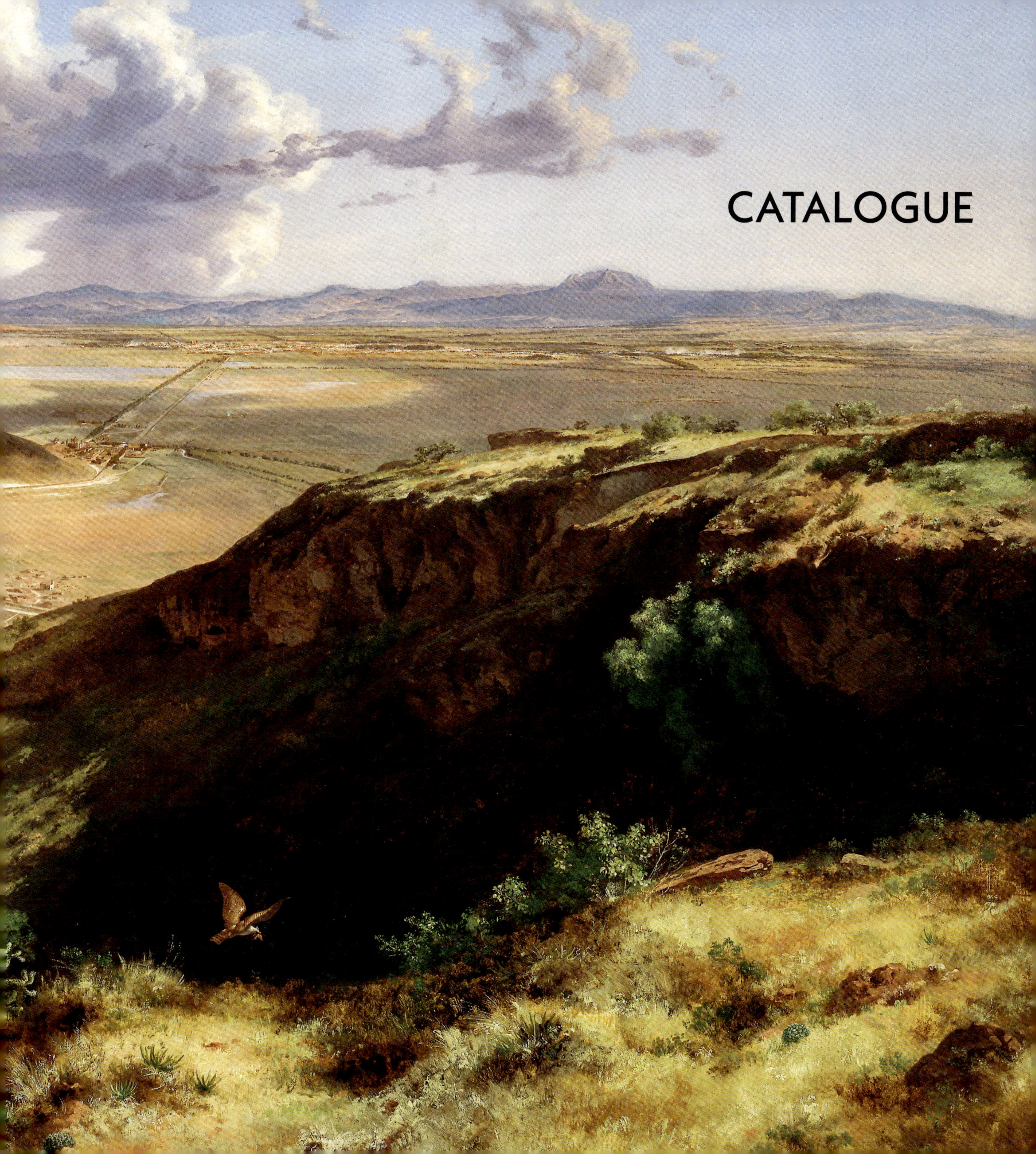
CATALOGUE

1

*THE GOATHERD OF
SAN ÁNGEL*

1861
OIL ON CANVAS, 32 × 43 CM
MUSEO NACIONAL DE ARTE, INBAL,
MEXICO CITY

2

*THE GOATHERD OF
SAN ÁNGEL*

1863
OIL ON CANVAS, 71.2 × 93.5 CM
MUSEO NACIONAL DE ARTE, INBAL,
MEXICO CITY

This pair of paintings, made in Velasco's student years, suggests the young artist's early but already decided interest in juxtaposing the rhythms of the natural world with the steady advance of industrialisation in the Valley of Mexico. When he painted these works the area of San Ángel – which included Tizapán, the small town whose textile factory these paintings depict – was far removed from the urban core, though it now lies well within Mexico City's south-western limits. The waterway at the centre of the compositions – trickling in the earlier painting and coursing through open sluice gates in the later – is the Magdalena River, which had been harnessed for the milling of flour, and later the generation of electricity. The puffing chimney and sheer stone wall on the far side of the ravine belong to La Hormiga, one of the country's first and most important textile factories, which was dedicated to the production of cotton.

Following the precepts for landscape painting set out by his teacher Eugenio Landesio, Velasco first made a study on site before elaborating his composition further in the studio. In the 1861 painting he seeks to capture his impression of the natural setting. The greens of the leafy trees and the ochre tones of the dry ground cover along the left bank are rendered with typical sensitivity, and he arranges the brown branches that hang over the gorge to form a dark void in the centre of the canvas. The factory building, by contrast, is represented in less detail, and the left foreground remains empty, with colour and contour only summarily indicated.

In the 1863 painting faithful observation of nature gives way, subtly, to narrative. The composition, of which he made two further variations, is larger than the on-site study and was brought to a much higher level of finish.[1] The left foreground has been filled with botanical and anecdotal incident: a large agave plant appears, as does – near the bottom of the canvas – an orange and black flower with three petals, native to Mexico and known in Nahuatl as an *oceloxóchitl*.[2] Closer to the gully a goatherd brandishes his whip, ushering his caprine charges up the bank, away from the precipice. Across the river, Velasco has increased the height of the factory and enlivened it with additional windows, giving it greater prominence and so making more emphatic the disjuncture between new and old. The traditional, age-old life of the goatherd contrasts with the modern industrial labour underway inside the high, angular walls of La Hormiga, whose chimney emits a continuous stream of grey fumes.[3] Looking over from the factory's roof, a man seems to gesture across to the goatherd, raising his arm in greeting, or perhaps warning him away from the ravine's edge.

The cascade of water pouring from the dam in the larger painting throws up a cloud of mist, generating a faint rainbow, which fills the area that had been a dark void in the earlier study with hazy colour. Velasco's interest in optics, suggested by his later annotated drawing of a rainbow (cat. 20), may have encouraged him to attempt to capture this phenomenon, which was apparently well known. The 'liquid prisms' of the falling water at Tizapán were admired at the end of the 1860s by the writer Justo Sierra, who exalted the location, noting that it possessed both enchanting natural beauty and the 'severe poetry of modern industry'.[4] *DSR*

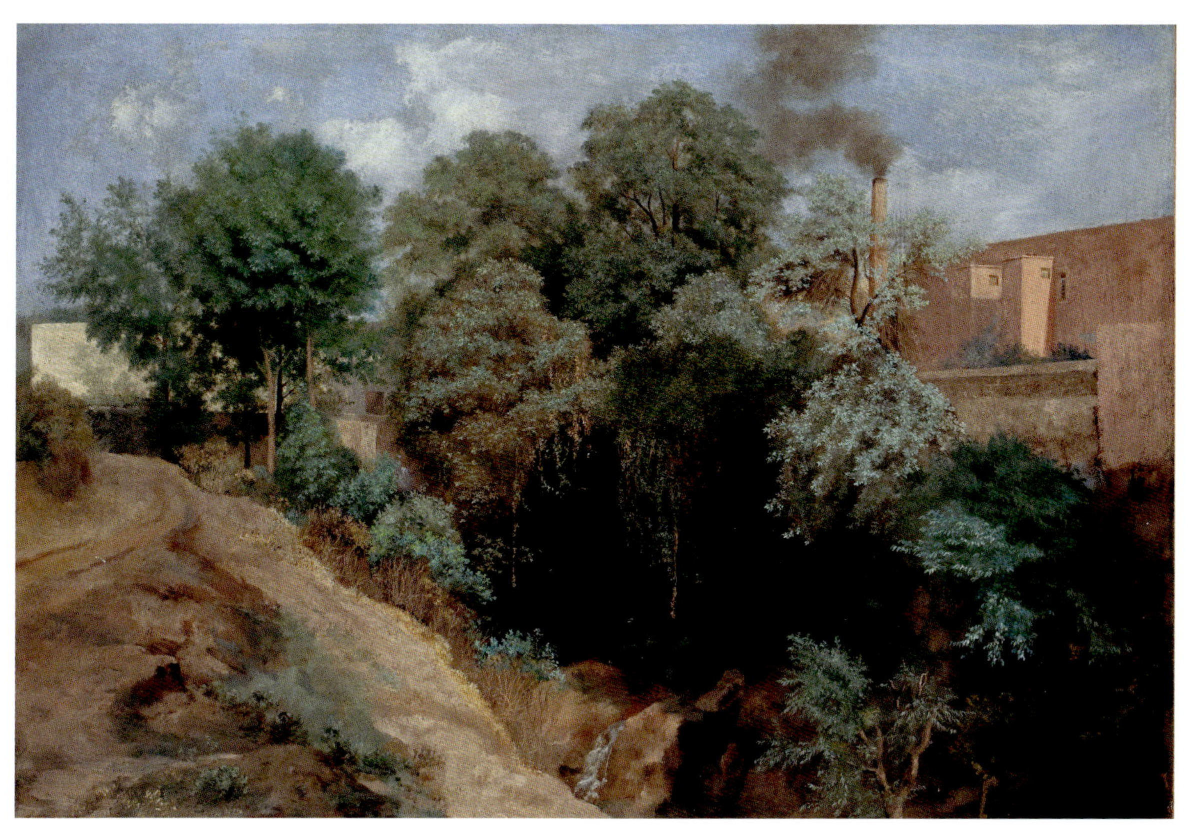

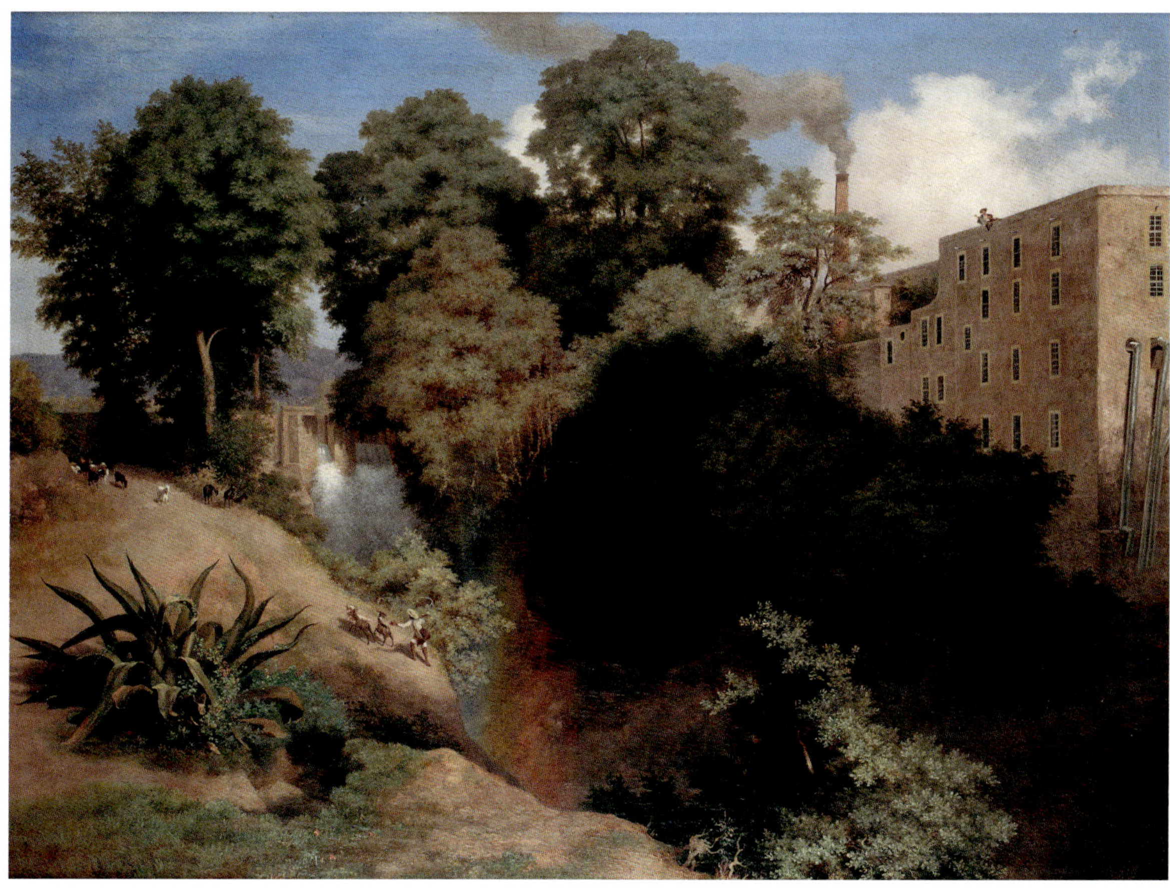

The soaring volcanic peaks that distinguish Mexico's *mesa central*, the elevated plateau in the middle of the peninsula, were among Velasco's perennial motifs, whether serving as the backdrop for his views of the Valley of Mexico or – like in these exceptionally well-preserved paintings – as his principal subjects. Both compositions, which are studio versions that the artist worked up from paintings made on site, originated during trips that took Velasco outside Mexico City – to Xalapa in 1875 and Oaxaca in 1887 – in search of new inspiration for his art.

The Pico de Orizaba, Mexico's tallest mountain, rises up more than five thousand metres at the far eastern end of the chain of volcanic peaks that runs across the centre of the country. The artist painted the dormant volcano, also known as Citlaltépetl, from outside the village of Coscomatepec, located high in its foothills. Velasco mentioned the town's beauty in a letter to his wife, remarking that 'it is filled with trees so that it looks like it is in a forest'.[1] In the painting, more vivid than the study on which it was based, diminutive white buildings peek out from under a verdant canopy, though the grandeur of the distant mountain – which Velasco represented using subtle gradations of purple-blue and mauve tones that give way at the snow-capped summit to crisp white – dominates the composition.[2]

On a return journey to Mexico City from Oaxaca just over a decade later, the artist painted a series of views in Puebla near the town of Atlixco, a regional centre of the textile industry.[3] Velasco oriented his view towards the north-west, where the volcanic cone of Popocatépetl is shadowed, in the far right background, by the hump-shaped outline of Iztaccíhuatl. These volcanoes had featured in many of his previous works, though they are usually seen from the other side, notably in both of his great paintings of *The Valley of Mexico from the Hill of Santa Isabel* (cats 15 and 17), in which the painter looked south-west across the Valley of Mexico. A textile mill, called La Carolina, is situated on the riverbank, partially obscured by lush vegetation. While there is no conspicuous trace of industrial activity near the factory, a single tendril of smoke rises in the middle distance.

Both these paintings were in the collection of František Kaska, who had come to Mexico with Emperor Maximilian I as a pharmacist and remained in the country until his death in 1907. Kaska, who hailed from Bohemia, was one of Velasco's most consistent patrons (owning eight of his paintings), as was Federico Semeleder, an Austrian doctor who had also arrived with the ill-fated emperor.[4] Velasco painted *Pico de Orizaba* for Semeleder, from whom it was later purchased by Kaska, while Kaska commissioned the artist to paint this larger version of *The Textile Mill of La Carolina, Puebla*. Kaska, who seems to have acted as an unofficial emissary of the Austro-Hungarian Empire, was among the numerous collectors of Velasco's work who maintained close ties with Europe and the United States (see pp. 28–9). After his death his entire collection – some 1,250 objects – was sent to Prague, where Velasco's paintings would wait more than sixty years before their importance was realised.[5] *DSR*

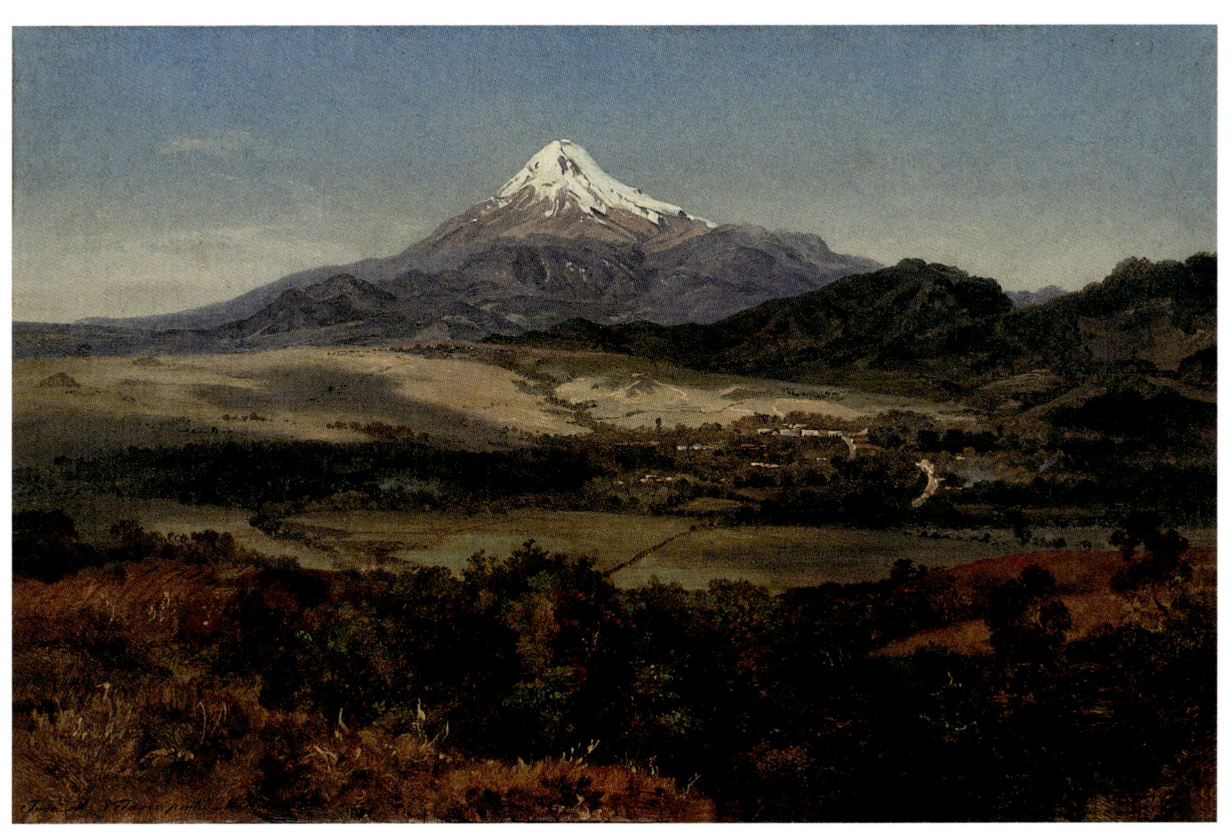

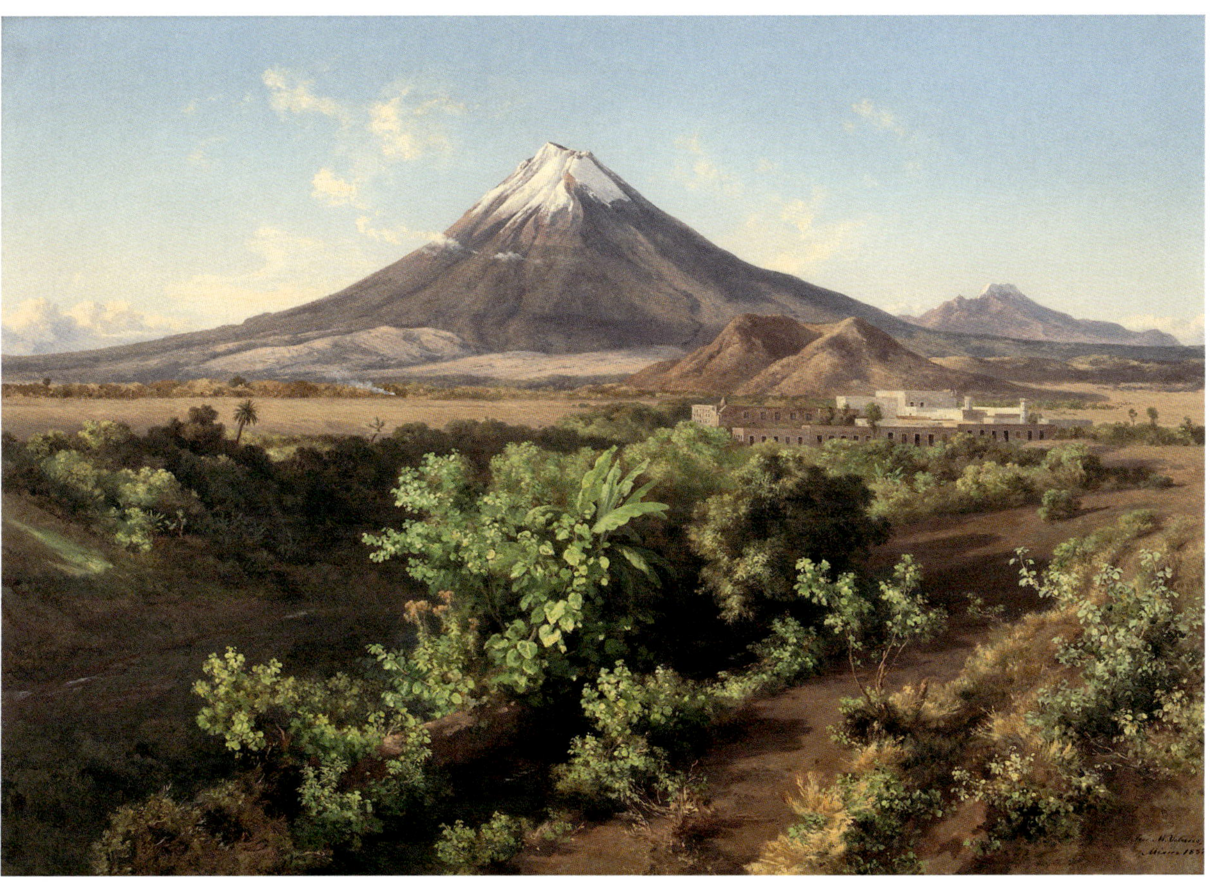

5

LAKE CHALCO

1885
OIL ON CANVAS, 49 × 71.6 CM
NATIONAL MUSEUM OF THE
CZECH REPUBLIC, PRAGUE

The landscape around Lake Chalco was undergoing significant transformation in the period when Velasco made this painting. Along with Lakes Texcoco and Xochimilco, it was part of the extensive lake system that once dominated the Valley of Mexico. For centuries the village of Chalco, shown in the middle of the painting, had served as a key lake port in the south-eastern part of the basin of Mexico, where goods arriving from the port of Veracruz would be stored before travelling by boat to Mexico City. However, the introduction of the Morelos railway in the early 1880s diminished Lake Chalco's commercial importance, leading to profound changes in the region. In 1895 the decision was made to drain the lake for the expansion of agricultural land, marking a significant shift in the area's landscape and economy.

A subtle detail in Velasco's painting hints at the impending transformation of the lake's surroundings: a train, emitting a plume of white smoke, traverses the plain behind the village. Unlike many of his other panoramic views, Velasco's perspective here is different, positioning the observer virtually in the lake rather than on top of a hill. This shift in viewpoint brings the dense, floating plant life, typical of Lakes Chalco and Xochimilco, into the foreground. This lush vegetation, which often complicated navigation, seems to serve as a reminder of traditional practices being replaced by newer, more efficient methods. The artist once again evokes the dichotomy between change and permanence, set against the background dominated by the enduring presence of the volcanoes Iztaccíhuatl and Popocatépetl.

According to Altamirano Piolle, there are at least four versions of this view of Lake Chalco.[1] One of them was shown at the 19th Exhibition of the Escuela Nacional de Bellas Artes in December 1879, described by Velasco himself in the exhibition catalogue as a studio copy of an earlier painting made on site. Altamirano Piolle does not specify the current locations of the other versions, but we know that the one exhibited in 1879 was acquired by Porfirio Díaz's government to be presented as a gift to the US president Ulysses S. Grant.[2] Two more versions of this view were created a few years later: one in 1882, commissioned by the civil engineer and architect Manuel Sánchez Facio, and this final one in 1885, commissioned by František Kaska.

A friend of Velasco, Kaska was a Czech pharmacist and officer in the Austro-Hungarian Army. He was enlisted in the Austrian Volunteer Corps to accompany Emperor Maximilian I to Mexico. Following the fall of Maximilian's empire, Kaska chose to remain in Mexico, where he devoted himself to scientific research and became an active member of various societies. He also amassed an extensive collection of historical artefacts related to the empire. On his death in 1907, his collection was donated to what became the National Museum of the Czech Republic in Prague, whose holdings include eight paintings by Velasco and three by his teacher and colleague Santiago Rebull. *VP*

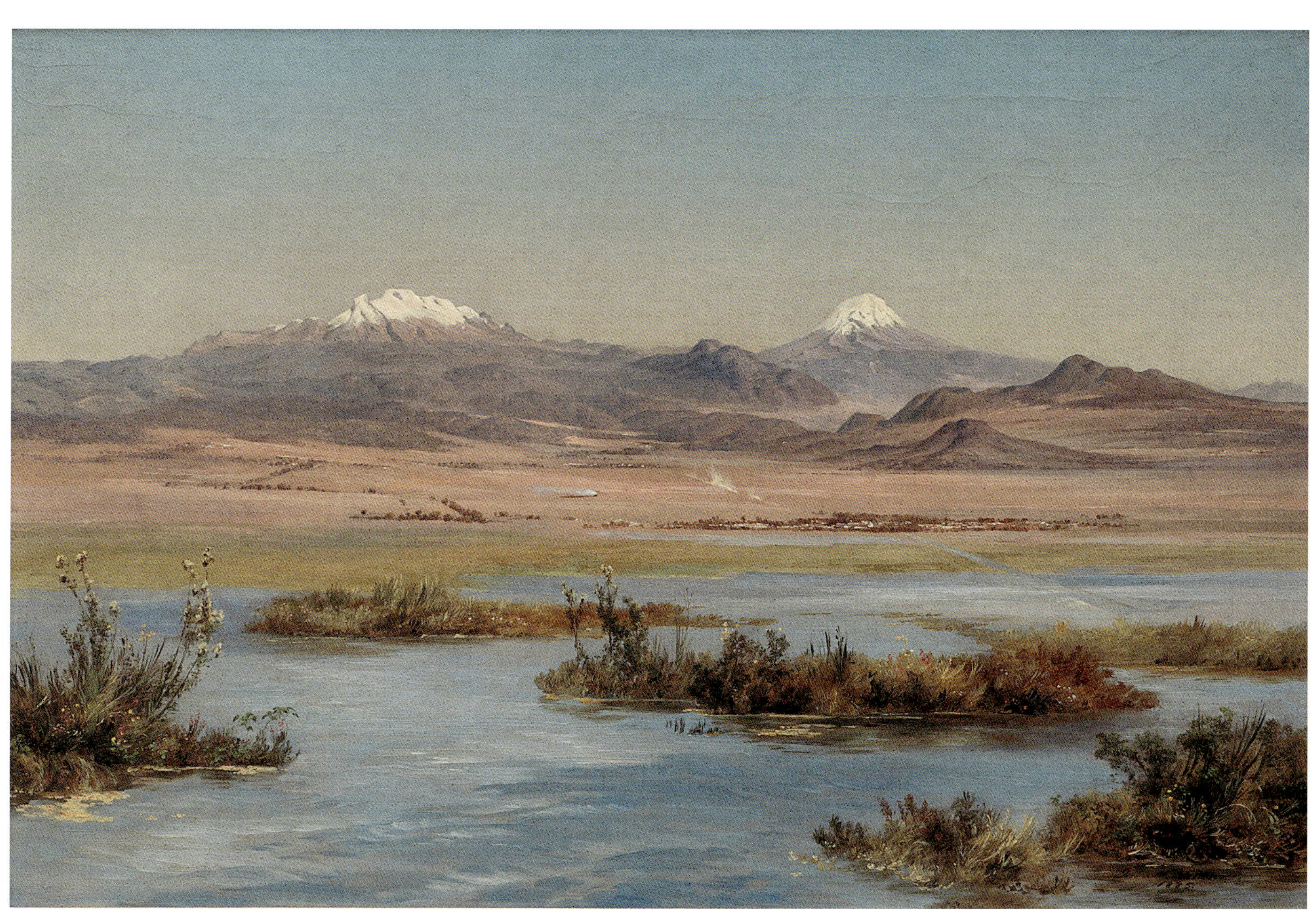

6

THE VALLEY OF MEXICO FROM THE MOLINO DEL REY

1895
OIL ON CANVAS, 45.5 × 61.5 CM
PRIVATE COLLECTION

Velasco's vantage-point, despite the painting's title, is actually west of Molino del Rey, a small industrial precinct presided over by a smoking chimney and the distinctive seventeenth-century gable-roofed mill from which the area takes its name. This was the site of a major battle during the Mexican–American War in 1847, which took place just before the infamous Battle of Chapultepec, when the *Niños Héroes*, six young cadets from the national military academy, gave their lives defending the academy's campus, then located in the Castle of Chapultepec, the white building perched atop the wooded hill. Ordered built as the summer residence of the Spanish viceroys, the castle later became the palace of Emperor Maximilian I of Mexico and later still, when Velasco made this painting, was home to Porfirio Díaz. Stretching out in the distance beyond, towards Mexico City – where the towers of the Baroque cathedral rise up, just visible – are the wooded boulevards of Reforma and Tacubaya. Velasco idealised the vista: by the 1890s the city, although it appears here with tidy boundaries, had already begun to sprawl out between the urban centre and the woodland of Chapultepec, which had been a place of recreation for city-dwellers since pre-Hispanic times, famous for its springs and *ahuehuetes*.

The artist positioned himself on the higher ground of Tacubaya, a district scattered with the villas and summer retreats of the aristocracy and rising middle class by the end of the nineteenth century. This area was favoured in part because, unlike the centre of Mexico City, it was not prone to flooding and enjoyed fresh breezes free from the marshy odours of the valley's lakes. This elevated location also allowed Velasco to capture the massive sweep of the volcanoes that encircle the Valley of Mexico, some rising more than five thousand metres above sea level, and the expansive vault of the sky. Before the urban and industrial changes of the twentieth century that led to the Valley of Mexico becoming one of the most polluted places on the planet, it was often referred to as *la zona más transparente del aire* or 'the area with the clearest air'.

Many of the views of the Valley of Mexico that Velasco painted in the 1890s, including this one, as art historian Fausto Ramírez observed, are governed by a particular compositional scheme. In them, a long diagonal, here an ill-defined dirt track, proceeds from one of the painting's bottom corners before encountering an obstacle in the middle ground, in this case the wall surrounding the buildings of Molino del Rey. The viewer's gaze is then directed upwards through a succession of horizontal planes, eventually reaching the snow-capped heights of Iztaccíhuatl and Popocatépetl in the far distance.[1] Velasco made several versions of this composition at different sizes, incorporating different foreground elements in each.[2] Some of these canvases include prominent groups of figures, but in others, such as this one, the artist elected instead to emphasise the plant life of the valley, observed with his characteristic botanical acuity. *DSR and PAV*

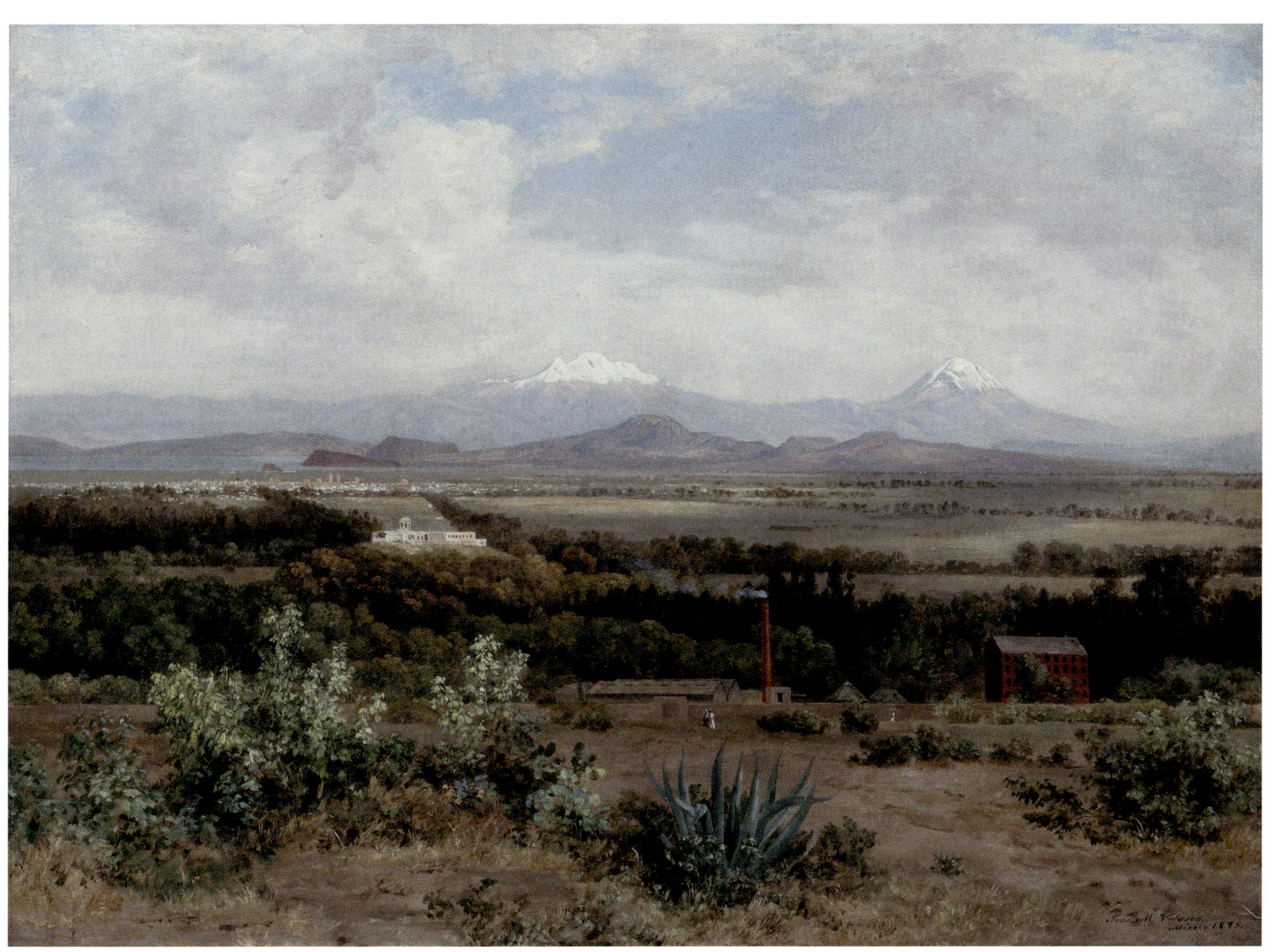

7

A RUSTIC BRIDGE
IN SAN ÁNGEL

1862
OIL ON PAPER LAID DOWN ON
CANVAS, 45.5 × 33 CM
MUSEO NACIONAL DE ARTE, INBAL,
MEXICO CITY

Painted during Velasco's student years at the Academia de San Carlos, this small canvas suggests his emerging interest in the scrupulous representation of the natural world as well as his debt to Eugenio Landesio, his teacher. The young artist, working near the colonial church of San Sebastián in Chimalistac, an area adjacent to San Ángel, to the south-west of the centre of Mexico City, selected a charismatic, ageing alder tree as the focus of his composition. The tree is rooted in the muddy bank of a slow-flowing stream, which is bridged by a crude span of planks that rests on its lower boughs. The painting, made on site, served as the model for a slightly larger composition dedicated to the same subject that Velasco exhibited in 1865.[1]

The work reflects the devotion with which the artist absorbed Landesio's rigorous pedagogy for landscape painting, which prized studious observation from nature, developed first through drawing.[2] Velasco's precise rendering of the alder's leaves and lichen-covered branches, and the surrounding vegetation – also evident in *The Goatherd of San Ángel* (cat. 1), painted some two kilometres away the year before – presages the methodical approach that would inform the botanical illustrations he made at the end of the 1860s, when he became a founding member of the Sociedad Mexicana de Historia Natural.

This canvas, however, evinces Velasco's interest in Landesio's art as much as in his teaching, and particularly in the Italian's *Trunk of a Holm Oak* (1844, Museo Nacional de San Carlos). The protagonist of that work is a blasted trunk, isolated near a stream, that sprouts shoots of new, green growth, just as the alder does in Velasco's composition. He may have also had in mind Landesio's *Apennines and Sub-Apennines* (see fig. 10), whose pendant, *Vallinfreda*, he had copied in 1861.[3] In orientation and attitude Velasco's gnarled tree, leaning to the left out over a brook, parallels the one his teacher had represented decades earlier in the hills east of Rome, though he forgoes the incidental human figures that populate Landesio's painting.

A Rustic Bridge in San Ángel numbers among the small group of works that Velasco made in the area during the early 1860s, when his distinctive approach to landscape painting was still in its infancy. If other works from this period, like *The Goatherd of San Ángel* (cats 1 and 2), highlight the contrast between traditional rural life and the emergence of industrial modernity in the Valley of Mexico with relative clarity, in this painting a gentle harmony still prevails: the improvised, slipshod bridge conforms and adapts to the branches of the stooping tree beneath. *DSR*

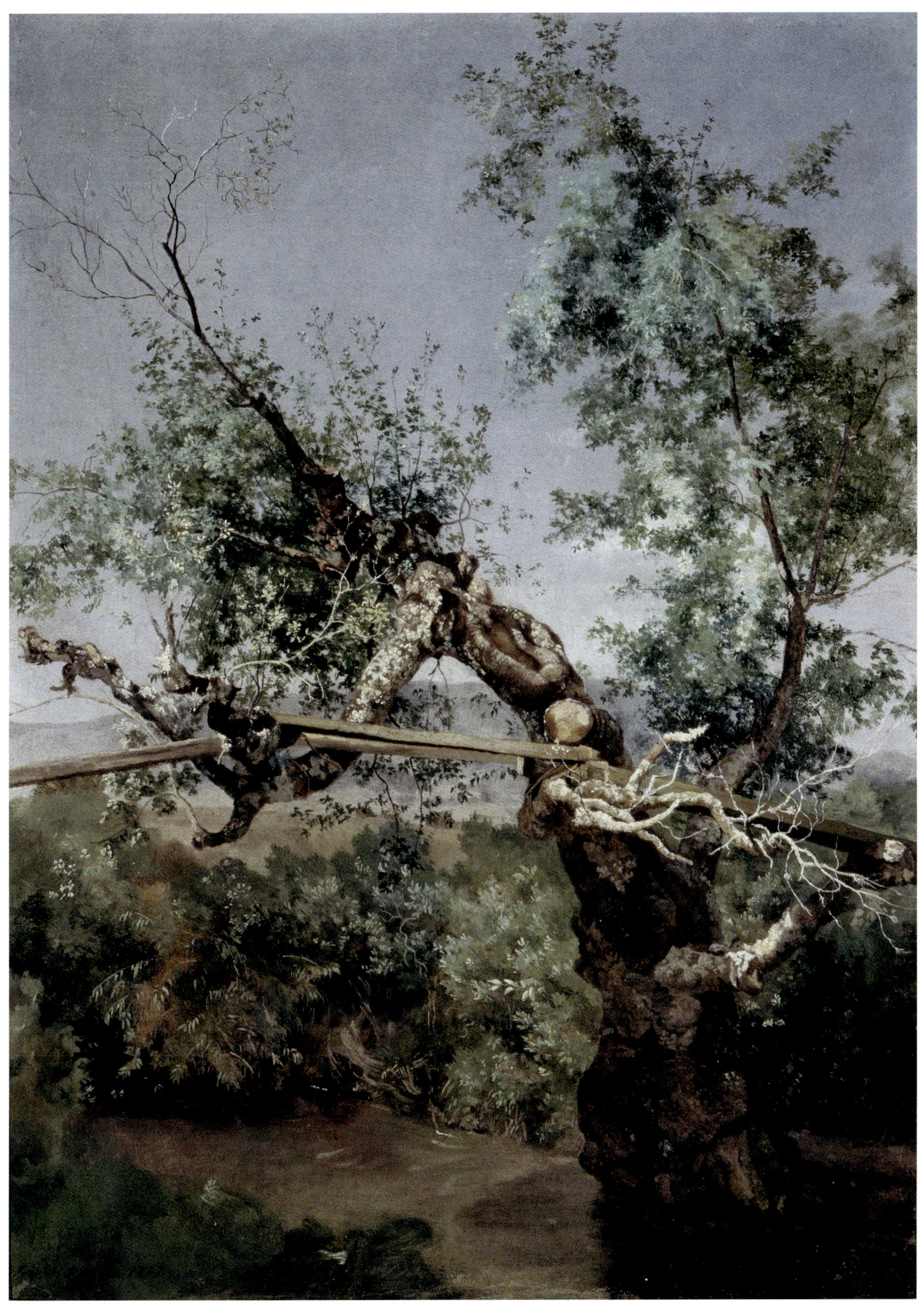

8

THE FOREST OF PACHO

1875
OIL ON CANVAS, 43.5 × 32.5 CM
MUSEO NACIONAL DE ARTE, INBAL,
MEXICO CITY

9

STUDY OF A SHRUB

DATE UNKNOWN
PENCIL ON PAPER, 10.9 × 16.5 CM
MUSEO NACIONAL DE ARTE, INBAL,
MEXICO CITY

In 1874 and 1875 Velasco made painting excursions in the highlands of the province of Veracruz, which lie some three hundred kilometres from Mexico City on the eastern slope of the ring of volcanic mountains that encircle the capital. Influenced by the climate of the Gulf of Mexico, the area is warm and moist, with teeming, evergreen foliage, even at considerable altitude. These tropical forests – whose close, almost stifling atmosphere Velasco conveys in this painting – boast various species of tree ferns that captured the imagination of nineteenth-century naturalists and botanists, as well as mosses, lichens, bromeliads and orchids. Throughout his career the artist had an unremitting interest in the plant life of Mexico, expressed several years earlier in his short-lived publication *Flora del Valle de México* (see pp. 45–7), which he also made the subject of several paintings.

The artist made *The Forest of Pacho* during his second trip to the region, later developing another version of the composition in his studio.[1] *Pacho* is the traditional name for tree ferns in this region, as well as the name given to a hill south of the city of Xalapa, which then belonged to a plantation called the Hacienda de Pacho. The chapel of this venerable estate, whose origins can be traced back to the colonial period, was represented in an oil study by the German traveller-artist Johann Moritz Rugendas in 1831.[2] In the early nineteenth century the property was purchased by José Julián Gutiérrez y Fernández,

in whose family it still remains.[3] In 1874 the Mexican writer Antonio García Cubas described the surrounding forest, where Velasco probably painted this picture a year later, as one of the area's 'most picturesque and pleasant places'.[4]

Velasco's canvas transmits the claustrophobic density of the tropical forest, a thick tapestry of varied green tones unrelieved by any sense of distance or horizon. His study of a shrub, by contrast, isolates a single clump of vegetation in a manner not unrelated to scientific illustration, with which he was intimately familiar. Of uncertain date, the drawing exemplifies the artist's practice of visual note-taking. He returned to studies like this one when developing larger paintings, incorporating elements from them to enrich the detail of his compositions.

The artist's travels in Veracruz, like García Cubas's, were facilitated, and perhaps even spurred, by the long-awaited opening of the railway that connected the high central plateau of Mexico to the lowlands of the eastern coast, which was inaugurated in 1873. The following year Velasco painted near the town of Orizaba, depicting a series of waterfalls and – from the village of Coscomatepec – Mexico's tallest mountain, the Pico de Orizaba, also known by its Nahuatl name, Citlaltépetl (see cat. 3). An additional branch of the railway opened in 1875, extending its reach northwards to Xalapa, whose verdant forests Velasco would soon depict. *DSR and PAV*

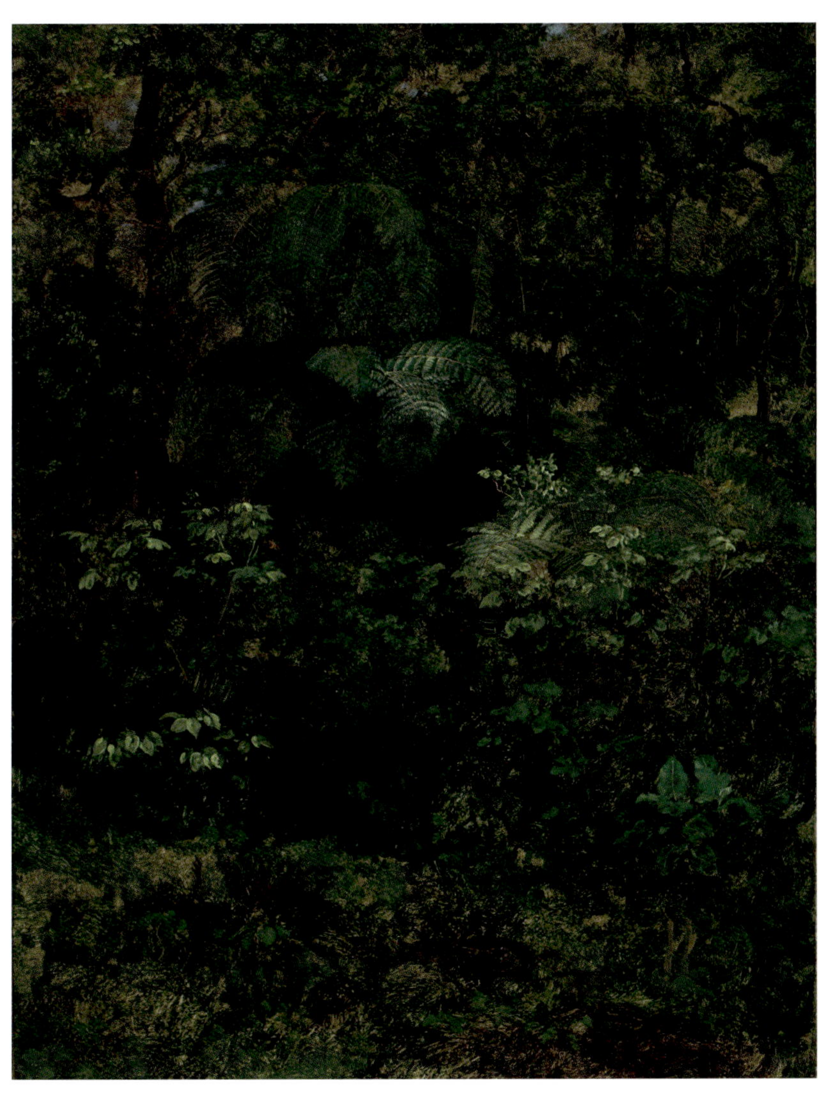

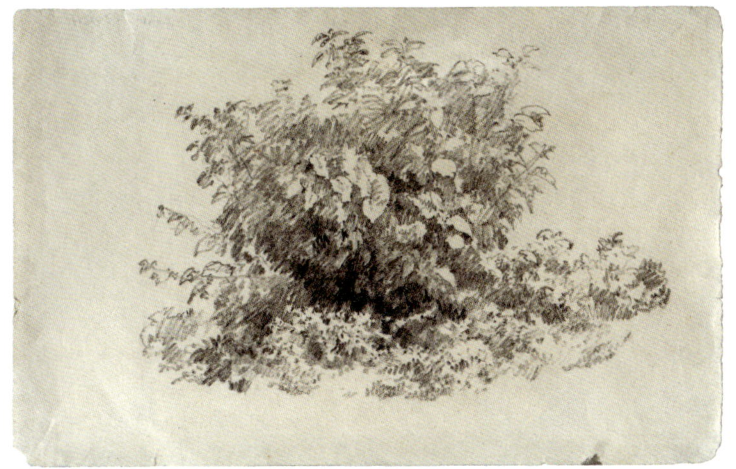

DATE UNKNOWN
OIL ON PAPER, 30 × 40 CM
JOSÉ MARÍA VELASCO ARCHIVE,
MUSEO KALUZ, MEXICO CITY

This vivid study of a mafaffa plant (*Xanthosoma sagittifolium*), perhaps made in the early 1880s, demonstrates Velasco's ongoing interest in Mexico's rich and diverse flora as well as his systematic approach to developing larger landscape compositions. The impressive plant that he depicts, also called a tannia, has broad, arrow-shaped leaves and is common to tropical zones in the Americas, where it is often found in warm, wet areas, like the forests surrounding Orizaba, where this work may have been painted. If Velasco's careful attention to the mafaffa's distinctive morphology reflects his scientific training, the roughed-in background reveals part of his artistic practice, in which subsidiary details are eliminated in favour of a singular focus.

The study exhibits the abilities that made Velasco an accomplished botanical illustrator. He was capable of precise observation and meticulous attention to the play of light across and through leaves, which allowed him to capture both the specific characteristics of a species and its aesthetic qualities. Working on paper – a medium that was easy to transport – Velasco has rendered the mafaffa's broad leaves with particular sensitivity to their waxy surfaces and distinctive vein patterns. The painting's unfinished state offers insight into his working method: the mafaffa is rendered with great care, but the rest of the right side of the composition remains largely untouched, with the underlying paper showing through in places and the foliage to the left only described with summary strokes. In 1882, around the time he painted this work, he proposed two new botanical publication projects, a 'Flora de los alrededores de México' and a 'Flora universal iconográfica', though neither came to fruition (see p. 46).[1]

Altamirano Piolle has suggested that this study could relate to one of Velasco's great representations of a railway, *The Curved Bridge of the Mexican Railway over the Metlac Ravine* (see fig. 13), which he painted in 1881.[2] In that large canvas, a foreground teeming with tropical greenery, including a prominent mafaffa, gives way to an expansive view of a newly constructed iron railway bridge.[3] If the study is indeed preparatory to the painting – a celebration of Mexico's technological advances that was owned by Porfirio Díaz – it serves as further evidence that Velasco developed his most ambitious compositions through the careful preliminary investigation of individual elements, uniting botanical accuracy with grand pictorial effect. *DSR*

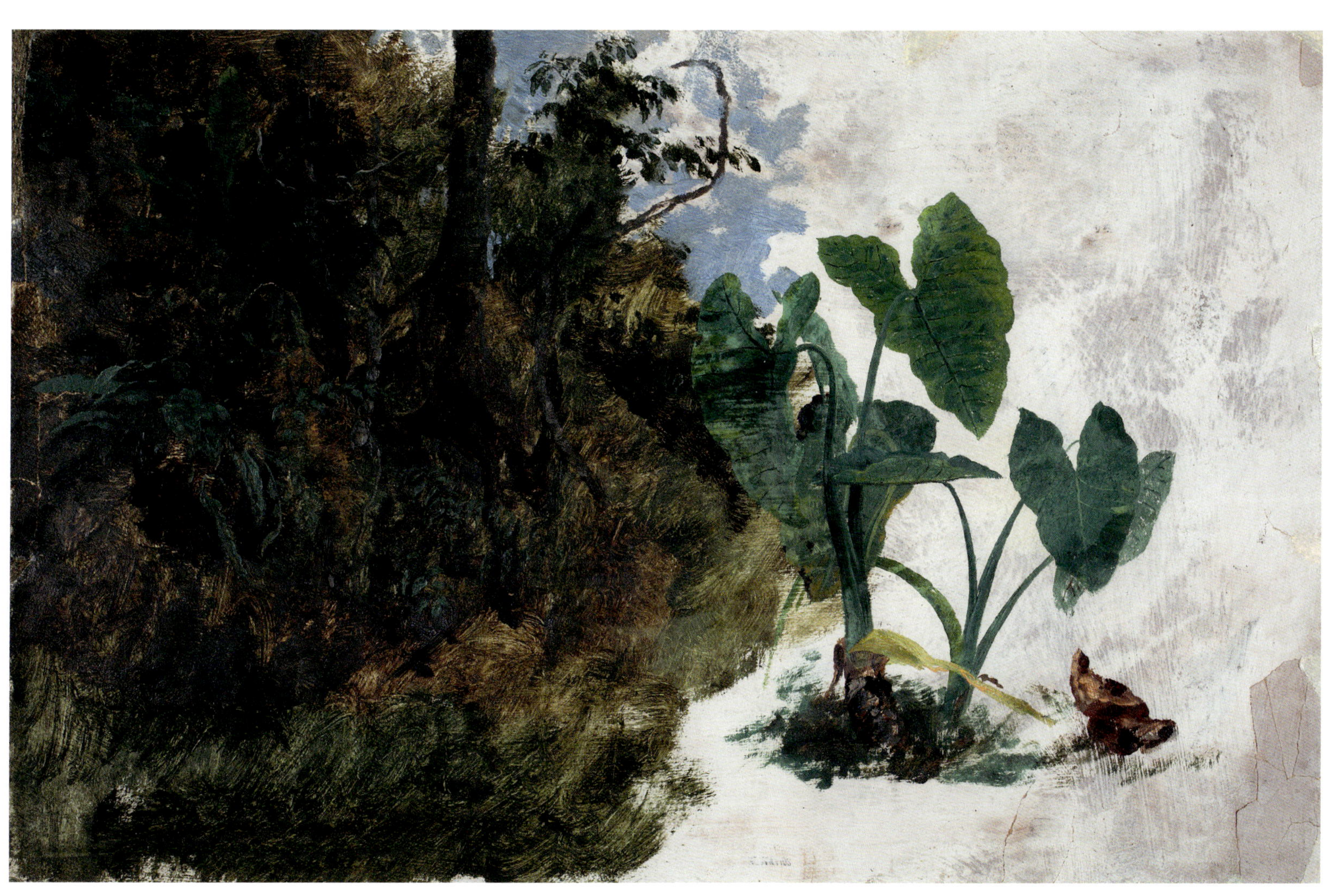

1887
OIL ON CANVAS, 61 × 46 CM
MUSEO NACIONAL DE ARTE, INBAL,
MEXICO CITY

The focal point of this painting is a towering Mexican giant *cardón* (*Pachycereus weberi*), which rises majestically from the slope of a hill. The immense cactus dominates the scene, its grandeur accentuated by the diminutive figure of a man in a sombrero standing in its shadow. Depicted in profile, he gazes to the right of the painting as if contemplating a view the observer can only imagine.

This work is connected to Velasco's visit to the southern Mexican state of Oaxaca in December 1887, where he was commissioned by the archbishop Eulogio Gillow y Zavalza to paint the colonial cathedral. As well as fulfilling his commission, Velasco took the opportunity to capture the surrounding landscape, painting views of Mitla, Guelatao and Oaxaca itself. He also documented the region's flora and geological features. The *cardón* was painted on location while Velasco was passing through the village of Tecomavaca, north-west of the city of Oaxaca. The canvas is dominated by earth tones that reflect the arid, rugged beauty of the Mexican countryside. These tones are applied with loose brushstrokes, while the plant's branches are meticulously rendered in varying shades of green against a deep blue sky.

Velasco focuses on the *cardón*'s impressive sculptural qualities. As is evident in many of his studies, the artist had a keen interest in distinctive plants, including the emblematic nopal cactus, which featured in his later composition *The Valley of Mexico from the Hill of Santa Isabel* (1877, cat. 17), and the *ahuehuetes* of Chapultepec (see fig. 4). Another notable example is his painting of a giant banana tree, discussed by Altamirano Piolle, who writes that the species was brought to Mexico and grown in the garden of the composer José María Reponti, and was 'considered one of the most beautiful ornamental species of the vegetable kingdom for its enormous leaves 4 to 5 metres in length'.[1] The composition of this painting closely mirrors that of the *cardón*, with the tree dominating the canvas and the figure of a boy added close by to highlight its impressive scale.

A similar giant cactus had previously been portrayed by Velasco's mentor Eugenio Landesio in a painting dated 1857. In *The Hacienda of Matlala*, depicting architect Lorenzo de la Hidalga's estate south-east of Mexico City, with his family in the foreground, Landesio includes a towering *cardón* in front of the aqueduct that dominates the scene (see fig. 11). Interestingly, Velasco never incorporated the *cardón* into any other paintings, though the work remained in his studio. He revisited the subject in later life, however, in a 1909 postcard painting, where the cactus appears by a stream with a mountain in the distance.[2] *VP*

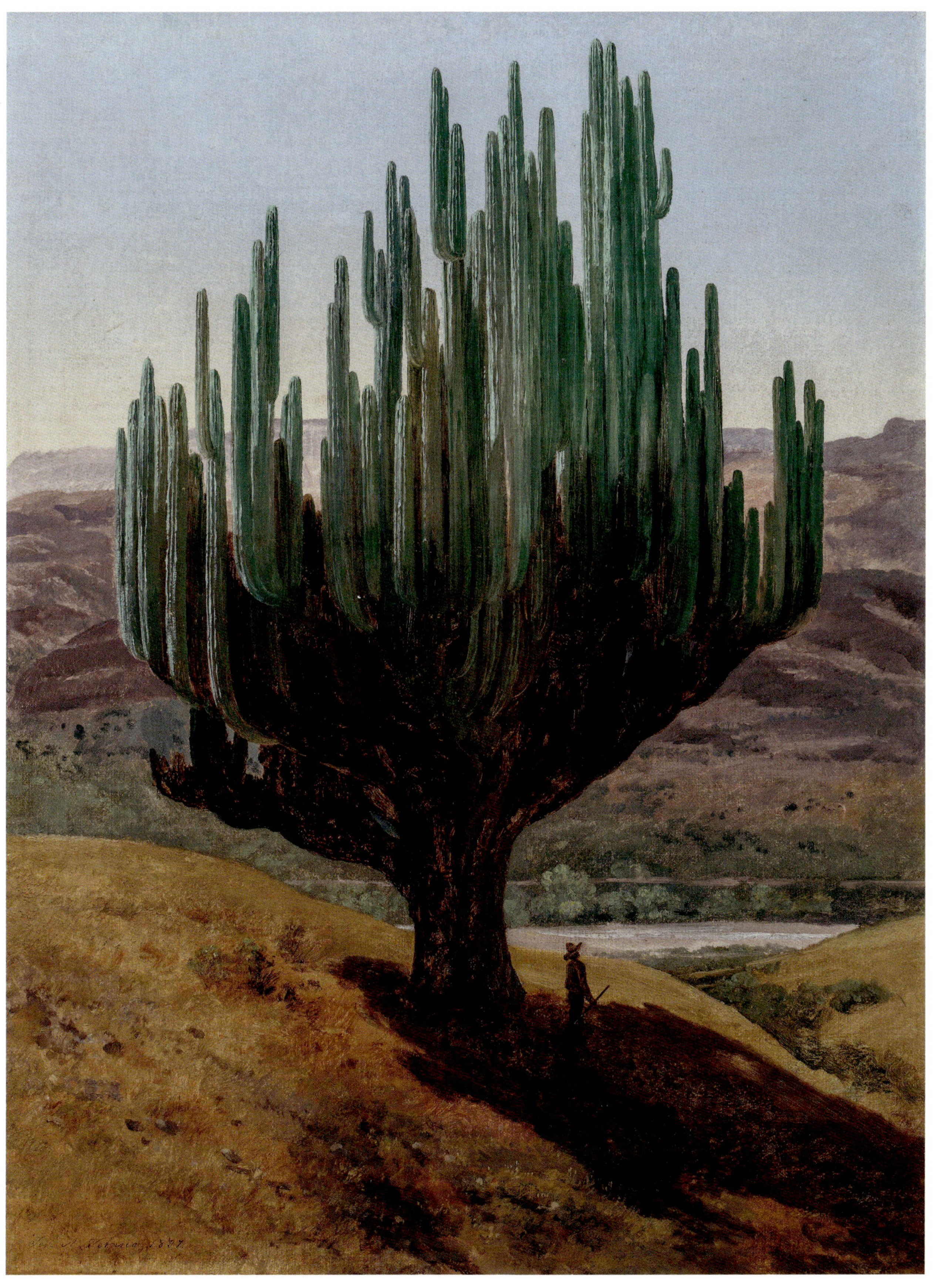

12

*THE PYRAMID OF THE
SUN IN TEOTIHUACÁN*

1878
OIL ON CANVAS, 31.4 × 46.2 CM
MUSEO NACIONAL DE ARTE, INBAL,
MEXICO CITY

13

*THE PYRAMIDS OF THE
SUN AND THE MOON*

1878
OIL ON CANVAS, 18.5 × 26.3 CM
COLECCIÓN PÉREZ SIMÓN

In these two paintings Velasco represents the monumental Pyramids of the Sun and the Moon, part of the temple complex of the ancient Mesoamerican city of Teotihuacán, located some fifty kilometres north-east of Mexico City. At its height Teotihuacán was one of the most populous cities in the world, and its great pyramids (constructed between AD 100 and 450) awed all who encountered them, from the Mexica to the Spanish conquistadors and later European travellers. Their immense size meant they were never truly lost, even after the city was abandoned around AD 700 for reasons that are still unclear: they remained touchstones in the cultural imagination of the Valley of Mexico. When Velasco painted the pyramids in 1878, early in his collaboration with the Museo Nacional, they were still overgrown, though state-sponsored excavations began in the mid-1880s, overseen by the archaeologist Leopoldo Batres.[1]

The two works offer different prospects of the temple precinct. In the larger painting, *The Pyramid of the Sun in Teotihuacán*, made on site, Velasco positioned himself on top of the Pyramid of the Moon, the smaller of the two pyramids, which is aligned with the long processional road that formed the principal north–south axis of the ancient city, known as the Avenue of the Dead. The Pyramid of the Sun appears on the left, its steep sides dotted with vegetation. *The Pyramids of the Sun and the Moon* records the archaeological site from a different vantage-point, though Velasco's depiction of the faltering light of the sun, which glows through a bank of clouds low on the horizon, gives the composition a poetry that transcends its ostensibly documentary function.

This version of *The Pyramids of the Sun and the Moon* is a smaller, jewel-like variation of the original painting that Velasco made at Teotihuacán of the same dimensions as *The Pyramid of the Sun in Teotihuacán*. This smaller painting, commissioned by Gumersindo Mendoza, director of the Museo Nacional, was perhaps used by Velasco to prepare the lithograph – equal in size to the small painting – that illustrated Mendoza's article about the pyramids in the museum's journal.[2] A lithograph of *The Pyramid of the Sun in Teotihuacán* also accompanies the text, and Velasco made a reduced oil version of that composition at the same scale.[3]

These views of Teotihuacán, along with *The Baths of Nezahualcóyotl* (cat. 14), were among the first works that Velasco made for the Museo Nacional, where he took up an official position in 1880. In his capacity as draughtsman, he was responsible for providing precise drawings of significant pre-Hispanic objects for the museum's publications, including famed monolithic Mexica sculptures like the Piedra del Sol and the immense statue of the goddess Coatlicue. Velasco had long been interested in the Mesoamerican past, participating in 1865 in an archaeological expedition to ruins that had been discovered in the area of Huauchinango. On his return journey, he noted in his report on that excursion, he passed by 'the great pyramids of Teotihuacán'.[4] *DSR and PAV*

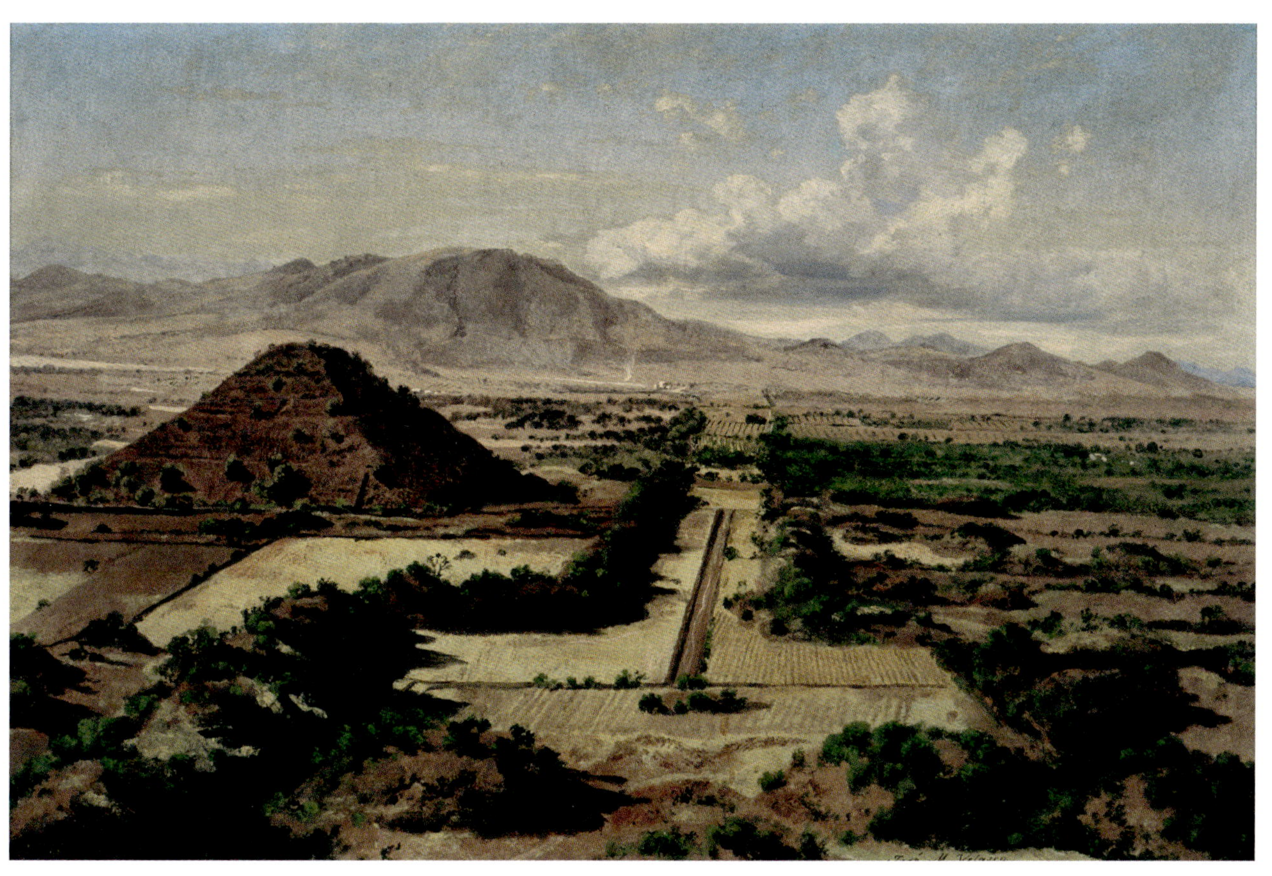

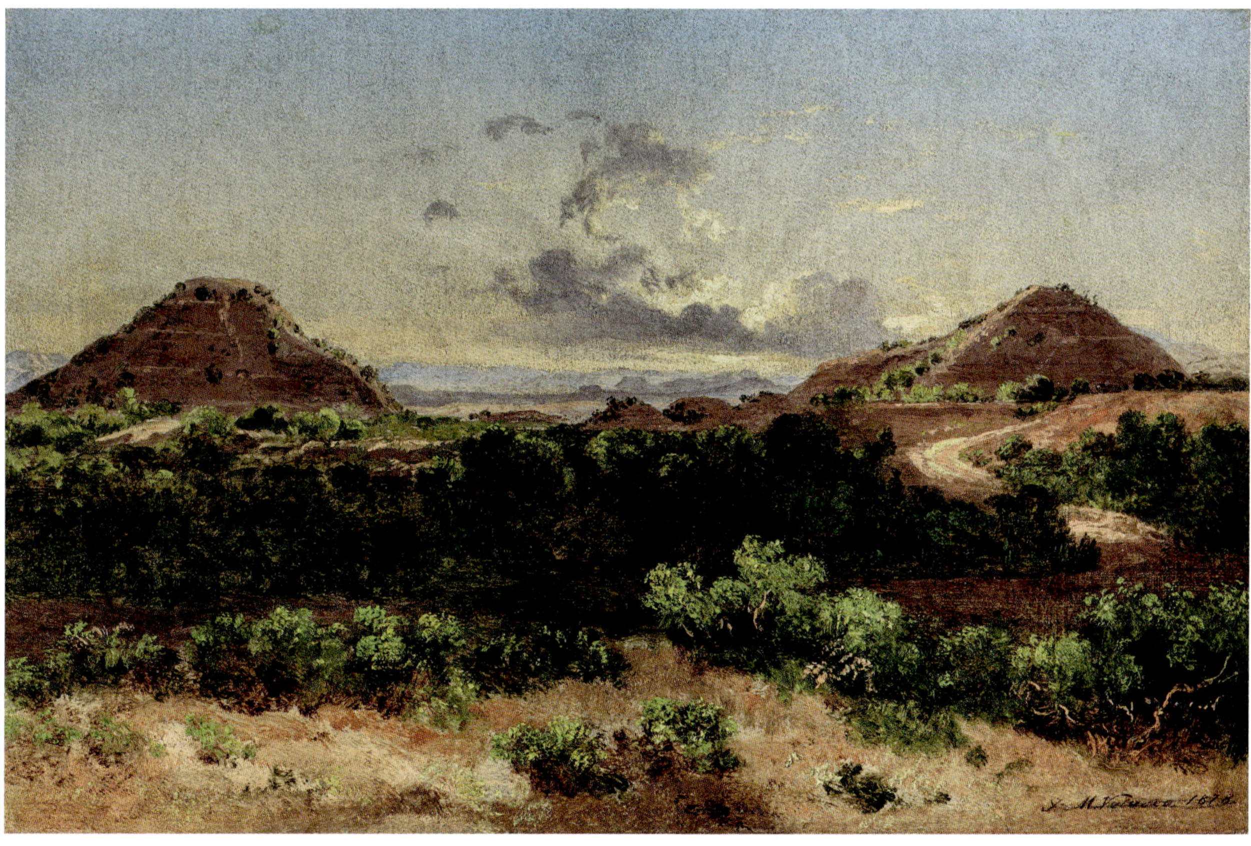

14

*THE BATHS OF
NEZAHUALCÓYOTL*

1878
OIL ON PAPER LAID DOWN ON
CANVAS, 62.7 × 46.4 CM
MUSEO NACIONAL DE ARTE, INBAL,
MEXICO CITY

This painting was made during an expedition
to the archaeological site of Texcotzingo, near
Texcoco, organised by Gumersindo Mendoza,
director of the Museo Nacional. It is signed and
dated 2 November 1878. Velasco accompanied
the expedition as the museum's draughtsman,
a position he held officially from 1880 until his
death in 1912. In this capacity, he worked under
Mendoza's guidance, producing illustrations
of ancient monuments, sculptures and
Mesoamerican codices for use in research and
the museum's journal, *Anales*. Velasco painted
the pyramids of Teotihuacán on the same
excursion (cats 12 and 13).

The archaeological site of Texcotzingo includes
the remains of a complex of pools known
as the Baños de Nezahualcóyotl, or Baths of
Nezahualcóyotl. This elaborate complex was built
in the mid-fifteenth century by the eponymous
tlahtoani or dynastic ruler of the city-state of
Texcoco, known for his love of poetry, philosophy
and nature. It was surrounded by luxurious
gardens that featured an extensive collection
of medicinal, ornamental and edible plants,
as well as exotic fauna. The building of such
installations demanded an extraordinary facility
for hydraulic engineering, notably the complex
task of channelling water from nearby springs to
sustain the gardens, the pools and the city. As
Ramírez noted, if Velasco's views of Teotihuacán
were a testament to ancient achievements in

monumental urban design and architecture,
the baths exemplified their refinement centuries
later under Nezahualcóyotl.[1]

In the painting Velasco represents the pool of
Nezahualcóyotl, carved into the rock with a fissure
through which the water would cascade into the
gardens below. As is typical in Velasco's works,
the main subject is positioned at the centre of the
composition and is seen from a slightly elevated
viewpoint. Blue skies and lilac mountains appear in
the background, while warmer yellow and ochre
tones, enriched by the green of the surrounding
vegetation, dominate the composition. The artist's
depiction of the site has a clear documentary
purpose, combining the location's natural features
with the markers of human intervention, and
showcases Velasco's ongoing dedication to the
intertwining of nature, science and history.

Velasco made this version of the painting
on site during the expedition. According to
Altamirano Piolle he would later produce
two copies: one commissioned by Mendoza
for the Museo Nacional and another for the
archaeologist Alfredo Chavero, to be included
in his *Historia antigua y de la conquista*, the first
volume of *Mexico a través de los siglos* (*Mexico
Through the Centuries*), a compendium of the
history of Mexican civilisation organised by
the liberal politician and historian Vicente Riva
Palacio and published in instalments between
1884 and 1889.[2] *VP*

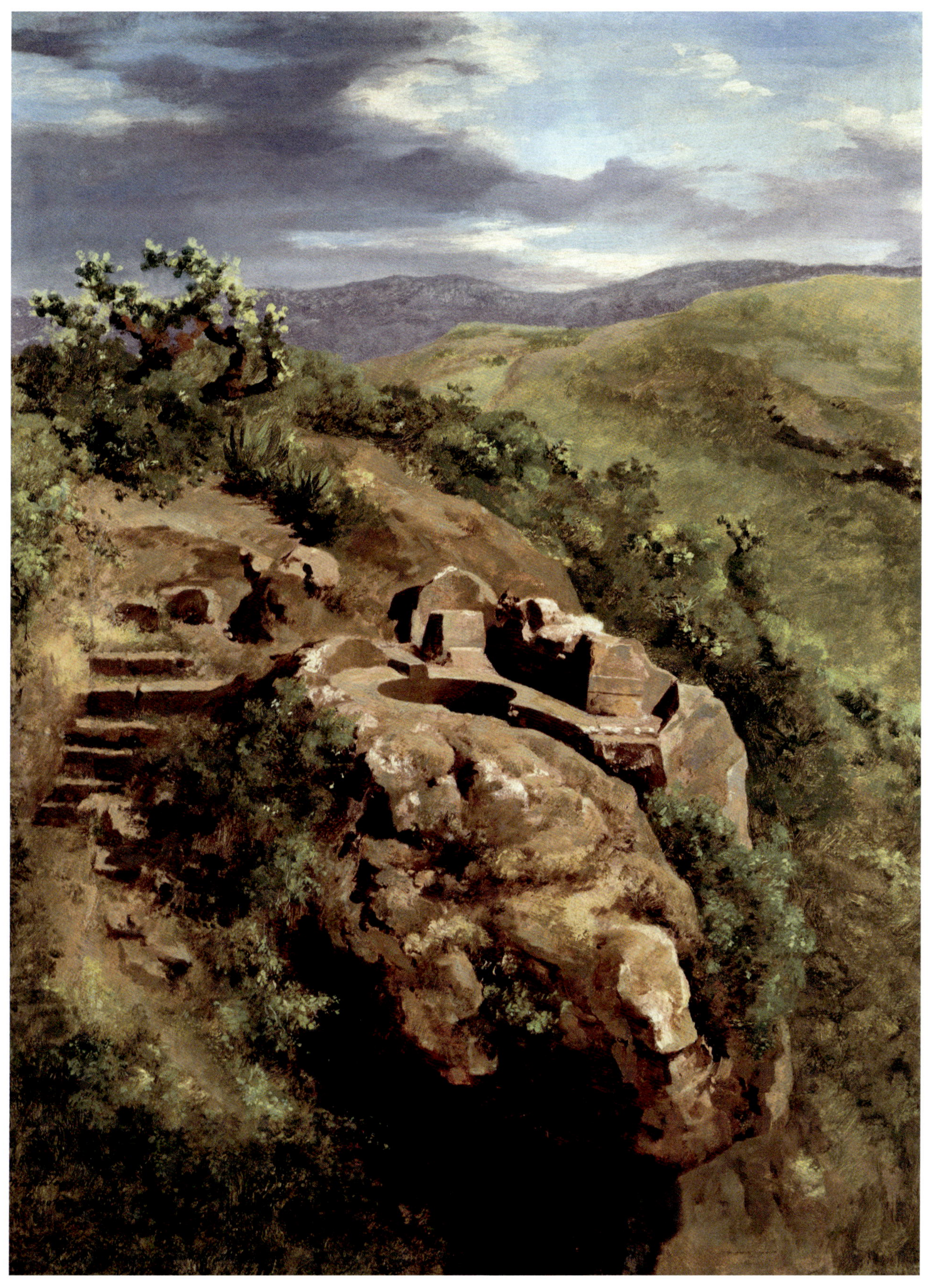

15

The mountains of the Sierra de Guadalupe, seen in the foreground of this painting, and the hill of Tepeyac – the small rise at the centre of the composition, with the town of Villa de Guadalupe nestled at its base – are prominent in dozens of Velasco's paintings of the Valley of Mexico as well as in the artist's own life. Tepeyac was where Juan Diego, an indigenous convert to Christianity, witnessed in 1531 the apparition of the Virgin of Guadalupe, who quickly became one of Mexico's most potent cultural icons. A deeply religious man, Velasco was devoted to the Virgin, and resided from 1884 until his death near the basilica in which her image is venerated in Villa de Guadalupe, where his house still stands today.[1]

Santa Isabel is one of the foothills of the Sierra de Guadalupe, which bordered the shore of Lake Texcoco, the largest of the five lakes that still covered parts of the Valley of Mexico in the 1870s. Velasco painted this canvas from the top of the hill during the months of March, April and May in 1875, a period of time that would have allowed him to observe seasonal changes to the lake in the distance, and the lagoon in the middle ground which receded and filled with the rains, as well as the effects of changing atmospheric conditions on the view to the south-east.[2] While Velasco avowed that he painted the work entirely on site, the inclusion of figures in the foreground, for which preparatory drawings survive, suggests that some refinements were probably made in the studio.[3]

The south-eastern promontories of the Sierra de Guadalupe were significant to the city's history long before the Virgin's miraculous appearance, having previously been associated with the goddess Tonantzin, a Nahuatl name that was used to describe several pre-Hispanic female deities. The area was also the destination of one of the four causeways that connected the Mexica city of Tenochtitlan, founded in 1325 in the middle of Lake Texcoco, to the shore. This route was repurposed by the Spanish, who erected monuments to the Mysteries of the Rosary along its length during the late Baroque period, from which the road – visible in the painting – took the name by which it is still known, the Calzada de los Misterios. An important pre-Hispanic hydraulic mechanism, the Albarradón de Nezahualcóyotl, was also located nearby: this was a dike designed and constructed during the reign of its namesake, ruler of the city of Texcoco. The Mexica and their allies used the barrier, which stretched some seventeen kilometres from the hill of Tepeyac in the north to Iztapalapa in the south, to control flooding and separate the brackish waters of Lake Texcoco from the spring-fed freshwater lakes to the south of Tenochtitlan, Xochimilco and Chalco.

This painting – the second of the artist's monumental views of the Valley of Mexico – was unveiled in Mexico City in December 1875 before being sent to the 1876 Centennial Exposition in Philadelphia, held to mark the centenary of American independence. Velasco's selection of such a significant location in the history of Mexico – whether conceived as valley, city or nation – was no coincidence for a painting intended to be shown abroad. The work intertwines natural and human history, themes to which Velasco returned in many of his paintings, to remind viewers

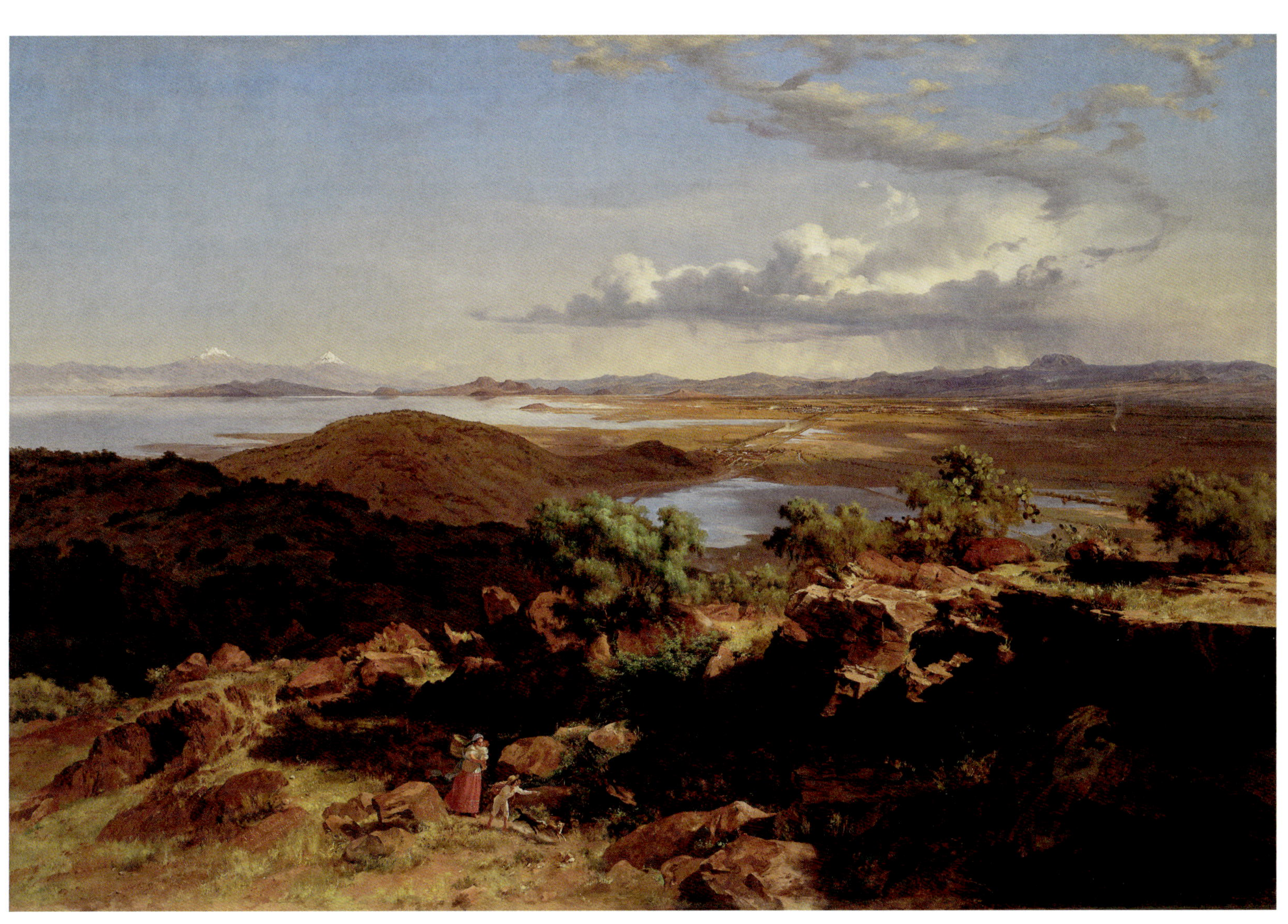

of Mexico's long historical past as compared, perhaps, to the relatively brief existence of the republic on its northern border. The episode in the foreground, with a woman carrying a basket of nopal pads and two young children, bridges past and present by evoking the indigenous communities that, though central to the nation's history, had suffered persistent marginalisation since the arrival of the Spanish.[4]

In his first large-scale view of the Valley of Mexico, *The Valley of Mexico from the Hill of Atzacoalco* (see fig. 5), which he painted in 1873 in the studio, Velasco included a number of figures venerating an image of the Virgin, though these do not appear in this precise preparatory drawing for the composition.[5] While similar studies for his later large views of the valley are not known, this scrupulous sheet – with annotations for significant buildings, peaks, and even colours to be used – demonstrates the artist's desire to capture, with an almost cartographic precision, the view from behind the complex of buildings dedicated to the cult of the Virgin of Guadalupe.[6]

The Valley of Mexico from the Hill of Santa Isabel, of which Velasco made fourteen variations in reduced sizes, expressed national pride through the painting of landscape.[7] It might also be considered a manifestation of Mexico's attempts to reassert itself in the face of the American empire. The Mexican–American War, which had led to the loss of more than half of Mexico's territory, was painful for Velasco personally as his family was forced to leave Mexico City, but it was also a traumatic moment in the national consciousness. The complex relationships between Mexico and other nations during the nineteenth century – alternating between admiration and resentment – are an unspoken presence in this painting, which the artist signed, on a rock at lower left, with both his name and his nationality. *DSR and PAV*

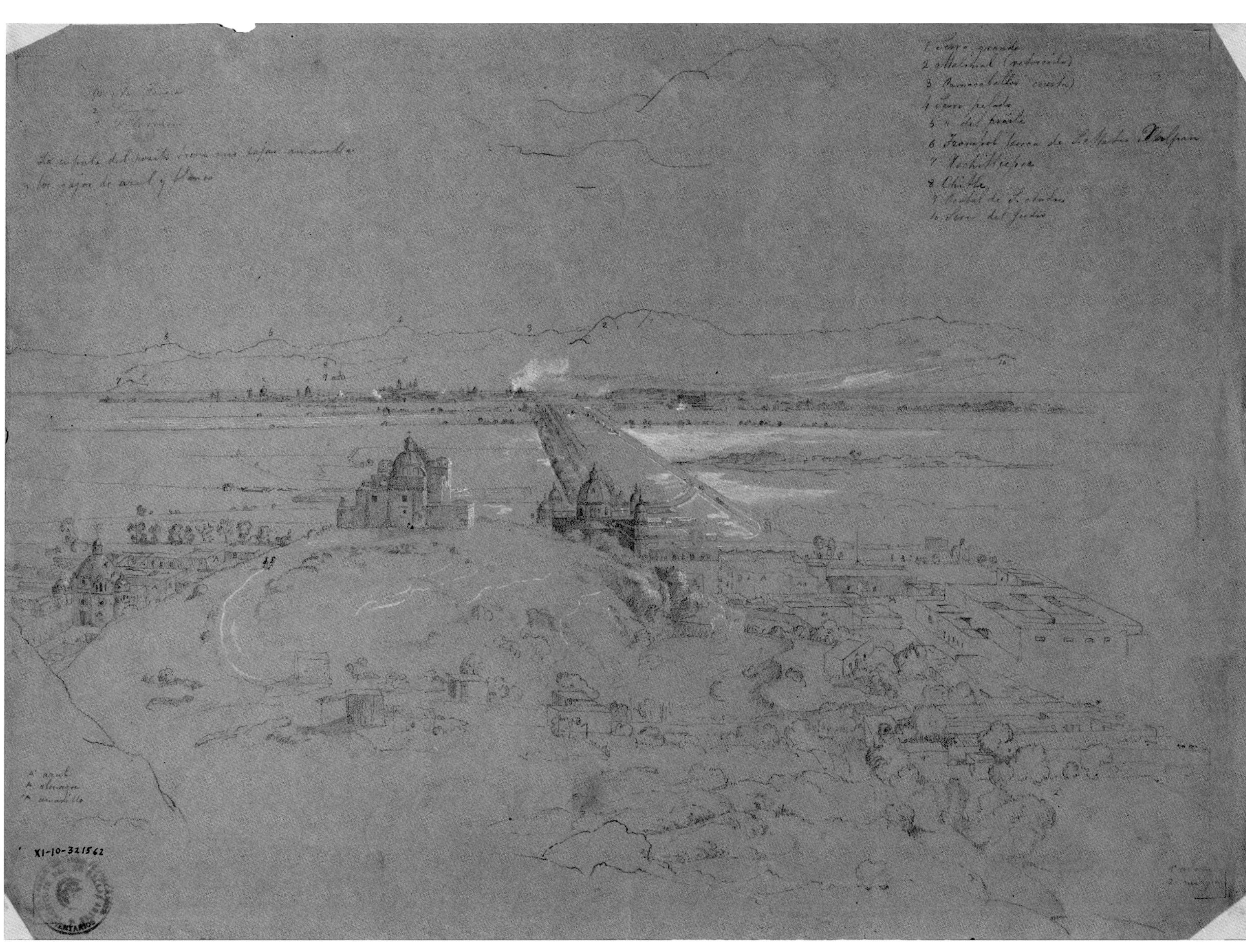

1 Cerro grande
2 Molinal (reducido)
3 Buenavista (cerrito)
4 Cerro pelado
5 " del Fraile
6 Frontol cerca de S.ta Maria Tultepan
7 Xochitepec
8 Chikile
9 Cerrito de S. Andres
10 Sierra del fierro

La cupula del pueblo viene mas bajas amarillas
los gajos de azul y blanco

azul
almagra
amarillo

XI-10-32/562

This monumental painting, Velasco's undisputed masterpiece, represents the culmination of his artistic development and, with it, his definitive transcendence of the influence of his teacher Eugenio Landesio. While his earlier large-scale views of the Valley of Mexico, painted in 1873 and 1875 (see fig. 5 and cat. 15), incorporated human figures in the foreground – in accordance with Landesio's pictorial conventions – in this painting Velasco eschews prosaic narrative devices in favour of an austere composition that draws its epic power from precise observation, superb control of atmospheric effects and, not least, a subtle but profound historical theme.

Painted during the late spring months of 1877 from the same vantage-point he had adopted two years earlier, the large canvas was first exhibited at the annual exhibition of the Escuela Nacional de Bellas Artes. In a long text that Velasco contributed to the catalogue, he described the scene with punctilious accuracy, noting that 'the effect of the light in the picture is from one of the first days of June at three o'clock in the afternoon' before naming many of the geographical features in the vista.[1] He also pointed out the stone aqueduct, just visible at the centre of the composition, that carried water to the Villa de Guadalupe and enumerated the different cloud formations he had depicted, including cumulus, nimbus and cirrus. The artist's evident concern with accuracy, or the pretence of it, however, did not preclude his rearranging and improving the view with borrowings from other paintings he had made previously, as Altamirano Piolle has observed.[2]

In his carefully structured painting Velasco brings together three historical eras, as he had in his 1875 painting: the pre-Hispanic past, the centuries of the Spanish viceroys, and contemporary Mexico. In the far distance, the capital of the modern republic – linked by rectilinear avenues and railways to the rest of the nation – has begun to expand across the plain of the Valley of Mexico, whose lakes would continue to be drained away in the decades to come. In the months that Velasco was at work on the painting, the United States – opposed to the new president, Porfirio Díaz – began to amass troops at the border, raising the spectre of an invasion that did not occur.[3] Closer to the picture plane but further away in time is the basilica dedicated to the Virgin of Guadalupe, seen at the centre of the painting at the foot of the hill of Tepeyac, which recalls the early sixteenth-century appearance of the sacred figure. The cult of the Virgin, often connected to female Mesoamerican deities, was a significant symbol of Mexico's mestizo identity, in which Spanish and indigenous traditions commingled.

In the foreground, replacing the figures that had appeared in his previous large paintings, Velasco depicted a nopal cactus, at lower left, and an eagle with a bird clasped in its beak. These emblems, whose significance surprisingly seems not to have been realised in the nineteenth century, refer to the mythical establishment of Tenochtitlan, capital of the Mexica and the forerunner of Mexico City, in the early fourteenth century. According to an ancient prophecy, an eagle with a snake in its beak would alight on a cactus at the site where

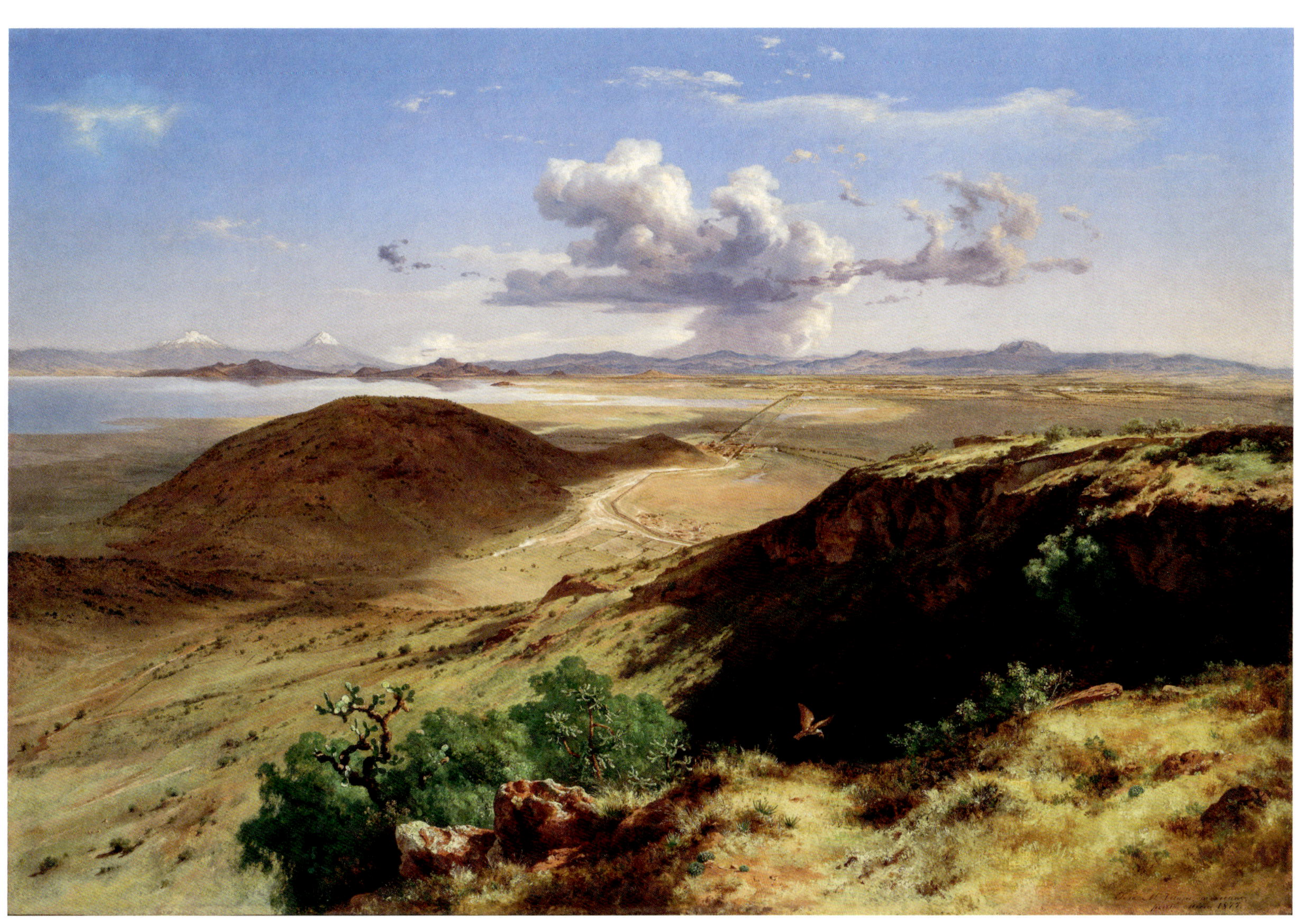

the city of the Mexica would stand. While no snake appears, other accounts of Tenochtitlan's founding, with which the artist must have been familiar, mention that the auspicious eagle feathered its nest with the colourful plumage of its avian prey.[4] The eagle and nopal, whose allusive importance to the painting were first noted by Justino Fernández in 1952, had been adopted as the nation's seal after independence and emblazon the centre of the Mexican flag.[5]

In his preparatory drawing of the eagle, Velasco seeks to capture the powerful beat of the raptor's wings, one of which he has rendered from a different angle at the bottom of the sheet. While the rough working drawing of the nopal cannot be definitively associated with this painting, the white heightening and careful shading suggest the pains that Velasco took in his representations of Mexico's plant life. Technical examination of the painting has revealed that the foreground was reworked extensively: Velasco painted over a mass of green vegetation with ochres and yellows, joining the foreground to the vista beyond and, at the same time, giving greater emphasis to its meaningful individual elements.[6] The incorporation of these symbols of Mexican identity as subtle natural details, rather than through overt historical reference, marks a signal development in Velasco's artistic vision.

Velasco painted the work, which garnered him first prize at the exhibition in Mexico City and a medal awarded by Díaz himself, with the intention of sending it to the Exposition Universelle in Paris in 1878, arranging for its transportation and display at his own expense (see p. 30). The success of this painting – of which he later made seven variations at smaller scale – established a template that Velasco would follow, with some exceptions, in subsequent decades, balancing precise observation with symbolic resonance.[7] More than any other painting in his oeuvre, this view from Santa Isabel, acquired by the government several years after it was made, cemented Velasco's status as the pre-eminent painter of Mexico in the late nineteenth century. *DSR*

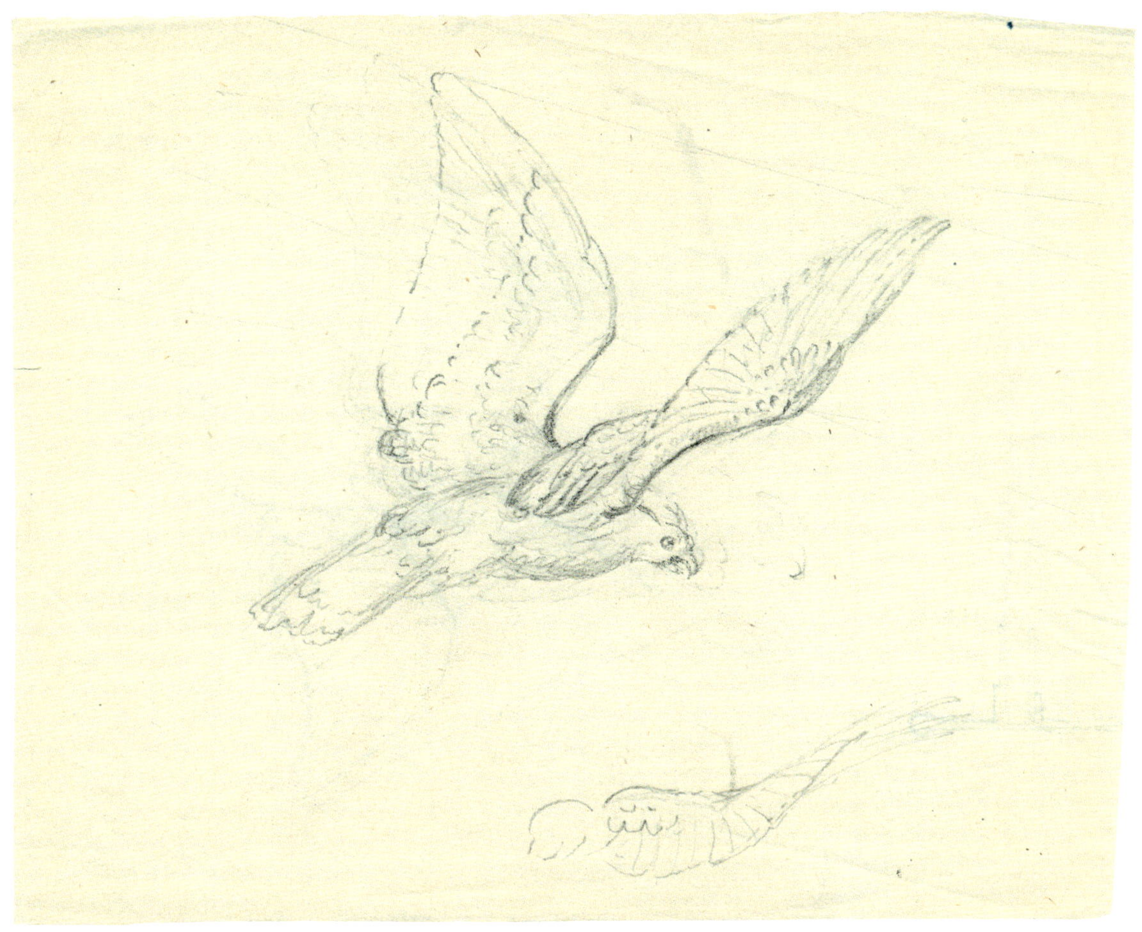

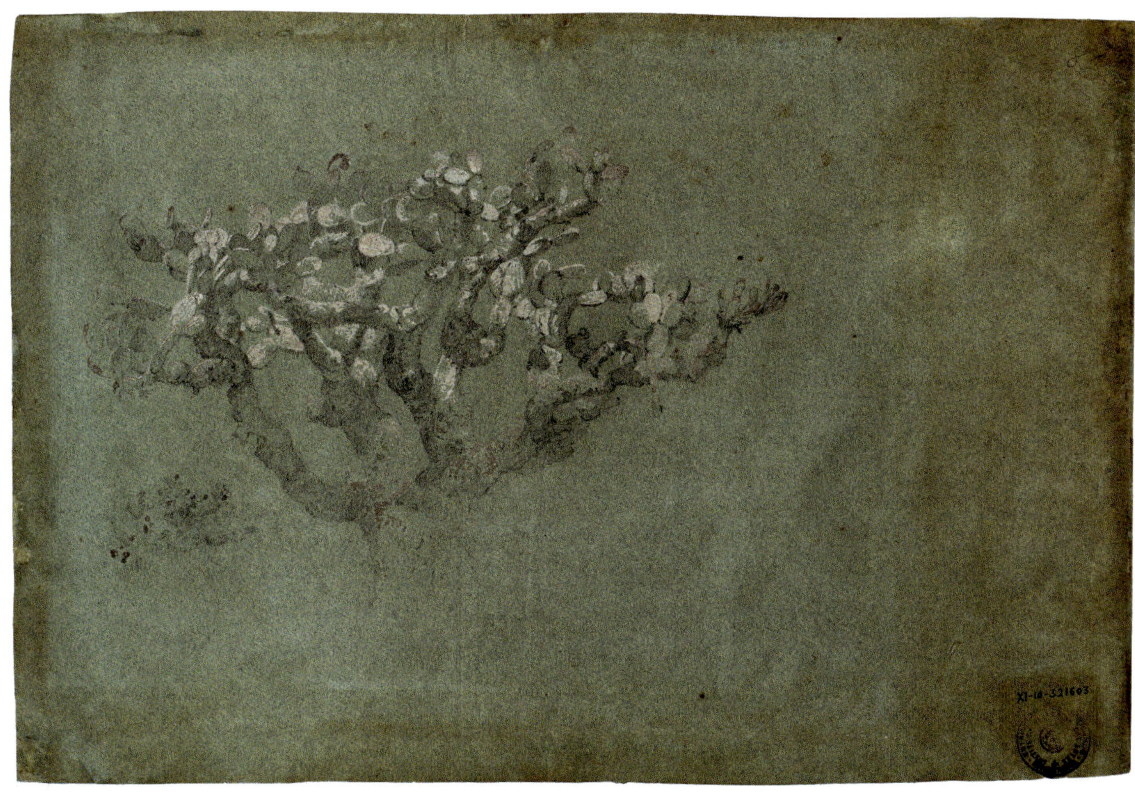

STUDY OF RAINBOWS

1884
PENCIL AND COLOURED PENCIL
ON PAPER, 24.5 × 31.8 CM
MUSEO NACIONAL DE ARTE, INBAL,
MEXICO CITY

On a scientific expedition to the Mesa de Metlaltoyuca near Puebla in 1865, Velasco noted: 'The artist needs to do little and observe much to enrich the imagination with the variety of objects that nature presents to us.'[1] This study of rainbows reflects the artist's commitment to his former teacher Eugenio Landesio's compositional method for landscape paintings, which stated that every single element of nature should be submitted to meticulous observation before they could be integrated into a cohesive whole.

The study is divided into three sections. The upper section depicts a rainbow set against the sky and encircled by clouds. The lower part of the drawing is split into two: on the left, Velasco concentrates on the colours of the rainbow and how the eye perceives them, the handwritten inscription detailing: 'The brightest and most visible is the yellow; followed by the orange and the green; blue and violet are less noticeable, while red is somewhat more apparent. Everything stands out because it is light.'[2]

On the right-hand section of the lower half, the artist plays with the inverted image of the rainbow, perhaps evoking the use of optical devices such as a camera, with a written note: 'The mirror or reflection of the rainbow has its colours inverted.'[3]

The work is dated 17 July 1884. The collection of the Museo Nacional de Arte includes at least one more study of clouds by Velasco bearing the same date, and throughout his life the artist executed many similar studies that demonstrate his interest in capturing atmospheric phenomena. While rainbows do not appear often in his paintings, weather conditions are always a special feature, used to lend a sense of drama or tranquillity to the composition. In some of the panoramic views of the Valley of Mexico heavy clouds gather on the horizon, announcing an imminent rain shower, while works like *Lumen en coelo* (*Light in the Sky*), which exists in different versions dating from 1892 to 1894, powerfully illustrate the dramatic effects of a stormy sky looming over a serene pasture. The last painting Velasco worked on before his death in 1912 (cat. 28), which remained unfinished, serves as a final testament to the artist's longstanding interest in depicting the heavens. *VP*

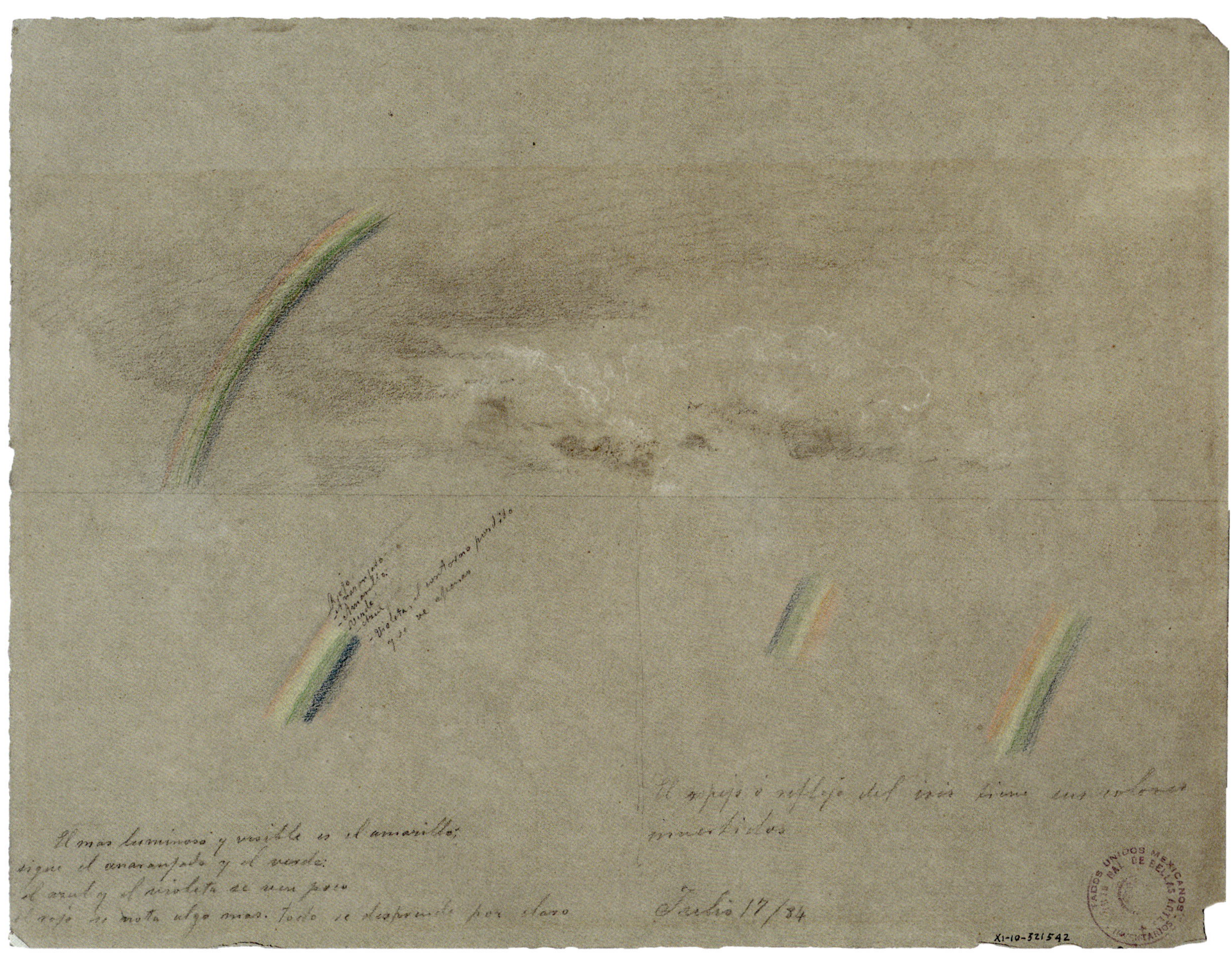
Rojo
Anaranjado
Amarillo
Verde
Azul
Violeta es un tono mas
que se apenas

El espejo ó reflejo del iris tiene sus colores
invertidos

El mas luminoso y visible es el amarillo:
sigue el anaranjado y el verde:
el azul y el violeta se ven poco
el rojo se nota algo mas. todo se desprende por claro

Julio 17/84

*ROCKS ON THE HILL
OF ATZACOALCO*

1874
OIL ON CANVAS, 31.5 × 44 CM
MUSEO NACIONAL DE ARTE, INBAL,
MEXICO CITY

22

STUDY OF ROCKS AND
FOLIAGE

DATE UNKNOWN
PENCIL ON PAPER, 10 × 13 CM
MUSEO NACIONAL DE ARTE, INBAL,
MEXICO CITY

Beginning in 1873, Velasco made a series of paintings of the outcrops, escarpments and boulders of the hill of Atzacoalco, which rises up to the north of the town of Villa de Guadalupe.[1] These meticulous depictions of rocks belong to Velasco's sustained investigation of the geological features of the Valley of Mexico, a project that occupied him throughout his career and overlapped with significant developments in scientific understanding of the region's geology. Like his conscientious renderings of cloud formations, they demonstrate the artist's interest in combining scientific observation with artistic representation, uniting precise records of geological phenomena with explorations of light, form and texture.

Velasco approached these landscapes as he did most others, making a small sketch outdoors to capture the scene and then elaborating in his studio a larger and more finished painting, which often entailed the inclusion of figures. In the study for *Rocks on the Hill of Atzacoalco* (private collection), the artist painted the imposing stones – which are perhaps porphyritic rhyolites – with care, but left the foreground unresolved.[2] In the version made in the studio, he added three ascending figures: a young man gestures to a veiled woman, while another woman, balancing a basket on her head, brings up the rear. Their presence emphasises the rocks' massive scale while suggesting the unequal relationship between natural and human forces. The composition is further enriched by Velasco's scrupulous observation of local flora, which include on the far left what appears to be a native variety of kidneywood tree, as well as the grasses and colonies of lichen that populate the rock faces, only suggested in the on-site study.[3] The pencil drawing, of uncertain date, also represents an isolated geological formation on a slope, which Velasco has sketched with considerable attention to the play of light and shadow across the uneven, craggy surfaces of the rocks.

Velasco's series of observations of the hill's massive rock formations – his 'mineral paintings' in Ramírez's phrase – reflect contemporary scientific understandings of these large stones, known as erratics, as evidence of a period of ancient glaciation.[4] This theory, proposed by the renowned geologist Louis Agassiz in 1840, had important implications for the Valley of Mexico, which often experienced flooding and was connected by some Mexican geologists to the great inundation described in the Bible.[5] These works, therefore, relate to an emerging nineteenth-century understanding of landscape as historically contingent, shaped by both natural processes and human intervention. Velasco's attentiveness to the rocks' layering and erosion suggests that they were notable records of geological processes, visible remnants of deep time. *PAV and DSR*

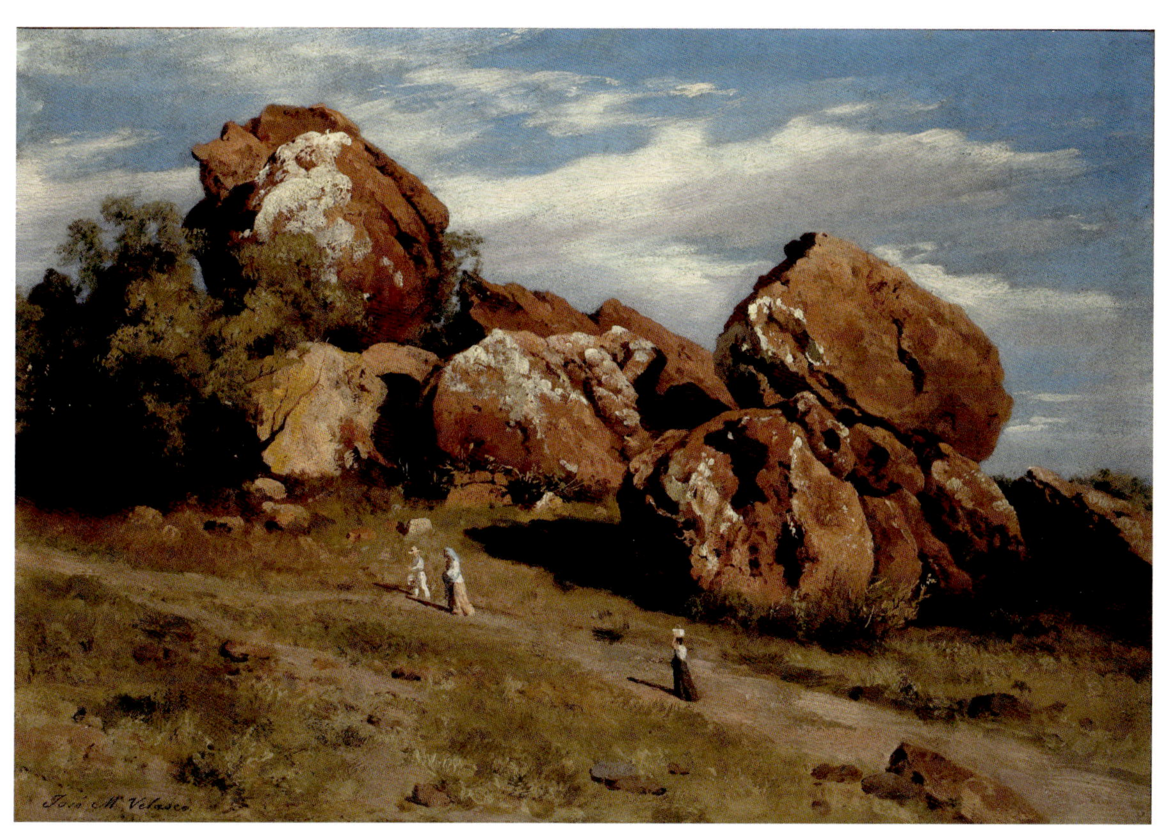

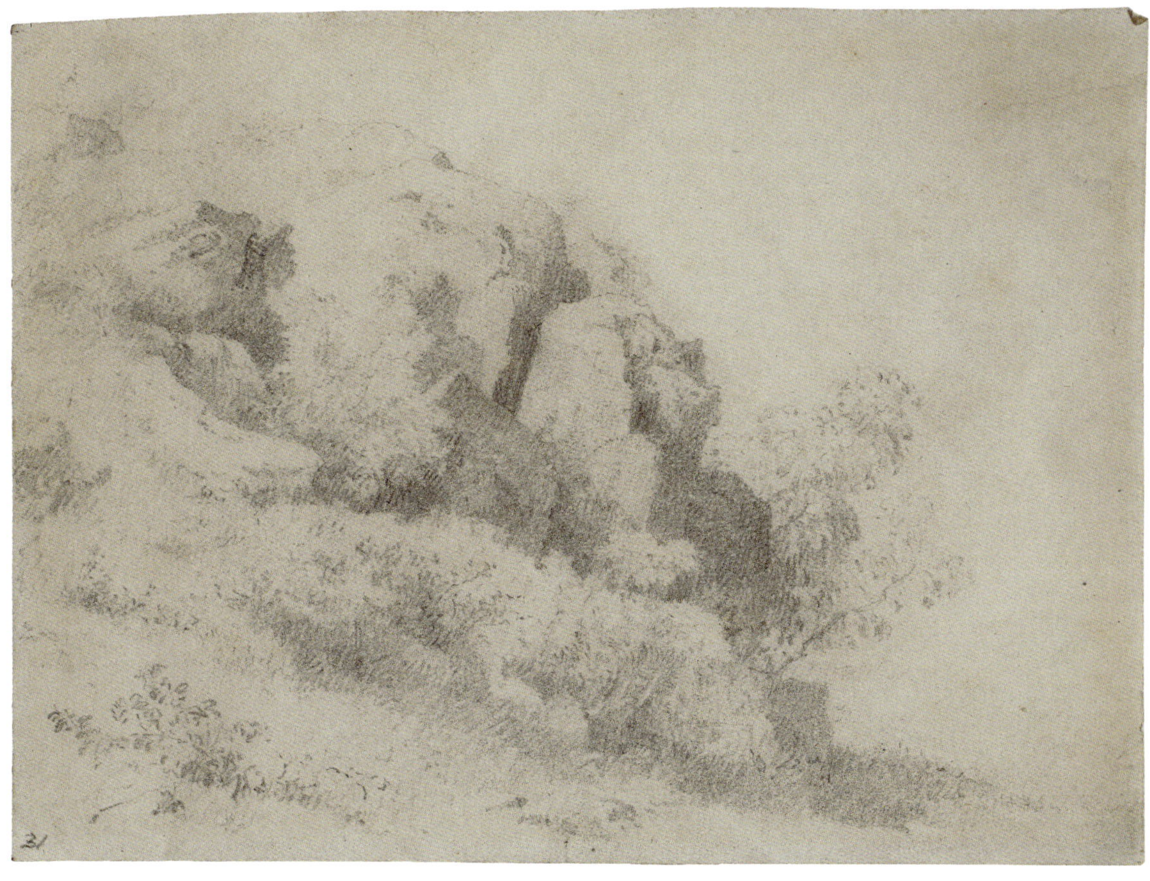

23

ROCKS

1894
OIL ON CANVAS, 163 × 105.5 CM
MUSEO NACIONAL DE ARTE, INBAL,
MEXICO CITY

Velasco first depicted this rock in a small oil painting (now lost), which served as a reference point in the creation of two larger canvases.[1] Alternatively titled *Porphyries of Tepeyac* after the purplish igneous rock that it depicts, the version shown here is one of these larger works. Altamirano Piolle notes that Velasco mentioned the porphyries in his personal documents ('these rocks had a cross on the top, placed there by stonecutters exploiting the rock; as of now, it no longer exists'),[2] while Ramírez comments on the way in which the artist imbued some of his paintings with religious symbolism, stating that in one of the three versions Velasco painted a cross on top of the rock.[3]

Religious symbolism was not a new phenomenon as far as the hill of Tepeyac was concerned, as it is believed to have been for centuries the site of worship for a female Mexica deity. However, it is no coincidence that in this same place the Virgin Mary would appear in December 1531 to a recently converted indigenous man. After four consecutive apparitions, the Virgin Mary is said to have left her own image imprinted on his *tilma* or tunic. This image of the *Virgen morena* or 'brown-skinned Virgin' is, according to tradition, the same one that is still venerated in one of the most visited Catholic shrines in the world, the Basilica of Our Lady of Guadalupe, built at the base of the hill of Tepeyac.

In *Rocks* Velasco positions the porphyry squarely at the centre of the composition, to ensure its position as the painting's focal point. The use of an oblique light source accentuates the intricate patterns on its rugged surface. The work captures the rock's facets in precise detail, almost as if the artist intended to paint its portrait. In fact, Ramírez describes Velasco's studies of rocks and plants as 'portraits of inanimate things', highlighting their focus on isolated elements of nature stripped of broader narrative context.[4]

This large depiction of a rock, a result of volcanic activity whose shape was carved over centuries by relentless meteorological forces, invites viewers to contemplate the vast expanse of geological time. Both the studies of isolated rock formations and his more extensive panoramic compositions can be seen as important indications of Velasco's fascination with geology, shared by many other artists during his lifetime. In the second half of the nineteenth century, geological knowledge equipped landscape painters with the ability to understand the history and processes that had shaped their surroundings. In a way, landscape painting became comparable to history painting, depicting the history of the Earth rather than human events.[5] The fascination with geology was such that artists relied on the work of palaeontologists and geologists to reconstruct scenes of life in prehistoric times, as in Velasco's panels for the new building of Mexico's Instituto de Geología in 1906.

By the time Velasco created *Rocks*, he was likely very familiar with the geology of the hill of Tepeyac. He had moved with his family to the village of Guadalupe in 1884, and from this hill, north of present-day Mexico City, he produced at least eight views of the Valley of Mexico between 1894 and 1895. *VP*

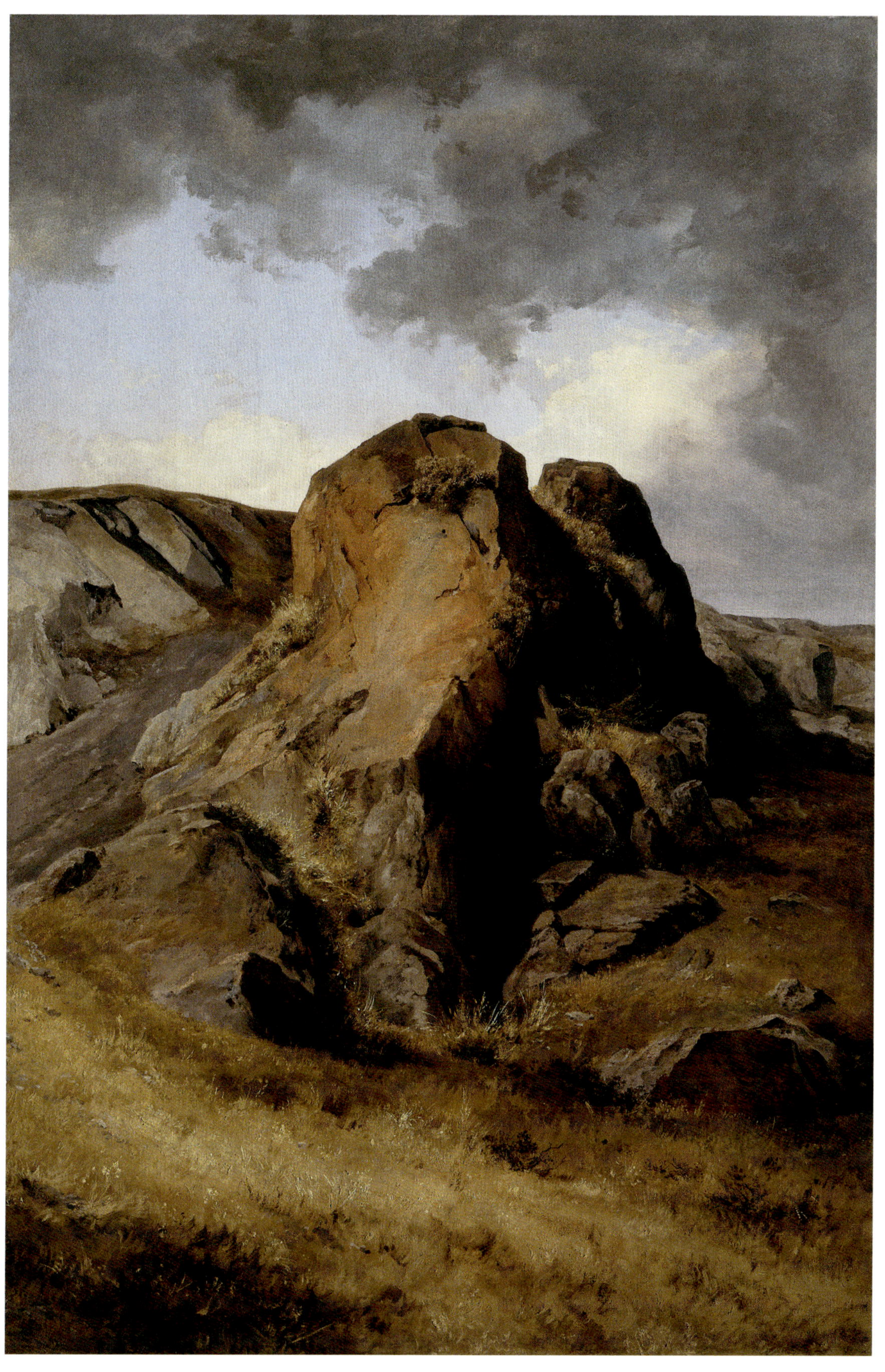

24

TEMASCALCINGO

1909
OIL ON CANVAS, 30 × 40 CM
ELDA MARGARITA CAPETILLO PONCE

Velasco depicted his birthplace San Miguel Temascalcingo twice in his career. He first painted the town from life in 1878 and later created this second version, dated 1909, building on the initial work. His personal connection to the subject is noted in the inscription: 'San Miguel Temascalcingo. View taken from La Joya. The maker was born in this village in 1840.'[1]

The panoramic view, captured from halfway up the hill of La Joya, looks south-west over the arid valley where Temascalcingo is situated, surrounded by volcanic mountains. A green strip running through the centre of the painting indicates that the town was built along the edge of a waterway. Dominating the town's skyline is the church of San Miguel Arcángel, founded by Franciscan monks in the sixteenth century. While the composition of the two paintings is very similar, the 1909 version reflects Velasco's later style, featuring a more simple treatment of the subject with fewer elements in the foreground.

According to Ramírez, Velasco depicted more places with historical associations in the period after his appointment as professor of landscape painting at the Escuela Nacional de Bellas Artes in 1877 and his close collaboration with the Museo Nacional.[2] The first painting of Temascalcingo is contemporary with his views of the archaeological sites of Teotihuacán and the Baths of Nezahualcóyotl (cats 12, 13 and 14). It seems reasonable to imagine that, apart from his own connection with the place, the artist would have wanted to bring attention to Temascalcingo's history. The town's name has its origins in the Nahuatl language, meaning 'the place of the small *temazcal*' (steam bath), alluding to traditional pre-Hispanic practices of body and soul purification. Not far from the town one can still find the so-called Spring of Jesus, or 'El Borbollón', a natural spring of volcanically heated water. The surrounding region contains archaeological sites with many cave paintings, indicating that occupation of this area on the edge of the River Lerma can be dated back around ten thousand years.

Like many of Velasco's paintings, this work intertwines the location's history with contemporary life, suggested by the smoke rising in the upper right-hand section of the canvas. This may indicate the nearby mountain known as La Pedrera (The Quarry), whose limestone was used for construction. *VP*

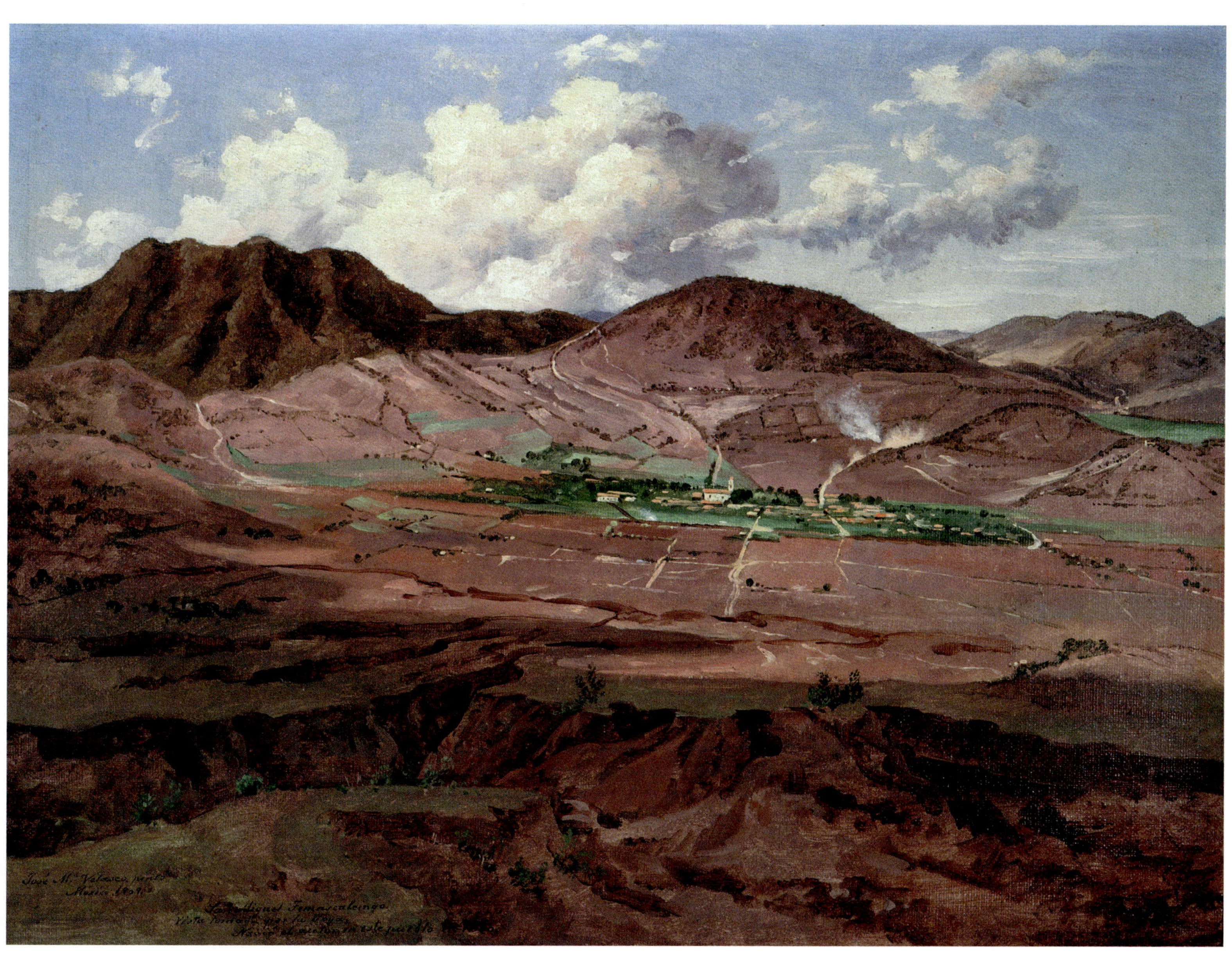
José Mª Velasco, pintó
México 1897
San Miguel Temascalcingo
Vista tomada por la tarde
Nació el autor en este pueblo

1910
OIL ON CANVAS, 121 × 81 CM
ACERVO DE LA SECRETARÍA DE
CULTURA DE VERACRUZ

In this late work, painted just two years before his death, Velasco recalls a celestial event that he had witnessed nearly three decades earlier, noting in an inscription near the bottom of the canvas that the composition was 'taken from life' on 4 October 1882.[1] The artist must refer to an original on-site sketch, however, because this painting – one of the largest that he made during the last decade of his life – is dated 1910 in the lower right corner.[2] In Velasco's elegiac canvas the pale white sweep of the comet's luminous, dispersing tail, reflected in the dark waters of the lake below, stands out on a background that gradates from an ash blue to the faint warm tones of the day's first light.

The Great Comet of 1882, visible during the autumn of that year, was one of the group of comets now called Kreutz sungrazers, some of which are among the brightest comets ever recorded. Juan Nepomuceno Adorno, a writer and inventor, observed the comet from Mexico City in late September, writing that it 'has such marvellous grace in its outline and so much vigour in its light that one never tires of contemplating it, and it is no wonder that it has made so many lazy people get up early in the morning to see such a splendid celestial phenomenon'.[3] Velasco painted several small nocturnal landscapes as well as studies of the sun, the moon and shooting stars in the years after 1900, and while they can be regarded as further expressions of his indefatigable interest in contemporary scientific discourse, *The Great Comet of 1882*, in particular, seems to bear both astronomical and political meanings.[4]

Comets had long held a special significance in Mexican culture, presaging conflict and change. In sixteenth-century accounts, like the *Durán Codex* (see fig. 32) and the *Florentine Codex*, the appearance of a shooting star augured ill for Moctezuma, the ruler of Mexico City, whose kingdom would soon be invaded by the Spanish. In spring 1910, the year Velasco painted this canvas, Halley's Comet, as predicted, glowed bright in the skies over Mexico. After a French astronomer, Camille Flammarion, was understood to have claimed that the comet's tail would infuse the Earth's atmosphere with lethal gas, panic ensued, and churches filled as the comet approached. The government of Porfirio Díaz also began to disintegrate. Attempting to avoid electoral defeat, the 79-year-old dictator imprisoned his opponent, an act that sparked the internecine conflict that grew into the conflagration of the Mexican Revolution.

Velasco's decision to paint this retrospective view of the comet of 1882 in 1910, the year that marked the end of the Porfiriato and the beginning of a decade of civil war, suggests not only his awareness of this venerable visual tradition, which had its roots in pre-Hispanic culture, but also his astute understanding of contemporary Mexican politics. Just as the subject was a departure from the norm, so was the format, vertical rather than horizontal, which lends this austere painting – the artist's last great achievement – its portentous, almost mystical quality. *DSR*

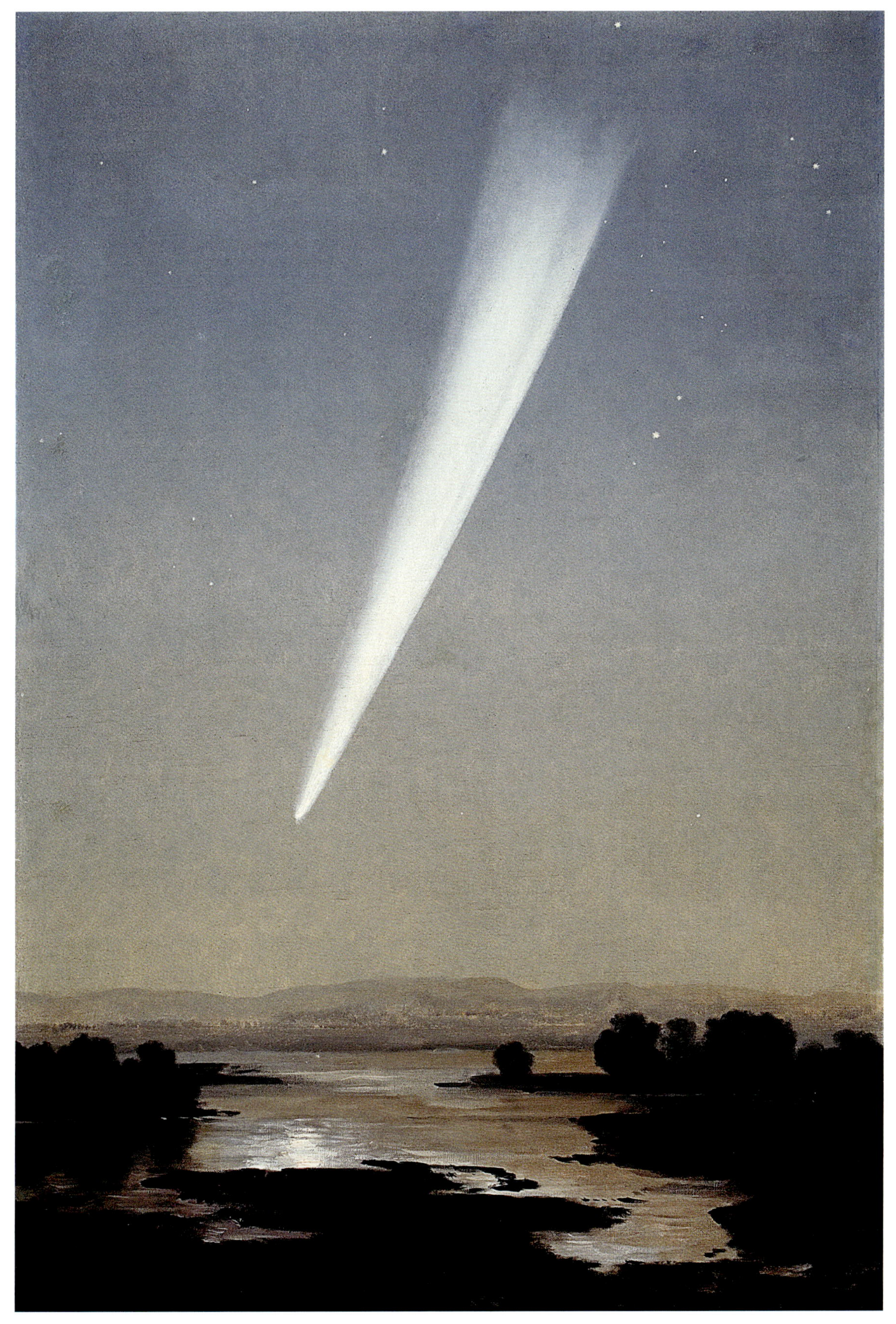

1910
OIL ON CARD, 14 × 9 CM
MUSEO NACIONAL DE ARTE, INBAL,
MEXICO CITY

Created during the later years of Velasco's life, this painting does not depict a real event but is instead an imagined scene. Alongside other small works exploring astronomical phenomena, nocturnal landscapes and dramatic atmospheric effects, the painting reflects the intense experimentation – in both subject matter and style – that characterised the last decade of the artist's life. During this time, Velasco experienced a significant decline in both his artistic reputation and his status at the Escuela Nacional de Bellas Artes, as well as his health. His creative imagination, which had long been captivated by the tectonic forces that shaped the landscapes he painted, now seemed to aim for a larger scale, tackling either cosmological subjects or the most threatening and uncontrollable forces of nature.

The painting captures a volcanic eruption with striking intensity. Minimal context is provided for the surroundings, with the focus solely on the eruption itself. The violent explosion of lava in the foreground is rendered with thick layers of yellow and red paint, while the dark column of smoke, which rises and blends with the greyish sky above, is rendered with loose, fast brushstrokes. Overall, the work offers a stark contrast to the smooth, finished views and tranquil atmosphere of Velasco's earlier works.

Volcanic eruptions were not entirely new to Velasco's artistic repertoire. As Altamirano Piolle notes, as a member of the Sociedad Mexicana de Historia Natural he had earlier made two prints of volcanic eruptions as illustrations to articles published in the journal *La Naturaleza* (see fig. 23). According to Altamirano Piolle, one of them was created from descriptions of an eruption that had taken place in 1855. The other, the eruption of the volcano Ceboruco in the state of Nayarit, was 'drawn by Velasco during its spectacular moments of eruption, capturing the dangerous emissions of gas and steam from four columns hundreds of metres high, which the wind carried in all directions'.[1] This painting is executed in the postcard format that Velasco used frequently in the last five years of his life. *VP*

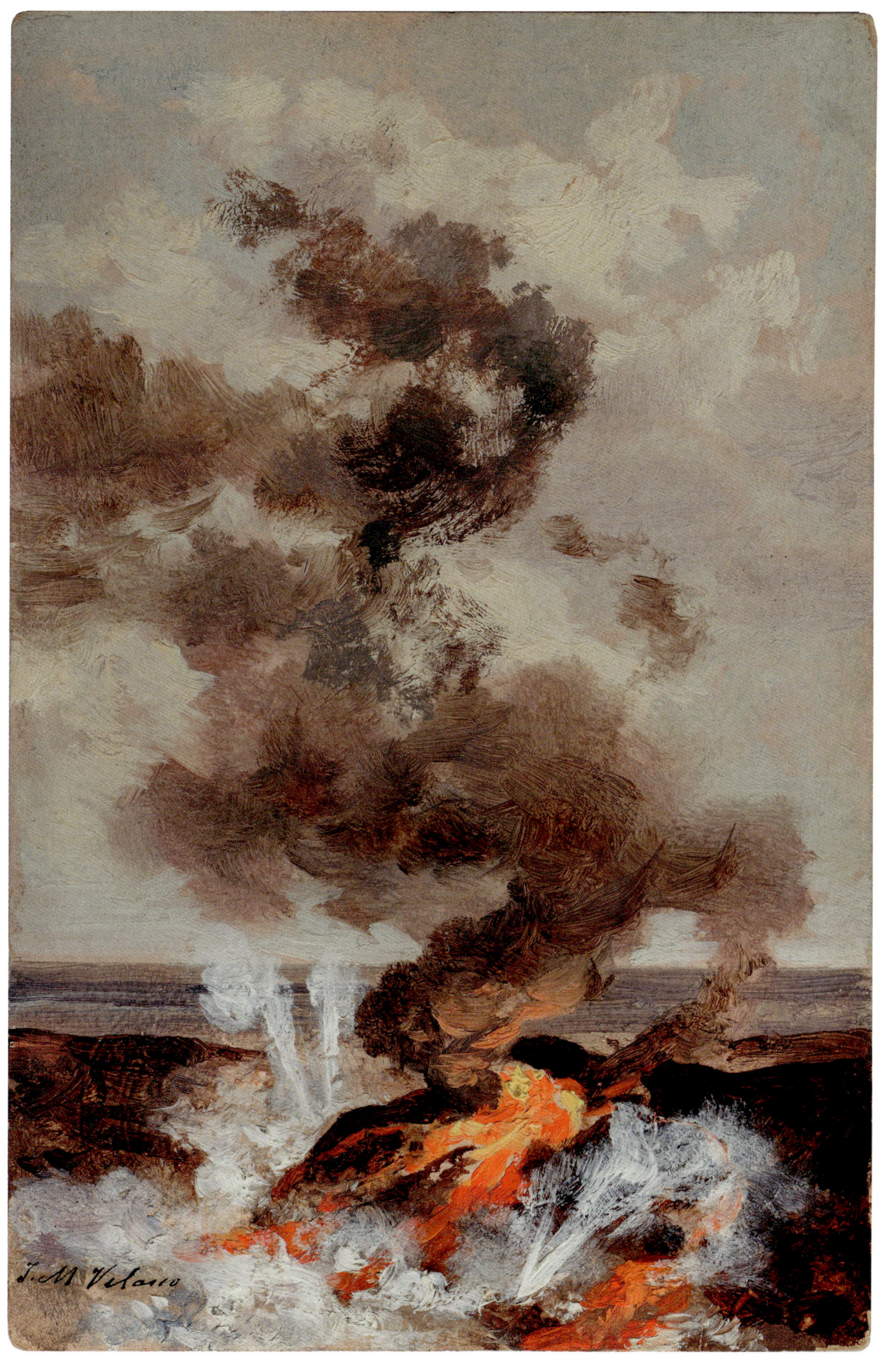

J. M. Vilasó

Following a train accident in 1901, which limited his mobility, and the gradual curtailment of his teaching duties over the following decade, imposed on him against his will, Velasco began to work at a more intimate scale. Particularly during the final few years of his life, he sometimes made small paintings on postcards: the embossed seal of Mexico, which depicts an eagle with a snake in its beak perched on a nopal, appears in the top left corners of both these works. While these late paintings have been interpreted through the lens of the ageing artist's presumed melancholy, they also testify to his persistent desire to continue depicting the world around him in whatever way he could.[1]

In *Aerial Perspective, Clouds and Space* Velasco returns to his enduring fascination with meteorological observation. The light of the sun's rays, reflected on the lake below, bursts through clouds, an effect reminiscent of his small painting of the pyramids of Teotihuacán (cat. 12), made some thirty years earlier. Velasco made cloud studies throughout his career and the postcard paintings, in which the sky usually occupies more than half of the image, can be understood in relation to these, though the later works – with their spiritual sensibility – depart from his earlier, more documentary studies, probably intended for use in other compositions. The loose handling and light palette that characterise the postcard paintings, which were never intended for exhibition, perhaps suggest Velasco's awareness of the artistic developments associated with Impressionism, though if he engaged with these innovations at all he did so selectively and on his own terms.[2]

This study, believed to be his last work, occupies a poignant place in Velasco's oeuvre, having been left unfinished on the morning of his death on 26 August 1912.[3] Above the ruled line that divides the card in two he indicated the rolling contours of the mountains of the Valley of Mexico with faint strokes of blue, though the forms of the white clouds overhead, through which glimpses of the support emerge, were the focus of his attention. The space below, where he might have intended to complete the landscape with one of his habitual motifs – a winding dirt track, a stand of trees or an expanse of shimmering water – remains untouched. *DSR*

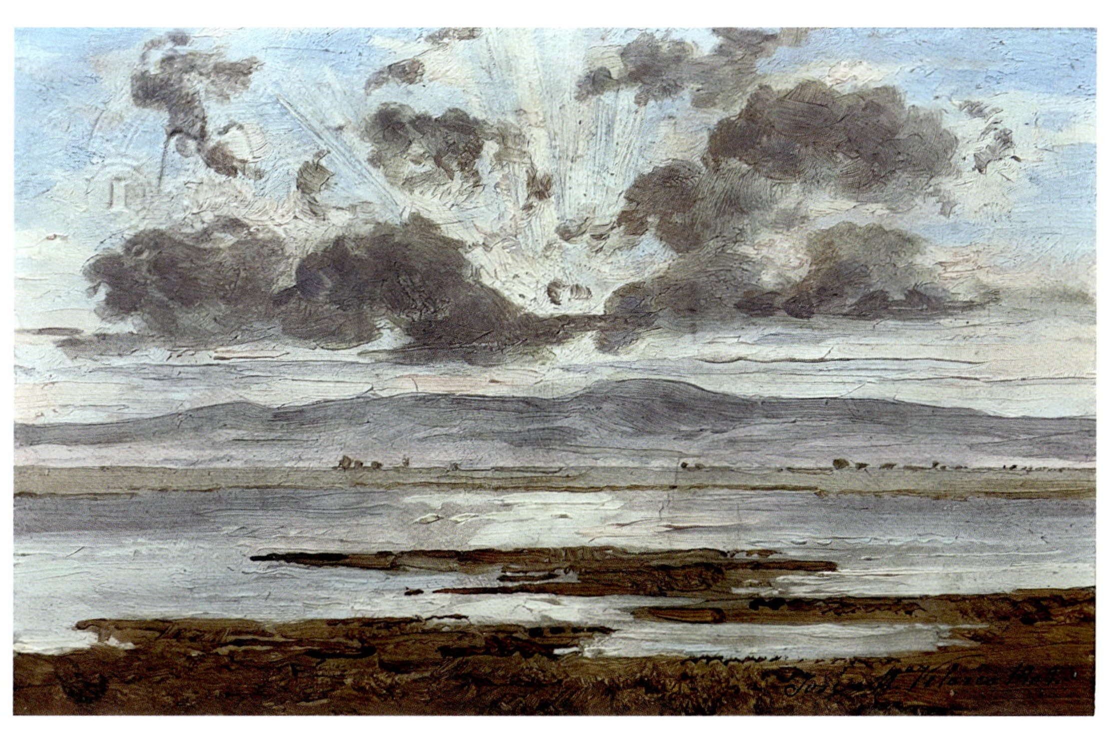

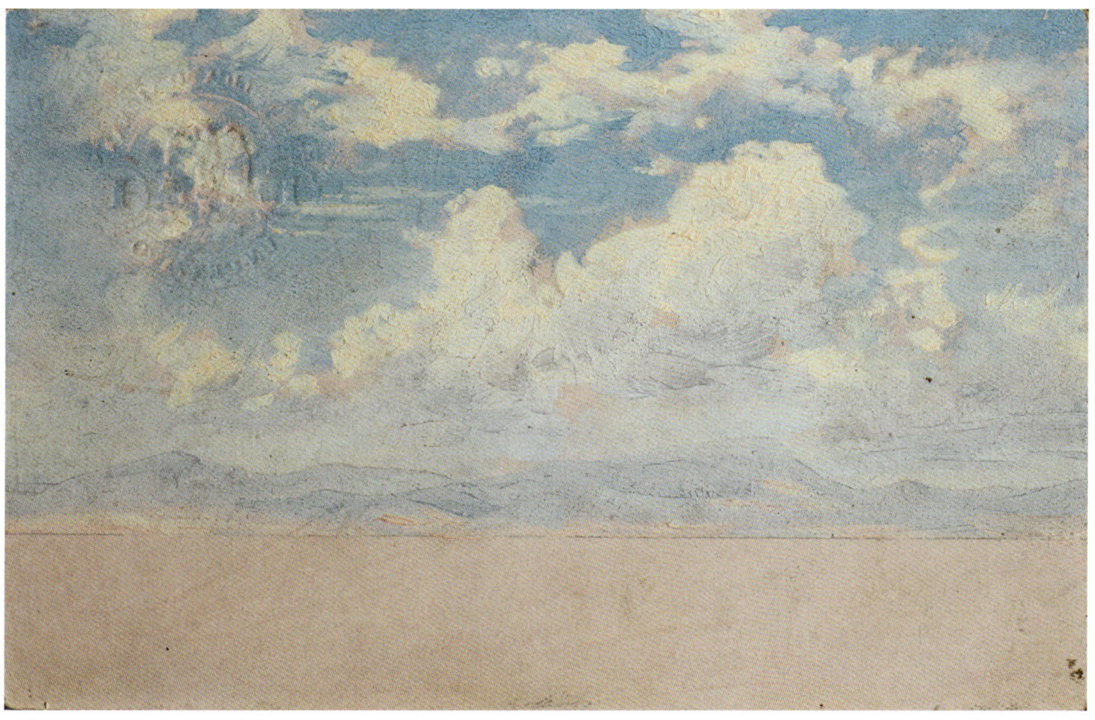

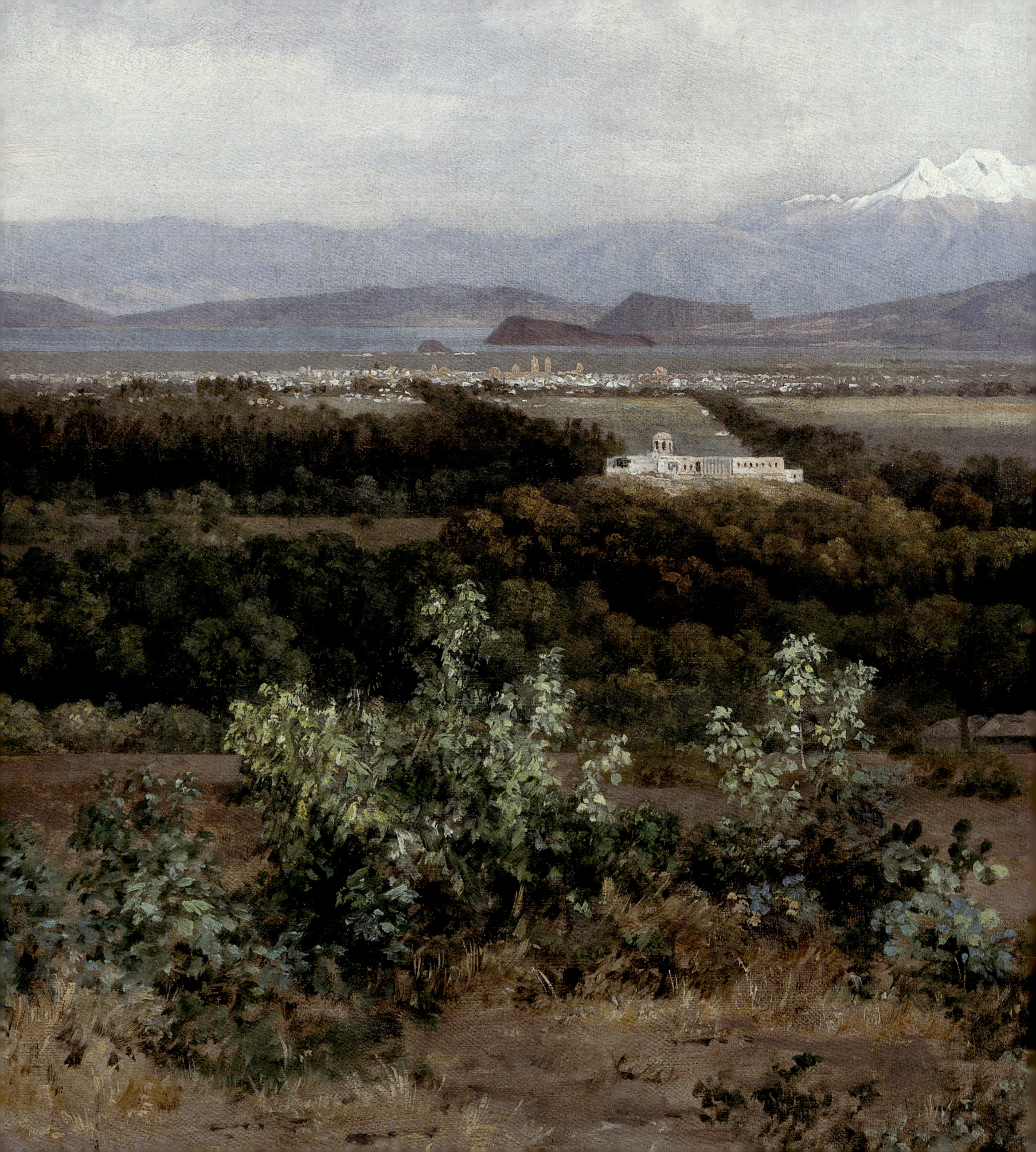

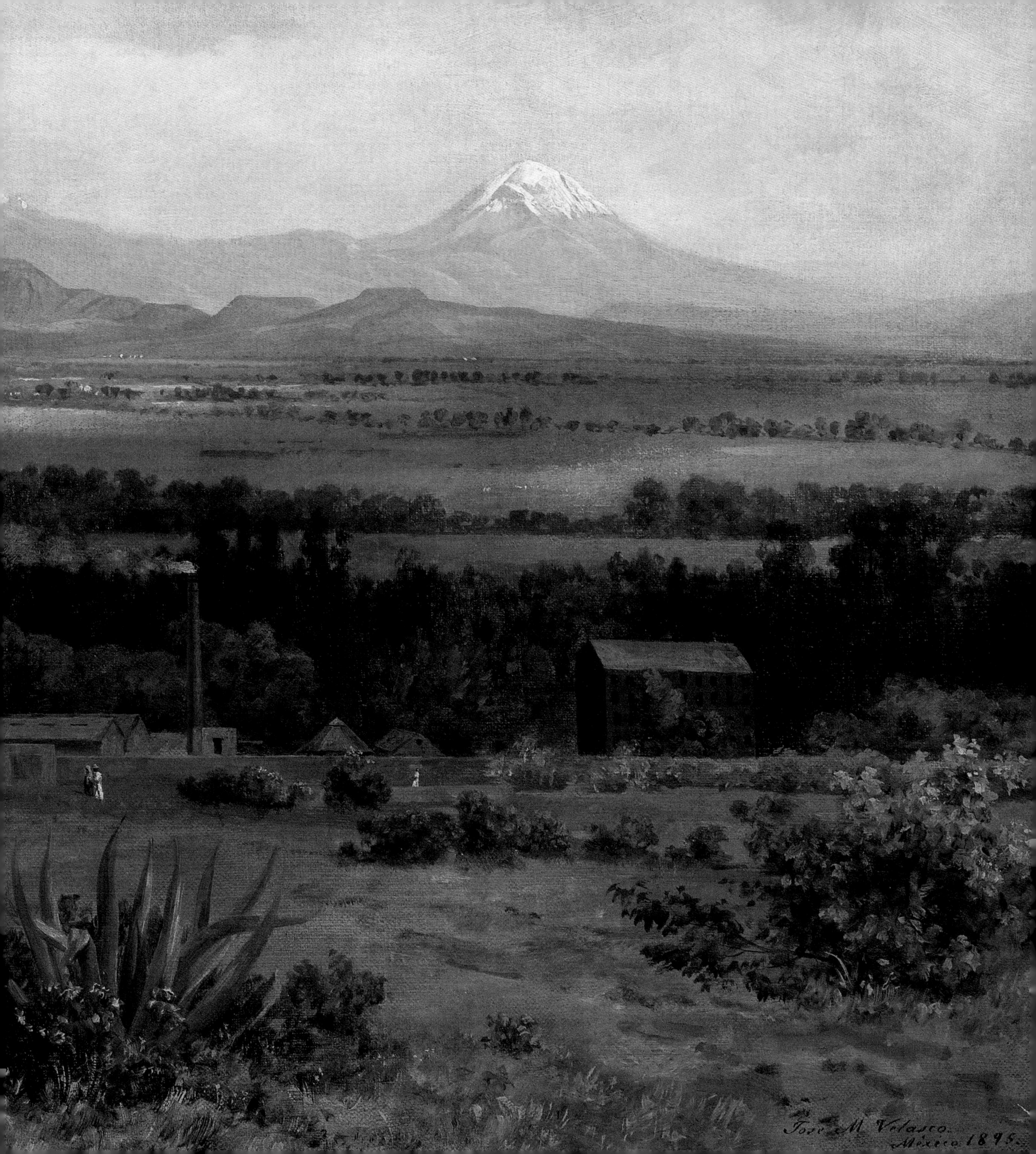
José Mª Velasco
México 1895.

NOTES

PREFACE
DAWN ADES

1   Global, before it was contaminated by multinational capitalism, was a term that sought free and neutral, non-nationalist cultural interchange.
2   Ades 1989, p. 101.
3   Romero de Terreros 1963, p. 483, citing Mexico City 1877.
4   Ignacio Manuel Altamirano (1834–1893), cited in Pérez de Salazar y Solana 1982, p. 94.
5   See, for example, Ruskin's drawing, Fragment of the Alps, about 1854–6 (Harvard Art Museums, inv. 1919.506).
6   The National Gallery, London (NG538).
7   The French painter Claude (1604/5?–1682) established a manner of painting ideal landscapes, using trees and hills to frame distant vistas.

MASTER OF THE FAR HORIZON
MARÍA ELENA ALTAMIRANO PIOLLE

1   José María Velasco, 'Apuntes genealógicos de la familia Velasco de Temascalcingo', p. 1 (undated), Velasco Archive (in the Museo Kaluz, Mexico City).
2   Drawing of a young man, about 1853, pencil on paper, 46 × 31 cm, private collection.
3   The Academia de San Carlos was referred to by various names throughout its long history. These changed often, especially during the turbulent 1860s. It was officially known as the Escuela Nacional de Bellas Artes from late 1867 until the Mexican Revolution, but was still referred to by Velasco and others as the 'Academia' or 'San Carlos'.
4   José María Velasco, 'Autobiografía', pp. 1–2 (undated), Velasco Archive.
5   Altamirano Piolle 2006, pp. 35–9. This book provides a detailed account of Velasco's life and work.
6   Eugenio Landesio, 'Programa para el año de 1865. Pintura general llamada de paisaje', private archive.
7   *The Courtyard of the Former Convent of San Agustín*, 1860, oil on canvas, 32 × 43 cm, private collection.
8   José María Velasco, 'Autobiografía', pp. 2–3 (undated), Velasco Archive.
9   Altamirano Piolle 2006, pp. 159–63.
10   José María Velasco, 'Cuadros originales de paisajes pintados por José María Velasco', pp. 54–5 (undated), Velasco Archive.
11   The Mexica, sometimes referred to as the Aztecs, were a Nahuatl-speaking people who founded the city of Tenochtitlan. The term 'Aztec', popularised in the nineteenth century by Alexander von Humboldt and still common, was not used by the Mexica to refer to themselves.
12   Velasco 1908, pp. 1–2.
13   José María Velasco, 'Hoja de servicios', p. 2 (undated), Velasco Archive.

VELASCO BEYOND MEXICO
DANIEL SOBRINO RALSTON

1   Velasco to María de la Luz Sánchez Armas Galindo, 29 May 1889, Velasco Archive. Excerpts from many of these letters were first published and translated in Altamirano Piolle's authoritative monograph, which served as the catalogue of the encyclopaedic Velasco exhibition held at the Museo Nacional de Arte in 1993. For the Chicago and Paris letters, see Altamirano Piolle 1993, vol. 2, pp. 331–54, 401–10. Unless otherwise noted, all other translations are my own.
2   Velasco's perceived similarities to European and American artists have often been mentioned but are not usually substantiated. For an early example, see Juan de la Encina's florid study, De la Encina 1943. The most rigorous and critical scholarship interprets Velasco's art primarily through reference to the history and culture of Mexico. See especially Ramírez 1989 and Ramírez 2017.
3   Archer 2010, pp. 285–97.
4   For an introduction to the Mexican–American War, see Vázquez 2010; Guardino 2017. For Santa Anna, see Fowler 2007.
5   Altamirano Piolle 1993, vol. 1, pp. 53–4.
6   For a comprehensive account of Napoleon III's plans for Mexico, see Cunningham 2001.
7   For a novelistic but deeply researched history of Maximilian's empire in Mexico, see Shawcross 2022.
8   For an overview of the institution's history, see Báez Macías 2009. See also Cuadriello 2014.
9   For the concept of *buen gusto*, see Niell 2013. For the plaster cast collection, see Bargellini and Fuentes Rojas 1989, pp. 60–87.
10   Landesio has never been the subject of a book-length monograph. For the foundational biography, see Revilla 1908. For studies of the painter, see Moyssén 1963; Nulman Magidin 2009; Larrucea Garritz 2016, pp. 142–7; Nulman Magidin 2015, pp. 356–66; Nulman Magidin 2021.
11   For an introduction to Markó's oeuvre, see Budapest 2011.
12   The painting was exhibited in 1854 in Mexico City and later owned by Pelegrín Clavé. Dragon 2007, pp. 192–3. For Clavé, see Mexico City 2019–20.
13   The painting, sometimes confused with a painting of near-identical size that was likely its pendant, *Vallinfreda*, was purchased by the Academia de San Carlos in 1852, along with four others by Landesio. Curatorial files, Museo Nacional de San Carlos, Mexico City. I am grateful to Mireida Velázquez Torres for details regarding the work's provenance and to Alberto Nulman Magidin for clarification of the work's title. For consideration of the two paintings and Landesio's association with the Deutschrömer, a group of German artists in Rome, see Nulman Magidin 2018.
14   Altamirano Piolle 1993, vol. 1, p. 105. These autobiographical notes are part of the Velasco Archive. Velasco's copy of *Vallinfreda* was displayed at the Academia de San Carlos's annual exhibition in 1862. Romero de Terreros 1963, p. 331.
15   Landesio's nomination came either through an association with Clavé in Rome, where they had overlapped in the 1840s, or on the recommendation of Markó himself, with whom Clavé began to correspond in 1852. For the varying accounts of Landesio's appointment, see Dragon 2007, pp. 193–6.
16   Revilla 1908, p. 293.
17   For the traveller-artists, see M.A. Fernández 2017; Fernández de Calderón 1996; Romero de Terreros 1959.
18   Landesio published a series of four articles explaining his pedagogical methods and artistic ideas in July 1866 in the periodical *El Mexicano*. These were collated by Fausto Ramírez, who also provided a brief introduction. See Ramírez 1992.
19   The De la Hidalga family, whose wealth derived from sugar production, were prominent patrons of the arts in Mexico. See Valderrama Negrón 2014.
20   For a detailed account of Velasco's progress through Landesio's teaching programme, see Altamirano Piolle 1993, vol. 1, pp. 65–99.
21   Bustamante and Altamirano Piolle 1974, p. 17; Altamirano Piolle 1993, vol. 1, p. 147.
22   The liberal writer Ignacio Manuel Altamirano was an outspoken critic of Landesio and Velasco. For a summary of his opposition to the painters, which arose from ideological differences, see Altamirano Piolle 1993, vol. 1, pp. 199–202.
23   For Maximilian and the Second Mexican Empire, see Pani 2012 and Pani 2017.
24   For Manet's paintings and related studies, see New York 2006–7.
25   Velasco's annotated list of his paintings was published by Altamirano Piolle. See Altamirano Piolle 1993, vol. 2, pp. 509–15. The original document is in the Velasco Archive.
26   For Semeleder, see Martínez Guzmán 2003, pp. 17–19.
27   Kaska bequeathed them, along with the rest of his collection, to the institution that became the National Museum of the Czech Republic, where the paintings languished unrecognised until 1970. See Štěpánek 1971 and Štěpánek 1985.
28   Altamirano Piolle 1993, vol. 2, p. 509. The painting's present location is not known.
29   Altamirano Piolle 1993, vol. 2, pp. 511–12. On the Boker family, see Buchenau 2013.
30   One of the paintings acquired by Barge, likely Benjamin Franklin Barge (1832–1902), is the *Valley of Oaxaca*, painted in 1888, now in the collection of the Philadelphia Museum of Art (inv. 1949-56-1). See Altamirano Piolle 1993, vol. 2, p. 513. Velasco's paintings apparently enjoyed a certain reputation in the United States, even after his death. For many years a painting that hangs in Fallingwater, one of

the architect Frank Lloyd Wright's most celebrated buildings, was attributed to Velasco. The painting was purchased by the Kaufmann family, the owners of the house, in the late 1930s. James Oles recently proposed that the work, which bears a signature that purports to be Velasco's, was in fact painted by his student Adolfo Tenorio. See Oles 2025, pp. 166–7.

31 For a brief consideration of foreign collectors' interest in Velasco's paintings, see Garrigan 2024, p. 61.

32 Landesio was forced to resign on political grounds. He claimed that his being a foreign citizen as well as his religious beliefs precluded his support of the liberal Reform Laws, which enacted the seizure of ecclesiastical properties and greater separation between church and state. See Revilla 1908, p. 311; Ramírez 1989, p. 41, n. 56.

33 Paz 1942. For an account of Paz's later interest in Velasco, see Tomlinson 1990.

34 According to Velasco, the painting was purchased by the collector Manuel Ibarrola: 'He sent it to Europe and it was shown at the Mexican consulate in the United States.' Altamirano Piolle 1993, vol. 2, p. 510.

35 The symbolism of the eagle and nopal seems to have eluded nineteenth-century critics, who did not discuss its significance. The episode was first remarked on by the art historian Justino Fernández. See J. Fernández 1952 (1967), p. 91. For further discussion of this detail, see Ramírez 1989, pp. 47–8.

36 For this development in the Mexican context, see Widdifield 1996, pp. 70–1.

37 Altamirano Piolle 1993, vol. 2, p. 512.

38 Ramírez 1989, p. 50, n. 75.

39 For Rico's oeuvre, see Madrid 2012–13.

40 Dubosc de Pesquidoux 1881, vol. 1, p. 458.

41 Velasco to Landesio, 13 May 1878. Velasco Archive. He directed Landesio to call on Juan González Asúnsolo – the father-in-law of Velasco's brother Antonio – who was then residing in Paris. Velasco seems to have transcribed a number of the letters he sent to Landesio, González and Clavé in a copy book. The contents of this fascinating volume have not been published and await detailed investigation.

42 Bustamante and Altamirano Piolle 1974, p. 19. Revilla claimed that Landesio travelled to Paris, but makes no mention of him seeing Velasco's painting; Revilla 1908, p. 321. A letter recorded in the copy book makes clear that Clavé had seen Velasco's painting in Paris and written to him about it. Velasco to Clavé, 27 September 1878, Velasco Archive.

43 For an introduction to the Porfiriato, see Buffington and French 2010.

44 For accounts that associate Velasco with the Porfiriato and its economic and cultural policies, see Saborit 1986; Tenorio-Trillo 1996, pp. 112–16; Cañizares-Esguerra 2006, pp. 155–6; Ortega 2021; Garrigan 2024, pp. 57, 61–2. For a sympathetic view of Velasco's concern for Mexico's indigenous communities and relationship to the regime, see Ramírez 2015, pp. 31–3, 43–4.

45 Altamirano Piolle 1993, vol. 2, pp. 512–13.

46 Ibid., p. 511.

47 Velasco painted 14 versions of the 1875 *Valley of Mexico from the Hill of Santa Isabel* and 7 of the 1877 *Valley of Mexico from the Hill of Santa Isabel*. Altamirano Piolle 1993, vol. 1, pp. 219, 238.

48 Two of his paintings, including the 1877 *View of the Valley of Mexico* (cat. 17), were sent to New Orleans in 1884 for the World Cotton Centennial. Altamirano Piolle 1993, vol. 2, pp. 313–14. Fourteen drawings of the Mesoamerican ruins at Cempoala, numerous drawings of artefacts from the Museo Nacional, and three paintings, one of them perhaps identifiable with *The Baths of Nezahualcóyotl* (cat. 14), were sent to Madrid in 1892 for the Exposición Histórico-Americana. Madrid 1892, p. 11.

49 For the building's architecture and decoration, see Tenorio-Trillo 1996, pp. 64–80, 96–112. For studies of Mexico's contributions to the 1889 Exposition Universelle, see Ramírez 1988; Díaz y de Ovando 1990; Garrigan 2012, pp. 135–52; Uslenghi 2016, pp. 129–32.

50 Silva Barón 2010, p. 47.

51 Cahun 1889.

52 Manuel Payno to Vicente Riva Palacio, 5 November 1889, document 346, wallet 190, Vicente Riva Palacio Collection, Benson Latin American Manuscripts Collection, University of Texas Libraries, Austin, Texas.

53 For a summary of his reports with many quotations from them, see Altamirano Piolle 1993, vol. 2, pp. 355–61.

54 José María Velasco, 'Exposición internacional de París de 1889', second report, quoted in Altamirano Piolle 1993, vol. 2, p. 357.

55 J. Fernández 1952 (1967), pp. 96, 98–9; Koeninger 1976, pp. 16–18; Ades 1989, pp. 108–9.

56 For these trips, see Altamirano Piolle 1993, vol. 2, pp. 349–51.

57 Velasco to María de la Luz Sánchez Armas Galindo, 1 December 1889, Velasco Archive.

58 Velasco to María de la Luz Sánchez Armas Galindo, 13 December 1889, Velasco Archive.

59 González corresponded with Velasco on several occasions, sending him a card at New Year in 1901 from 128 Sutherland Avenue, an address in Paddington. Juan González Asúnsolo to José María Velasco, 22 January 1901, Velasco Archive. According to an obituary, González died in London in 1914 at the age of 87. *The Tablet*, 21 November 1914.

60 Altamirano Piolle 1993, vol. 2, p. 510.

61 'You can imagine what I would suffer in those museums of paintings, since for my father it is the only thing that has any importance, so he would spend whole days and I would stand next to him just yawning, because I was fed up with works of art.' Francisco Velasco Sánchez Armas to María de la Luz Sánchez Armas Galindo, 28 October 1889, Velasco Archive.

62 For his time in Chicago, see Altamirano Piolle 1993, vol. 2, pp. 401–9. Velasco's involvement in the World's Columbian Exposition was touched on in two exhibitions at Chicago's National Museum of Mexican Art, *Arte Diseño Xicágo* (2018) and *Arte Diseño Xicágo II: From the World's Fair to the Present Day* (2024).

63 I am grateful to Cesáreo Moreno of the National Museum of Mexican Art for his assistance in locating this engraving.

64 For Velasco's activities as a teacher, see Altamirano Piolle 1993, vol. 1, pp. 243–50.

65 For brief comparisons of Velasco to the Hudson River School painters, see Clifford 1944–5, p. 15; Koeninger 1976, p. 18; Manthorne 2014, pp. 181–2.

66 For a reflection on Velasco's relationship to Church, see Tomlinson 1990, pp. 87–91.

67 For Khevenhüller's letters during the Second Mexican Empire, see Hamann 1983 (2000). Relatives of the Mexican generals Miguel Miramón and Tomás Mejía, who were executed alongside Maximilian, also appear in the photograph.

68 I am most grateful to members of the Khevenhüller-Metsch family for their generous collaboration in attempting to learn more about this painting, which may have been destroyed or lost. I also thank them for identifying the man in the photograph as their ancestor Carl Khevenhüller. For the events of the Austrians' visit, see Altamirano Piolle 1993, vol. 2, p. 435.

69 Ramírez 2001, p. 291.

70 Islas García 1932, p. 10.

71 These tours included an exhibition held at the Tate Gallery in 1953, in which Velasco's 1877 *The Valley of Mexico from the Hill of Santa Isabel* (cat. 17) was displayed. London 1953, p. 78.

AT THE INTERSECTION OF ART AND SCIENCE
OMAR OLIVARES SANDOVAL

1 This relationship is discussed further in Olivares Sandoval (forthcoming 2025).

2 General approaches to Velasco's work and biography include Ramírez 2017 and Altamirano Piolle 1993. Velasco's scientific works are explored in Trabulse 2012.

3 Gudiño Cejudo 2015.

4 See Nulman Magidin 2021.

5 For Cezanne, see Princeton 2020; for Moran, see Bedell 2001.

6 Altamirano Piolle 1993, p. 511.

7 Bárcena 1874, p. 1.

8 Cuatáparo 1874, pp. 366–9.

9 Bárcena 1876.

10 Humboldt 1827, vol. 1, pp. 414–15.

11 Humboldt and Bonpland 1805.

12 Lobato 1875.

13 Volcanoes, 1870, pencil and watercolour on paper,

44 × 26.6 cm, Museo Nacional de Arte, INBAL, Mexico City.

14 See, for instance, Bárcena, Iglesias and Matute 1877.

15 The Royal Botanical Expedition to New Spain (1787–1803), sponsored by Charles III of Spain, was led by the Spanish naturalist Martín Sessé in collaboration with the Mexican naturalist Mariano Mociño. The Mexican artists Atanasio Echeverría and Juan de Dios Vicente de la Cerda accompanied the botanical expedition and produced thousands of drawings. For more information, see Bleichmar 2012.

16 Velasco 1870, pp. 201–3; Velasco and Velasco 1870, pp. 338–42.

17 This study was carried out in 2022 by the Laboratorio Nacional de Ciencias para la Investigación y Conservación del Patrimonio Cultural (LANCIC) at the Instituto de Biología, UNAM, Mexico City.

18 Velasco 1879.

19 Phaf-Rheinberger 2011. This subject is explored in greater detail in Olivares Sandoval 2021.

20 Churchill 2015.

21 Weismann 1880.

22 Velasco 1880, p. 82.

23 See 'Séance du 25 avril 1882', *Bulletin de la Societé zoologique de France*, 7 (1882), p. xviii.

24 Weismann 1882.

25 Reiß, Olsson and Hoßfeld 2015.

LANDSCAPE AS THE SITE OF CHANGE
DEXTER DALWOOD

1   This was a mostly foreign preoccupation for artists in the United States, where painters of the Hudson School focused largely on the immensity of the American landscape.

2   The National Gallery, London (NG538 and NG524).

3   The National Gallery, London (NG3908 and NG6479).

4   Causey 2020, p. 42.

5   Gasquet 2012, p. 154.

6   Paz 1942.

7   Casanova 2017, p. 37.

8   These were made by Velasco in the museum since he was not part of the expedition; Martínez Marín 1989, p. 213.

9   Quoted in Charlot 1962, p. 142.

10 'Pensaba en ti, Susana. En las lomas verdes. Cuando volábamos papalotes en la época del aire. Oíamos allá abajo el rumor viviente del pueblo mientras estábamos encima de él, arriba de la loma, en tanto se nos iba el hilo de cáñamo arrastrado por el viento'; English translation by Douglas J. Weatherford, Rulfo 1955 (2023).

11 An engraving by the influential graphic artist José Guadalupe Posada (1852–1913) was made in 1899, *El gran cometa Halley*, then interestingly repurposed for the reappearance of Halley's Comet in 1910.

CATALOGUE

1. *THE GOATHERD OF SAN ÁNGEL*, 1861
Museo Nacional de Arte, INBAL, Mexico City

2. *THE GOATHERD OF SAN ÁNGEL*, 1863
Museo Nacional de Arte, INBAL, Mexico City

Notes:
1. For the later variations, one of which was acquired by Landesio, see Altamirano Piolle 1993, vol. 1, p. 121.
2. For the identification of the flower, see Altamirano Piolle 1993, vol. 1, p. 123.
3. Ramírez 1989, pp. 25–7.
4. Sierra 1869.

3. *PICO DE ORIZABA*, 1876
National Museum of the Czech Republic, Prague

4. *THE TEXTILE MILL OF LA CAROLINA, PUEBLA*, 1887
National Museum of the Czech Republic, Prague

Notes:
1. Letter from José María Velasco to María de la Luz Sánchez Armas Galindo, 22 December 1875, Velasco Archive.
2. For the different versions, see Altamirano Piolle 1993, vol. 1, pp. 209–13.
3. For the series, see Altamirano Piolle 1993, vol. 2, pp. 321–5.
4. For Kaska's paintings, see Štěpánek 1971, Štěpánek 1985.
5. For Kaska's collection, sometimes called the 'Treasure of the Emperor Maximilian', see Prague 1999.

5. *LAKE CHALCO*, 1885
National Museum of the Czech Republic, Prague

Notes:
1. Altamirano Piolle 1993, vol. 1, p. 267.
2. The 18th President of the United States from 1869 to 1877, Grant was Commander General of the US Army during the American Civil War and served with distinction in the Mexican–American War between 1846 and 1848.

6. *THE VALLEY OF MEXICO FROM THE MOLINO DEL REY*, 1895
Private collection

Notes:
1. Ramírez 2017, p. 87.
2. For the different versions, see Altamirano Piolle 1993, vol. 2, pp. 428–35.

7. *A RUSTIC BRIDGE IN SAN ÁNGEL*, 1862
Museo Nacional de Arte, INBAL, Mexico City

Notes:
1. Romero de Terreros 1963, p. 384.
2. For Velasco's early drawings of the natural world, some copied from prints, see Altamirano Piolle 1993, vol. 1, pp. 81–93.
3. For the original and the copy, see Altamirano Piolle 1993, vol. 1, pp. 105–6.

8. *THE FOREST OF PACHO*, 1875
Museo Nacional de Arte, INBAL, Mexico City

9. STUDY OF A SHRUB, DATE UNKNOWN
Museo Nacional de Arte, INBAL, Mexico City
[London only]

Notes:
1. For the second version, painted for the Mexico City businessman Edmundo van den Wyngaert, see Altamirano Piolle 1993, vol. 1, p. 213.
2. See Berlin 2002, cat. 37, pp. 28, 42.
3. Marisa Moolick Gutiérrez at Hacienda de Pacho, email communication (3 August 2024).
4. Cubas 1874, p. 258.

10. *MAFAFFA LEAVES*, DATE UNKNOWN
José María Velasco Archive, Museo Kaluz, Mexico City

Notes:
1. See Olivares Sandoval 2019, p. 234.
2. See Altamirano Piolle 1993, vol. 1, pp. 275–9.
3. For Velasco's railway paintings, see Ramírez 1989, pp. 60–7.

11. *CARDÓN, STATE OF OAXACA*, 1887
Museo Nacional de Arte, INBAL, Mexico City

Notes:
1. *Banana Tree*, 1876, oil on canvas, 45 × 32 cm, private collection. See Altamirano Piolle 1993, vol. 1, no. 280, p. 227.
2. Private collection.

12. *THE PYRAMID OF THE SUN IN TEOTIHUACÁN*, 1878
Museo Nacional de Arte, INBAL, Mexico City

13. *THE PYRAMIDS OF THE SUN AND THE MOON*, 1878
Colección Pérez Simón

Notes:
1. For a history of archaeology during the Porfiriato, see Bueno 2016.
2. Mendoza 1877.
3. For mentions of the various versions, about whose dimensions there is some confusion, see Altamirano Piolle 1993, vol. 1, p. 223.
4. Gudiño Cejudo 2015, p. 1840.

14. *THE BATHS OF NEZAHUALCÓYOTL*, 1878
Museo Nacional de Arte, INBAL, Mexico City

Notes:
1. Ramírez 1989, p. 51.
2. Altamirano Piolle 1993, vol. 1, p. 261.

15. *THE VALLEY OF MEXICO FROM THE HILL OF SANTA ISABEL*, 1875
Museo Nacional de Arte, INBAL, Mexico City

16. STUDY FOR *THE VALLEY OF MEXICO FROM THE HILL OF ATZACOALCO*, ABOUT 1873
Museo Nacional de Arte, INBAL, Mexico City
[London only]

Notes:
1. For Velasco's homes in Villa de Guadalupe, see Altamirano Piolle 1993, vol. 2, pp. 308, 363–6.
2. Ibid., p. 511.
3. Altamirano Piolle 1993, vol. 1, pp. 214–16.
4. Ramírez 2015, pp. 31–3.
5. For the 1873 painting, see Altamirano Piolle 1993, vol. 1, pp. 183–8.
6. For the drawing, see Moyssén 1989, pp. 8–9.
7. For the variations, see Altamirano Piolle 1993, vol. 1, p. 219.

17. *THE VALLEY OF MEXICO FROM THE HILL OF SANTA ISABEL*, 1877
Museo Nacional de Arte, INBAL, Mexico City

18. HARPY EAGLE (STUDY FOR *THE VALLEY OF MEXICO FROM THE HILL OF SANTA ISABEL*), 1877
José María Velasco Archive, Museo Kaluz, Mexico City
[London only]

19. STUDY OF A NOPAL CACTUS, DATE UNKNOWN
Museo Nacional de Arte, INBAL, Mexico City
[London only]

Notes:
1. Romero de Terreros 1963, p. 483.
2. Altamirano Piolle 1993, vol. 1, pp. 233–5.
3. For an analysis of the political and intellectual context for the painting's creation, see Ramírez 2015, pp. 33–7.
4. Ramírez 1989, p. 47.
5. J. Fernández 1952 (1967), p. 90.
6. Ramírez 2004, p. 68.
7. For the later versions, see Altamirano Piolle 1993, vol. 1, p. 238.

20. STUDY OF RAINBOWS, 1884
Museo Nacional de Arte, INBAL, Mexico City
[London only]

Notes:
1. 'El Artista necesita más bien de hacer poco y de observar mucho para enriquecer la imaginación de la variedad de objetos que nos muestra la naturaleza'; Gudiño Cejudo 2015, p. 1841.
2. 'El más luminoso y visible es el amarillo; sigue el anaranjado y el verde; el azul y el violeta se ven poco, el rojo se nota algo más. Todo se desprende por claro.'
3. 'El espejo o reflejo del iris tiene sus colores invertidos.'

21. *ROCKS ON THE HILL OF ATZACOALCO*, 1874
Museo Nacional de Arte, INBAL, Mexico City

22. STUDY OF ROCKS AND FOLIAGE, DATE UNKNOWN
Museo Nacional de Arte, INBAL, Mexico City
[London only]

Notes:
1. For this group of works, see Altamirano Piolle 1993, vol. 1, pp. 178–83.
2. For the identification of the type of rock, see Altamirano Piolle 1993, vol. 1, p. 183.
3. Olivares Sandoval 2019, p. 116.
4. Ramírez 2017, p. 40.
5. Olivares Sandoval 2019, p. 115.

23. *ROCKS*, 1894
Museo Nacional de Arte, INBAL, Mexico City

Notes:
1. Altamirano Piolle 1993, vol. 2, p. 411.
2. Ibid.

3. Ramírez 1993, vol. 1, p. 32.
4. Ramírez 1989, p. 28.
5. Bedell 2009, p. 52.

24. *TEMASCALCINGO*, 1909
Elda Margarita Capetillo Ponce
[London only]

Notes:
1. 'San Miguel Temascalcingo. Vista tomada por La Joya. Nació el autor en este pueblo en 1840'.
2. Ramírez 1993, vol. 1, p. 31.

25. *THE GREAT COMET OF 1882*, 1910
Acervo de la Secretaría de Cultura de Veracruz

Notes:
1. The inscription reads, in Spanish, 'tomado del natural'.
2. For the related small painting, see Altamirano Piolle 1993, vol. 2, p. 493.
3. Adorno 1882, p. 12.
4. For the night scenes and celestial bodies, see Altamirano Piolle 1993, vol. 2, p. 494.

26. *ERUPTION*, 1910
Museo Nacional de Arte, INBAL, Mexico City

Notes:
1. 'fue dibujado por Velasco durante sus espectaculares momentos eruptivos, con las peligrosas emanaciones de gases y vapor de cuatro columnas de cientos de metros de altura, que el viento llevava en todas direcciones'; Altamirano Piolle 1997, p. 33.

27. *AERIAL PERSPECTIVE, CLOUDS AND SPACE*, 1909
Secretaría de Cultura del Gobierno del Estado de México, Museo del Paisaje José Maria Velasco

28. STUDY OF CLOUDS, 1912
José María Velasco Archive, Museo Kaluz, Mexico City

Notes:
1. See Altamirano Piolle 1993, vol. 2, pp. 482–3; Ramírez 2017, p. 117.
2. See Ramírez 2017, pp. 118–19.
3. See Altamirano Piolle 1993, vol. 2, pp. 498–9.

BIBLIOGRAPHY

Ades 1989
D. Ades, *Art in Latin America: The Modern Era, 1820–1980*, New Haven and London 1989

Adorno 1882
J.N. Adorno, *Memoria escrita por Juan Nepomuceno Adorno acerca de los tres fenómenos astronómicos*, Mexico City 1882

Altamirano Piolle 1993
M.E. Altamirano Piolle, *National Homage: José María Velasco (1840–1912)*, 2 vols and addendum, Mexico City 1993

Altamirano Piolle 1997
M.E. Altamirano Piolle, 'José María Velasco científico', *Ciencias*, 45 (January–March 1997), pp. 32–5

Altamirano Piolle 2006
M.E. Altamirano Piolle, *José María Velasco. Paisajes de luz, horizontes de modernidad*, Mexico City 2006

Archer 2010
C.I. Archer, 'Fashioning a New Nation', in W.H. Beezley and M.C. Meyer (eds), *The Oxford History of Mexico*, Oxford and New York 2010, pp. 285–318

Báez Macías 2009
E. Báez Macías, *Historia de la Escuela Nacional de Bellas Artes (Antigua Academia de San Carlos) 1781–1910*, Mexico City 2009

Bárcena 1874
M. Bárcena, 'Orología. Estudio sobre los pórfidos cenozoicos de México', *El minero mexicano*, 30 (5 November 1874), p. 1

Bárcena 1876
M. Bárcena, 'El señor ingeniero D. Mariano Bárcena', *El propagador industrial* (1 May 1876), pp. 1–5

Bárcena, Iglesias and Matute 1877
M. Bárcena, M. Iglesias and J.I. Matute, 'Informe sobre los temblores de Jalisco y la erupción del volcán "Ceboruco"', in *Anales del Ministerio de Fomento de la República Mexicana*, Mexico City 1877, pp. 115–96

Bargellini and Fuentes Rojas 1989
C. Bargellini and E. Fuentes Rojas, *Guía que permite captar lo bello: yesos y dibujos de la Academia de San Carlos 1778–1916*, Mexico City 1989

Bedell 2001
R. Bedell, *The Anatomy of Nature: Geology and American Landscape Painting, 1825–1875*, Princeton and Oxford 2001

Bedell 2009
R. Bedell, 'The History of the Earth: Darwin, Geology and Landscape Art', in D. Donald and J. Munro (eds), *Endless Forms: Charles Darwin, Natural Science and the Visual Arts*, New Haven and London 2009, pp. 49–79

Berlin 2002
R. Löschner, *Johann Moritz Rugendas no México (1831–1834): um pintor nas pegadas de Alexander von Humboldt*, exh. cat., Instituto Ibero-Americano, Patrimônio Cultural Prussiano, Berlin 2002

Bleichmar 2012
D. Bleichmar, *Visible Empire: Botanical Expeditions and Visual Culture in the Hispanic Enlightenment*, Chicago 2012

Buchenau 2013
J. Buchenau, 'Una empresa mercantil alemana en la ciudad de México, 1865–1900: la Casa Boker, la globalización y el inicio de una cultura de consumo', in S. Kuntz Ficker and L. Reinhard (eds), *Estudios sobre la historia económica de México desde la época de la independencia hasta la primera globalización*, Madrid and Frankfurt am Main 2013, pp. 145–69

Budapest 2011
B. Gábor (ed.), *Károly Markó and his Circle: From Myth to Image*, exh. cat., Magyar Nemzeti Galéria, Budapest 2011

Bueno 2016
C. Bueno, *The Pursuit of Ruins: Archaeology, History, and the Making of Modern Mexico*, Albuquerque, NM 2016

Buffington and French 2010
R.M. Buffington and W.E. French, 'The Culture of Modernity', in W.H. Beezley and M.C. Meyer (eds), *The Oxford History of Mexico*, Oxford and New York 2010, pp. 373–406

Bustamante and Altamirano Piolle 1974
M. de la L. Bustamante and C. Altamirano Piolle, 'José María Velasco', in D.F. Rubín de la Borbolla (ed.), *José María Velasco. Pintor del paisaje mexicano*, Toluca 1974, pp. 13–23

Cahun 1889
L. Cahun, 'L'Exposition Universelle. VII. Le Mexique (1er article)', *La Phare de la Loire*, 20 June 1889

Cañizares-Esguerra 2006
J. Cañizares-Esguerra, 'Landscapes and Identities: Mexico, 1850–1900', in *Nature, Empire, and Nation: Explorations of the History of Science in the Iberian World*, Stanford 2006, pp. 129–68

Casanova 2017
R. Casanova, 'El Museo Nacional, un espacio de la fotografía documental', *Gaceta de Museos*, 64 (2017), pp. 36–45

Causey 2020
F. Causey, 'Finds', in Princeton 2020, pp. 41–63

Charlot 1962
J. Charlot, *Mexican Art and the Academy of San Carlos 1785–1915*, Austin, TX 1962

Churchill 2015
F.B. Churchill, *August Weismann: Development, Heredity, and Evolution*, Cambridge, MA and London 2015

Clifford 1944–5
H. Clifford, 'Note on Velasco's Paintings', in *José María Velasco*, exh. cat., Philadelphia Museum of Art, Philadelphia 1944; Brooklyn Museum, New York 1945, pp. 15–16

Cuadriello 2014
J. Cuadriello, 'The Painting Department of the Royal Academy of San Carlos: Origins, Development and Epilogue', in L.E. Alcalá and J. Brown (eds), *Painting in Latin America: 1550–1820*, New Haven and London 2014, pp. 205–42

Cuatáparo 1874
J.N. Cuatáparo, 'Ligera exposición geológica relativa al valle de México leída en la Sociedad de Historia Natural y dedicada al Sr. Lic. D. Miguel T. Barron', *El minero mexicano*, 30 (5 November 1874), pp. 366–9

Cubas 1874
A.G. Cubas, 'Un paseo a Jalapa', in *Escritos diversos de 1870 a 1874*, Mexico City 1874, pp. 249–68

Cunningham 2001
M. Cunningham, *Mexico and the Foreign Policy of Napoleon III*, Basingstoke and New York 2001

De la Encina 1943
J. de la Encina, *El paisajista José María Velasco (1840–1912)*, Mexico City 1943

Díaz y de Ovando 1990
C. Díaz y de Ovando, 'México en la exposición universal de 1889', *Anales del Instituto de Investigaciones Estéticas*, 16, no. 61 (1990), pp. 109–71

Dragon 2007
Z. Dragon, 'Las 15 pinturas de Károly Markó en México', *Anales del Instituto de Investigaciones Estéticas*, 29, no. 90 (2007), pp. 189–226

Dubosc de Pesquidoux 1881
L. Dubosc de Pesquidoux, *L'art dans les deux mondes: peinture et sculpture* (1878), 2 vols, Paris 1881

J. Fernández 1952 (1967)
J. Fernández, *El arte del siglo XIX en México*, Mexico City 1967; first published as *Arte moderno y contemporáneo de México*, Mexico City 1952

M.A. Fernández 2017
M.A. Fernández (ed.), *Travelers in Paradise: Mexico, 19th Century*, Mexico City 2017

Fernández de Calderón 1996
C. Fernández de Calderón (ed.), *European Traveller-Artists in Nineteenth-Century Mexico*, Mexico City 1996

Fowler 2007
W. Fowler, *Santa Anna of Mexico*, Lincoln, NE 2007

Garrigan 2012
S.E. Garrigan, *Collecting Mexico: Museums, Monuments, and the Creation of National Identity*, Minneapolis 2012

Garrigan 2024
S.E. Garrigan, 'La movilidad del paisaje mexicano decimonónico', *Latin American and Latinx Visual Culture*, 6, no. 1 (2024), pp. 47–63

Gasquet 2012
J. Gasquet, *Cézanne*, Paris 2012

Guardino 2017
P. Guardino, *The Dead March: A History of the Mexican-American War*, Cambridge, MA 2017

Gudiño Cejudo 2015
M.R. Gudiño Cejudo, 'Expedición a la Mesa de Metlaltoyuca. El relato del pintor José María Velasco (1865)', *Historia Mexicana*, 64, no. 4 (April 2015), pp. 1807–43

Hamann 1983 (2000)
B. Hamann, *Con Maximiliano en México: del diario del príncipe Carl Khevenhüller 1864–1867*, Mexico City 2000; first published in German as *Mit Kaiser Max in Mexiko: Aus dem Tagebuch des Fürsten Carl Khevenhüller, 1864–1867*, Vienna 1983

Humboldt 1827
A. von Humboldt, *Ensayo político sobre la Nueva España*, 2 vols, Paris 1827 (2nd edn)

Humboldt and Bonpland 1805
A. von Humboldt and A. Bonpland, *Essai sur la géographie des plantes; accompagné d'un tableau physique des régions équinoxiales*, Paris 1805

Islas García 1932
L. Islas García, *Velasco. Pintor cristiano*, Mexico City 1932

Koeninger 1976
P. Koeninger, 'José María Velasco, Painter of the Valley of Mexico', in *José María Velasco 1840–1912*, exh. cat., Mexican Cultural Institute, San Antonio and University Art Museum, University of Texas at Austin, Austin, TX 1976, pp. 9–19

Larrucea Garritz 2016
A. Larrucea Garritz, *País y paisaje: dos invenciones del siglo XIX mexicano*, Mexico City 2016

Lobato 1875
J. Lobato, 'Meteorología de México', *Boletín de la Sociedad Mexicana de Geografía y Estadística*, 3, no. 2 (1875), pp. 11–15

London 1953
Mexican Art from Pre-Columbian Times to the Present Day, exh. cat., Tate Gallery, London 1953

Madrid 1892
Catálogo de la sección de México: Tomo I, exh. cat., Exposición Histórico-Americana de Madrid, Madrid 1892

Madrid 2012–13
J. Barón (ed.), *El paisajista Martín Rico (1833–1908)*, exh. cat., Museo Nacional del Prado, Madrid 2012–13

Manthorne 2014
K. Manthorne, 'Curating the Nation and the Hemisphere: Mexico and Brazil at the US Centennial Exposition, 1876', *Journal of Curatorial Studies*, 3, no. 2–3 (2014), pp. 175–93

Martínez Guzmán 2003
M. Martínez Guzmán, 'Cuatro médicos personales del Emperador Maximiliano de Habsburgo. 1864–1867', *Boletín Mexicano de Historia y Filosofía de la Medicina*, 6, no. 1 (2003), pp. 17–22

Martínez Marín 1989
C. Martínez Marín, 'José María Velasco y el dibujo arqueológico', in Ramírez et al. 1989, pp. 203–31

Mendoza 1877
G. Mendoza, 'Las pirámides de Teotihuacán', *Anales del Museo Nacional de México*, 1 (1877), pp. 186–95

Mexico City 1877
Catálogo de las obras presentadas a la 18ª Exposición Nacional de Obras de Bellas Artes, Mexico City 1877

Mexico City 2019–20
L.M. León (ed.), *Pelegrín Clavé. Origen y sentido (1811–1880)*, exh. cat., Museo Nacional de San Carlos, Mexico City 2019–20

Moyssén 1963
X. Moyssén, 'Eugenio Landesio: teórico y crítico de arte', *Anales del Instituto de Investigaciones Estéticas*, 8, no. 32 (1963), pp. 69–91

Moyssén 1989
X. Moyssén, 'El dibujo de José María Velasco', in Ramírez et al. 1989, pp. 1–13

New York 2006–7
J. Elderfield, *Manet and the Execution of Maximilian*, exh. cat., Museum of Modern Art, New York 2006–7

Niell 2013
P.B. Niell, 'Introduction', in P.B. Niell and S.G. Widdifield (eds), *Buen Gusto and Classicism in the Visual Cultures of Latin America, 1780–1910*, Albuquerque, NM 2013, pp. xiii–xxxv

Nulman Magidin 2009
A. Nulman Magidin, 'Eugenio Landesio y la historia natural', MA thesis, Universidad Nacional Autónoma de México, Mexico City 2009

Nulman Magidin 2015
A. Nulman Magidin, 'The Birth of the Liberal Project in Mexico and the Construction of a National Landscape (1867–1870)', in L. Noelle and D.M.J. Wood (eds), *Landscape Aesthetics in the Americas*, Mexico City 2015, pp. 333–66

Nulman Magidin 2018
A. Nulman Magidin in G. Capitelli and S. Cracolici (eds), *Roma en México, México en Roma: las academias de arte entre Europa y el Nuevo Mundo, 1843–1867*, exh. cat., Museo Nacional de San Carlos, Mexico City 2018, cat. VI.2, pp. 234–6

Nulman Magidin 2021
A. Nulman Magidin, 'Eugenio Landesio y la teoría del paisaje, teorías y prácticas del paisaje en Italia en los años de su formación y en México en sus años de magisterio', PhD dissertation, Universidad Nacional Autónoma de México, Mexico City 2021

Oles 2025
J. Oles, 'Memories of Mexico at Bear Run', in J. Gunther and S.W. Perkins (eds), *Fallingwater: Living with and in Art*, New York 2025, pp. 115–67

Olivares Sandoval 2019
O. Olivares Sandoval, 'Imagen y conocimiento científico en el siglo XIX: láminas y paisajes de José María Velasco', PhD dissertation, Universidad Nacional Autónoma de México, Mexico City 2019

Olivares Sandoval 2021
O. Olivares Sandoval, 'The Scientific Images of the Axolotl by José María Velasco and Their Role in Nineteenth-Century Evolutionary Thinking', *Nuncius*, 36 (2021), pp. 143–66

Olivares Sandoval (forthcoming 2025)
O. Olivares Sandoval, *Del paisaje a la anatomía: José María Velasco y el conocimiento científico del siglo XIX*, Mexico City (forthcoming 2025)

Ortega 2021
E. Ortega, 'The Mexican Picturesque and the Sentimental Nation: A Study in Nineteenth-Century Landscape', *The Art Bulletin*, 103, no. 2 (2021), pp. 129–55

Pani 2012
E. Pani (ed.), *La intervención francesa en la revista Historia Mexicana*, Mexico City 2012

Pani 2017
E. Pani, 'Juárez vs. Maximiliano: Mexico's Experiment with Monarchy', in D.H. Doyle (ed.), *American Civil Wars: The United States, Latin America, Europe, and the Crisis of the 1860s*, Chapel Hill, NC 2017, pp. 167–84

Paz 1942
O. Paz, 'Un gran pintor mexicano: José María Velasco', *Hoy*, 12 September 1942

Pérez de Salazar y Solana 1982
J. Pérez de Salazar y Solana, *José María Velasco y sus contemporáneos*, Monterrey 1982

Phaf-Rheinberger 2011
I. Phaf-Rheinberger, 'Darwin y la obra de José María Velasco. Una visión científico artística', in A. Barahona, E. Suárez and H.-J. Rheinberger (eds), *Darwin, el arte de hacer ciencia*, Mexico City 2011, pp. 225–44

Prague 1999
L. Sršeň and D. Stehlíková, *Mexické dobrodružství Maxmiliána Habsburského*, exh. cat., National Museum of the Czech Republic, Prague 1999

Princeton 2020
J. Elderfield (ed.), *Cézanne: The Rock and Quarry Paintings*, exh. cat., Princeton University Art Museum, Princeton 2020

Ramírez 1988
F. Ramírez, 'Dioses, héroes y reyes mexicanos en París, 1889', in *Historia, leyendas y mitos de México: su expresión en el arte. XI Coloquio Internacional de Historia del Arte*, Mexico City 1988, pp. 201–53

Ramírez 1989
F. Ramírez, 'Acotaciones iconográficas a la evolución de episodios y localidades en los paisajes de José María Velasco', in Ramírez et al. 1989, pp. 15–85

Ramírez et al. 1989
F. Ramírez et al., *José María Velasco. Homenaje*, Mexico City 1989

Ramírez 1992
F. Ramírez, 'La pintura del paisaje en las concepciones y en las enseñanzas de Eugenio Landesio', *Memoria*, 4 (1992), pp. 61–79

Ramírez 1993
F. Ramírez, 'On José María Velasco's Artistic Achievements', in Altamirano Piolle 1993, vol. 1, pp. 25–34

Ramírez 2001
F. Ramírez, 'La construcción de la patria y el desarrollo del paisaje en el México decimonónico', in S.G. Widdifield (ed.), *Hacia otra historia del arte en México*, Mexico City 2001, vol. 2, pp. 269–92

Ramírez 2004
F. Ramírez, 'La materia del arte: visión y color en los paisajes de José María Velasco', in *La materia del arte: José María Velasco y Hermenegildo Bustos*, exh. cat., Instituto Nacional de Bellas Artes, Mexico City 2004, pp. 55–70

Ramírez 2015
F. Ramírez, 'Velasco and the Valley of Mexico (1873–1908): Narrative Moment and Visual Rhetoric', in L. Noelle and D.M.J. Wood (eds), *Landscape Aesthetics in the Americas*, Mexico City 2015, pp. 21–50

Ramírez 2017
F. Ramírez, *José María Velasco: pintor de paisajes*, Mexico City 2017

Reiß, Olsson and Hoßfeld 2015
C. Reiß, L. Olsson and U. Hoßfeld, 'The History of the Oldest Self-Sustaining Laboratory Animal: 150 Years of Axolotl Research', *Journal of Experimental Zoology, Part B: Molecular and Developmental Evolution*, 324, no. 5 (2015), pp. 393–404

Revilla 1908
M.G. Revilla, 'Eugenio Landesio', in *Obras del Lic. D. Manuel G. Revilla. Biografías (Artistas)*, Mexico City 1908, pp. 291–322

Romero de Terreros 1959
M. Romero de Terreros, 'México visto por pintores extranjeros del siglo XIX', *Anales del Instituto de Investigaciones Estéticas*, 7, no. 28 (1959), pp. 33–46

Romero de Terreros 1963
M. Romero de Terreros (ed.), *Catálogos de las exposiciones de la antigua Academia de San Carlos de México, 1850–1898*, Mexico City 1963

Rulfo 1955 (2023)
J. Rulfo, *Pedro Páramo* (1955), trans. D.J. Weatherford, London 2023

Saborit 1986
A. Saborit, 'Cuaresmas porfirianas', *Historias*, no. 15 (1986), pp. 71–3

Shawcross 2022
E. Shawcross, *The Last Emperor of Mexico: A Disaster in the New World*, London 2022

Sierra 1869
J. Sierra, 'La cascada de Tizapán', *El Renacimiento*, 1, no. 22 (1869), pp. 294–5

Silva Barón 2010
M.A. Silva Barón, 'Pinturas mexicanas en París, 1889', in M.F. Matos Moctezuma (ed.), *México en los pabellones y las exposiciones internacionales, 1889–1929*, Mexico City 2010, pp. 42–55

Štěpánek 1971
P. Štěpánek, 'Pinturas de José María Velasco y de Santiago Rebull en Praga', *Anales del Instituto de Investigaciones Estéticas*, 10, no. 40 (1971), pp. 113–17

Štěpánek 1985
P. Štěpánek, 'José María Velasco y el tesoro de Kaska', *México en el arte*, 9 (1985), pp. 2–10

Tenorio-Trillo 1996
M. Tenorio-Trillo, *Mexico at the World's Fairs: Crafting a Modern Nation*, Berkeley, Los Angeles and Oxford 1996

Tomlinson 1990
C. Tomlinson, 'José María Velasco (1840–1912) en su época y la nuestra', in exh. cat., *Octavio Paz: los privilegios de la vista*, Centro Cultural Arte Contemporaneo, Mexico City 1990, pp. 85–93

Trabulse 2012
E. Trabulse, *José María Velasco: un paisaje de la ciencia en México*, Mexico City 2012

Uslenghi 2016
A. Uslenghi, *Latin America at Fin-de-Siècle Universal Exhibitions: Modern Cultures of Visuality*, New York 2016

Valderrama Negrón 2014
N. Valderrama Negrón, 'Las redes familiares de Lorenzo de la Hidalga en Nueva España. Una visión desde la historia del arte', in A. Garritz Ruiz and J. Sanchiz Ruiz (eds), *Genealogía, heráldica y documentación*, Mexico City 2014, pp. 159–88

Vázquez 2010
J.Z. Vázquez, 'War and Peace with the United States', in W.H. Beezley and M.C. Meyer (eds), *The Oxford History of Mexico*, Oxford and New York 2010, pp. 319–48

Velasco 1870
J.M. Velasco, 'Estudio sobre la família de las cactáceas de Mexico', *La Naturaleza*, 1 (1870), pp. 201–3

Velasco 1879
J.M. Velasco, 'Descripción, metamorfosis y costumbres de una especie nueva del género Siredón', *La Naturaleza*, 4 (1879), pp. 209–33

Velasco 1880
J.M. Velasco, 'Anotaciones y observaciones al trabajo del señor August Weismann, sobre la transformación del ajolote mexicano en Amblistoma', *La Naturaleza*, 5 (1880), pp. 58–84

Velasco 1908
J.M. Velasco, 'El arte de la pintura', Mexico 1908

Velasco and Velasco 1870
J.M. Velasco and I. Velasco, 'Estudios sobre una nueva espécie de falsa jalapa de Querétaro *Ipomoea triflora*', *La Naturaleza*, 1 (1870), pp. 338–42

Velasco Archive
José María Velasco Archive, Museo Kaluz, Mexico City

Weismann 1880
A. Weismann, 'Transformacíon del ajolote mexicano en Amblistoma', *La Naturaleza*, 5 (1880), pp. 31–57

Weismann 1882
A. Weismann, *Studies in the Theory of Descent*, 2 vols, London 1882

Widdifield 1996
S.G. Widdifield, *The Embodiment of the National in Late Nineteenth-Century Mexican Painting*, Tuscon 1996

PICTURE CREDITS

The works of José María Velasco are designated artistic monuments, forming part of the cultural heritage of the nation of Mexico. Their reproduction is authorised by the Instituto Nacional de Bellas Artes y Literatura.

BARCELONA
Museu Nacional d'Art de Catalunya, Barcelona © Artepics / Alamy Stock Photo: fig. 9.

LONDON
© The National Gallery, London: fig. 12.

MADRID
© Hispanic Digital Library, National Library of Spain: fig. 32.

MEXICO CITY
© Acervo Histórico de la Biblioteca del Instituto de Biología de la UNAM. Digitalization: Socorro Tapia: fig. 24.
© Colección Pérez Simón, Mexico. Photo: Oliver Santana: cat. 13.
© José María Velasco Archive, Museo Kaluz, Mexico City: figs 8, 15, 18; cat. 18. Photo: Jorge Vertiz: figs 3, 4; cats 10, 28.
Museo Nacional de Arte, Mexico City © Reproduction authorised by the Instituto Nacional de Bellas Artes y Literatura, 2025: figs 2, 6, 7, 19, 20, 21, 22, 30; cats 1, 2, 7, 8, 12, 14, 21, 23. Photo: Francisco Kochen: cats 9, 11, 15, 16, 17, 19, 20, 22, 26.
Museo Nacional de Historia, Castillo de Chapultepec © SECRETARIA DE CULTURA .- INAH. Reproduction authorised by the Instituto Nacional de Antropología e Historia: fig. 14.
Museo Nacional de San Carlos, INBAL © Photo: Eduardo Galindo Vargas: fig. 10.

NEW YORK
New York Botanical Garden, LuEsther T. Mertz Library. Images courtesy Biodiversity Heritage Library: figs 23, 25, 26.
© The Metropolitan Museum of Art, New York: fig. 27.

PRAGUE
© The National Museum of the Czech Republic, Prague. Photo: Denisa Dimitrovova: cats 3, 4, 5.

PRIVATE COLLECTIONS
Private Collections © Courtesy the owners: figs 1, 5, 13. Photo: Rafael Doniz: figs 17, 28.
Private Collection © DACS 2025: fig. 31.
Private Collection © Photo: Laura Cohen: cat. 6.
Elda Margarita Capetillo Ponce © Courtesy the owner: cat. 24.

PUEBLA
© Colección Fundación Amparo - Museo Amparo, Puebla, México: fig. 11.

TOLUCA
Museo del Paisaje José María Velasco © Secretaría de Cultura del Gobierno del Estado de México, Museo del paisaje José Ma. Velasco: cat. 27.

VERACRUZ
Acervo de la Secretaría de Cultura de Veracruz © Secretaría de Cultura de Veracruz, Colección Museo de Arte del Estado de Veracruz: cat. 25; © Album / Alamy Stock Photo: fig. 29.

WASHINGTON DC
© Smithsonian Institution / Bridgeman Images: fig. 16.

AUTHORS

Dawn Ades, Professor Emerita of Art History and Theory, University of Essex

María Elena Altamirano Piolle, independent scholar

Pablo Arredondo Vera, independent scholar

Dexter Dalwood, artist and curator

Omar Olivares Sandoval, Researcher, Instituto de Investigaciones Estéticas, Universidad Nacional Autónoma de México

Valéria Piccoli, Ken and Linda Cutler Chair of the Arts of the Americas and Curator of Latin American Art, The Minneapolis Institute of Art

Daniel Sobrino Ralston, CEEH Associate Curator of Spanish Paintings, The National Gallery, London

LIST OF LENDERS

MEXICO CITY
Colección Pérez Simón
Elda Margarita Capetillo Ponce
Museo Kaluz
Museo Nacional de Arte, INBAL

PRAGUE
National Museum of the Czech Republic

TOLUCA
Secretaría de Cultura del Gobierno del Estado de México, Museo del Paisaje José Maria Velasco

VERACRUZ
Secretaría de Cultura de Veracruz, Colección Museo de Arte del Estado de Veracruz

And those lenders who wish to remain anonymous

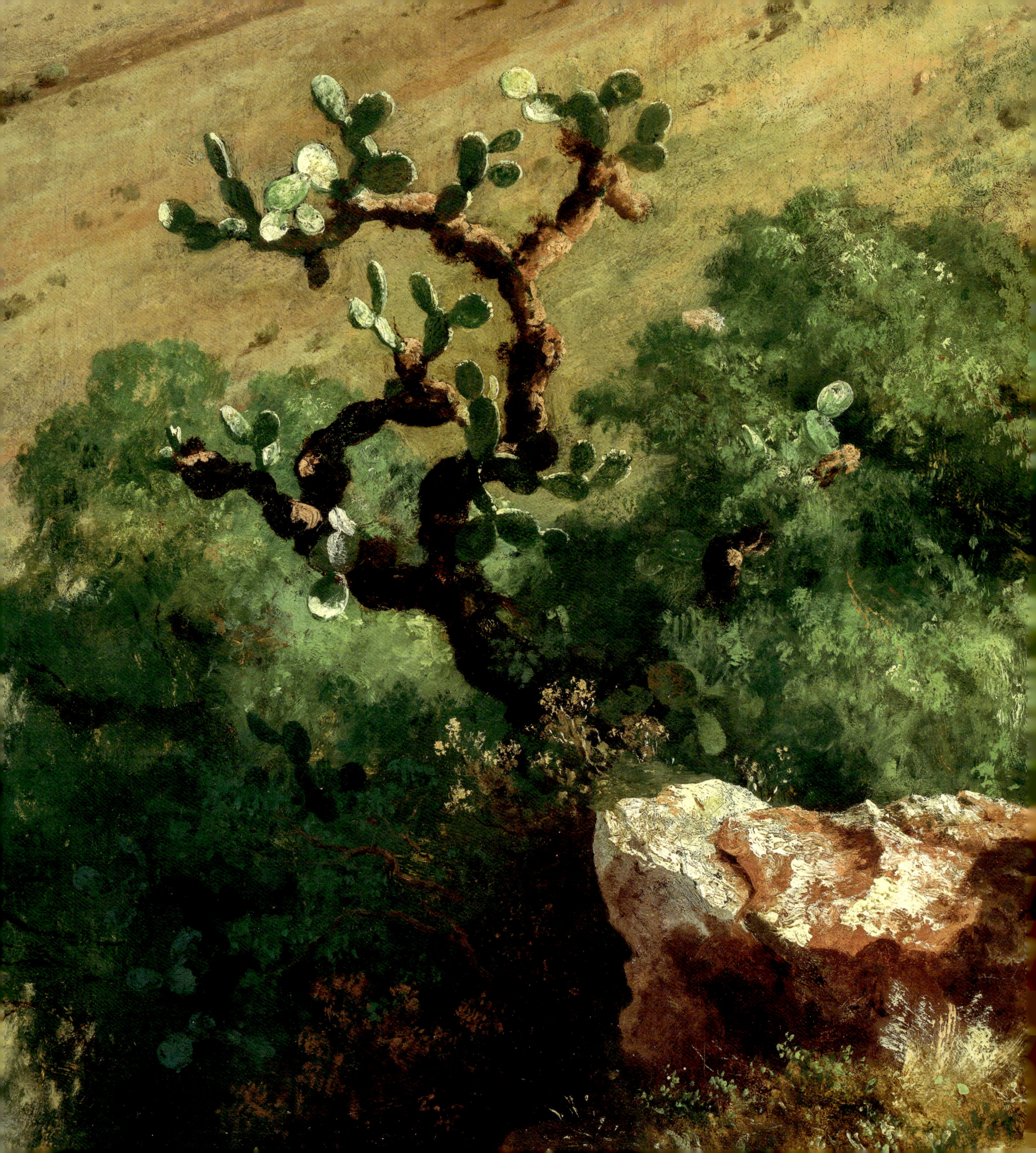

ACKNOWLEDGEMENTS

In the summer of 2022, I proposed an exhibition on José María Velasco to Gabriele Finaldi, Director of the National Gallery. My interest in Mexican history was first ignited by a 2017 residency in Mexico. This interest culminated in *Esto No Me Pertenece* ('This Doesn't Belong to Me'), an exhibition of my own work held at the Museo Nacional de Arte (MUNAL), Mexico City, in 2021 that included several Velasco paintings from the museum's collection. In early discussions with Francisco Berzunza, Mariana Munguía, Pablo Arredondo Vera and Elizabeth Calzado Michel, I discovered that Velasco's fascinating oeuvre occupied a central but static place in the history of Mexican art, where alternative perspectives were unusual or absent. Emboldened by Dawn Ades's encouragement and my familiarity with the National Gallery's collection, I felt that an exhibition of Velasco's work would serve to recontextualise the institution's late nineteenth-century holdings, prompting audiences to reflect on the connections between European landscape painting, Mexico and Velasco's singular artistic achievement.

Daniel Sobrino Ralston, the CEEH Associate Curator of Spanish Paintings at the National Gallery, soon joined me as co-curator. I am indebted to him for his tireless efforts and am pleased that we have collaborated closely, developing a shared vision for the exhibition.

This exhibition would not have been possible without the vital support of Mexico's Secretary of State for Culture, Claudia Curiel de Icaza, the Undersecretary of Cultural Development, Marina Núñez Bespalova, and the Instituto Nacional de Bellas Artes y Literatura (INBAL). We are grateful to INBAL's Director, Alejandra de la Paz Nájera, as well as Lluvia Sepúlveda Jiménez, Paulina de la Paz Egea, and Gerardo Cedillo Bolaños of the Coordinación Nacional de Artes Visuales. Their indefatigable efforts in securing loans were essential.

The majority of the works in this exhibition come from MUNAL, and we wish to extend our sincere gratitude to its Director, Mireida Velázquez Torres, Subdirector Ana Leticia Carpizo González, former Directors Héctor Palhares Meza and Carmen Gaitán Rojo, curators María Estela Duarte and Ramón Avendaño Esquivel, and librarian Diana Pérez Barrera.

We are grateful to the other institutional and private lenders, including the Secretaría de Cultura de Veracruz, with the valuable assistance of Sergio A. Rosete Xotlanihua and Isis Varinia Castro Ramos; the Museo Kaluz, where we were supported by Khery Cámara, Xavier de la Riva Ros and José Ignacio Aldama; and the Museo del Paisaje José María Velasco, where Paul Gregory Earle Ocampo proved crucial. Additionally, we wish to express our appreciation to Pavla Mikešová and Jakub Anderle at the National Museum of the Czech Republic in Prague. Finally, we thank the Pérez Simón collection and its curator, Graciela Téllez Trevilla, along with all the lenders who prefer to remain anonymous.

We owe a great debt to the contributors to the catalogue, particularly María Elena Altamirano Piolle, who shared her unparalleled, comprehensive knowledge of Velasco throughout the preparations for this exhibition. We are also grateful to Omar Olivares Sandoval, Dawn Ades, Valéria Piccoli and Pablo Arredondo Vera. Additionally, we would like to thank Stacie G. Widdifield, Nancy Ireson, Michael Snyder, Chiara Di Stefano, Pierre Von-Ow, and Edward J. Sullivan for their thoughtful and generous feedback.

We are grateful to the many other colleagues and friends who gave liberally of their expertise and advice, including Jeronimo Arrigunaga, Nancy Bryan, Elizabeth Calzado Michel, Lisa Cole, Fernando Elizundia, Jamie E. Forde, Kathleen Foster, Daniel Garza Usabiaga, José Ignacio González, Patricio González Caraza-Campos, Fernando Gutiérrez Champion, Jaqueline Gutiérrez Fonseca, Anne Higonnet, Claudia Hopkins, Cristobal Jácome-Moreno, Mayken Jonkman, Dylan Joy, Hemma Khevenhüller-Metsch, Brigitte E. Leidwein, Ramiro Martínez Estrada, Ricardo Mercado Ruiz, Cesáreo Moreno, Alberto Nulman Magidin, James Oles, Emmanuel Ortega, Tatiana Peralta, Scott Perkins, Paloma Porraz, David Pullins, Fausto Ramírez, Salvador Rueda Smithers, Pavel Štěpánek, Lisa Trever, Sergio Vela, Mireida Velázquez Torres and Darío Yazbek Bernal.

At the National Gallery, we thank Gabriele Finaldi, Jane Knowles, Christopher Riopelle and Sunnifa Hope for the enthusiasm with which they received the initial proposal. Hannah Hawksworth, Réka Vajda, Chris Oberon, Nicola Smith and Louise Nyborg have been invaluable in bringing the exhibition to life. The catalogue was edited by Daniel Sobrino Ralston, Flora Allen and Felicity Maunder, and assembled with the help of Rebecca Thornton, Diana Adell and Laura Lappin, with a wonderful design by Daniela Rocha.

Our deepest gratitude goes to Francisco Berzunza, whose dedication to and respect for Velasco and his art made this exhibition possible.

Dexter Dalwood and Daniel Sobrino Ralston

Published to accompany the exhibition
José María Velasco: A View of Mexico
The National Gallery, London, 29 March – 17 August 2025
The Minneapolis Institute of Art, 27 September 2025 – 4 January 2026

Curated by Dexter Dalwood and Daniel Sobrino Ralston, the National Gallery's CEEH
Associate Curator of Spanish Paintings, from an initial concept by Dexter Dalwood

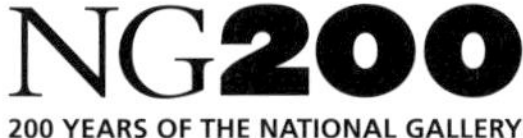 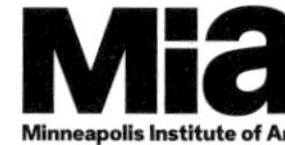

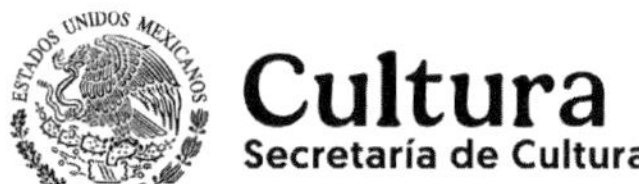 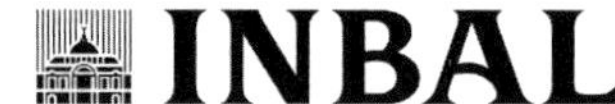 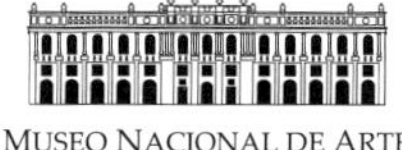

Exhibition supported by

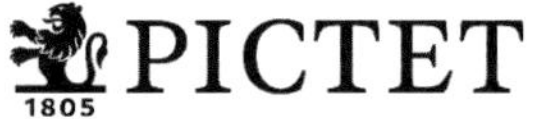

The Monument Trust

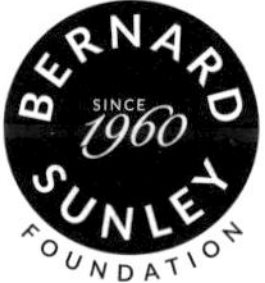

The Sunley Room exhibition programme is
supported by the Bernard Sunley Foundation

This exhibition has been made possible by the
provision of insurance through the Government
Indemnity Scheme. The National Gallery would
like to thank HM Government for providing
Government Indemnity and the Department
for Culture, Media and Sport and Arts Council
England for arranging the indemnity.

© National Gallery Global Limited 2025

Authorised Representative in the EU Details:
Easy Access System Europe
Mustamäe tee 50, 10621 Tallinn, Estonia
gpsr.requests@easproject.com

First published in 2025 by
National Gallery Global Limited
Trafalgar Square
London WC2N 5DN
www.shop.nationalgallery.org.uk

ISBN: 9781857097252
1054380

British Library Cataloguing-in-Publication Data
A catalogue record is available from the
British Library
Library of Congress Control Number:
2024951916

Publisher: Laura Lappin
Senior Project Editor: Flora Allen
Copy-editor: Felicity Maunder
Proofreader: Caroline Ellerby
Picture Researcher: Rebecca Thornton
Production: Davina Cheung

Designed by Daniela Rocha
Origination by DL Imaging
Printed in Belgium by Graphius

All works are by José María Velasco (1840–1912)
unless otherwise stated.

All measurements give height before width.

Front cover: *Cardón, State of Oaxaca*, 1887
(cat. 11)

Full-page details:
p. 2: detail from cat. 4
p. 4: detail from cat. 23
p. 6: detail from fig. 3
pp. 62–3: detail from cat. 17
pp. 106–7: detail from cat. 6
p. 118: detail from cat. 17